A Right
to
Bear Arms

Recent Titles in
Contributions in Political Science

A Right
to
Bear Arms

State and Federal Bills of Rights and Constitutional Guarantees

Stephen P. Halbrook

Contributions in Political Science, Number 243

GREENWOOD PRESS

New York • Westport, Connecticut • London

Library of Congress Cataloging-in-Publication Data

Halbrook, Stephen P.
  A right to bear arms : state and federal bills of rights and
constitutional guarantees / Stephen P. Halbrook.
    p. cm. — (Contributions in political science, ISSN
0147–1066 ; no. 243)
  Bibliography: p.
  Includes index.
  ISBN 0–313–26539–9 (lib. bdg. : alk. paper)
  1. Firearms—Law and legislation—United States—States—History.
I. Title. II. Series.
KF3941.Z95H35   1989
344.73′0533—dc20
[347.304533]   89–11722

British Library Cataloguing in Publication Data is available.

Library of Congress Catalog Card Number: 89–11722
ISBN: 0–313–26539–9
ISSN: 0147–1066

First published in 1989

Greenwood Press, Inc.
88 Post Road West, Westport, Connecticut 06881

Printed in the United States of America

The paper used in this book complies with the
Permanent Paper Standard issued by the National
Information Standards Organization (Z39.48–1984).

10 9 8 7 6 5 4 3 2 1

Contents

CONTENTS

Preface

The federal Bill of Rights was not a falling star that James Madison picked up off the ground in 1789 and introduced in Congress the next day. Nor was it simply the result of demands in the state ratifying conventions that the Constitution framed at Philadelphia two years earlier include a statement of individual liberties on which the new government could not infringe.

Beginning in the summer of 1776 when independence from Britain was declared, half of the states adopted bills of rights, much of the language of which would reappear in the federal Bill of Rights. And while none of the other states adopted bills of rights at that time, similar conceptions of personal liberty existed in those states as in the states with formal declarations. The articulation by the colonists of their grievances for rights violated in the decade before the war for independence, and the assertion of their rights in the state bills of rights, constitutions, and legislation as well as in newspapers and in the writings of the "founding fathers" of the individual states, are all sources of the federal Bill of Rights.

Moreover, the state bills of rights remain a primary barrier to overreaching governmental intrusions at the state and local levels. The state bills of rights and the sources of each are currently undergoing rediscovery as alternative grounds to the federal Bill of Rights to protect personal freedoms.

Perhaps the most controversial but least understood part of the federal Bill of Rights, the Second Amendment provides: "A well regulated Militia, being necessary to the security of a free State, the right of the people to keep and bear Arms, shall not be infringed." The philosophical origins, common-law background, and history of adoption of the Second Amendment were comprehensively treated by this author in *That Every Man Be Armed: The Evolution of a Constitutional Right*, published in 1984. Yet the major gap in that work is a topic which must be a book in itself, namely, the history and development of the right to keep and bear arms in the original states from the time when the grievances against British rule were generated through the epoch of the adoption of the Second Amendment.

No scholarly studies have hitherto been published on the attempts by the British to disarm the American inhabitants in the years leading to the American Revolution. Without referring to any original sources, a law review article confidently asserts: "In all the writings on the Revolutionary War and the turbulent times preceding it, there is no evidence showing that the colonists or their revolutionary leaders believed that they had a personal right to carry firearms, nor that the British were violating a personal right to carry firearms."[1]

Similarly, the courts have rarely, if ever, relied on original sources to construe guarantees for the right to bear arms under the state bills of rights. Construing the right-to-bear-arms guarantee of the Massachusetts Declaration of Rights, the highest court of that state wrote: "The meaning of such provisions is to be gathered from their history which is reasonably well known and need not be reviewed here in detail."[2] Without reference to any original sources, the court concluded that the right exists only in "the aggregate of citizens," today's National Guard, and is "not directed to guaranteeing individual ownership or possession of weapons."[3] The empirical validity of the court's version of history depends on original sources with which the court appears to have been unfamiliar. Ironically, as will be seen, the brunt of British efforts to disarm the colonists took place in Massachusetts, and the greatest protests by the patriots on that policy originated in that state.

Besides legal scholars and the courts, professional historians have all but ignored the pre-Revolutionary background and the first state bills of rights on the issue of the right to keep and bear arms. There has been an apparent fixation on the period of the ratification of the federal Constitution and the debate on whether a federal bill of rights was necessary to protect rights such as bearing arms.[4] This narrow focus insufficiently accounts for the historical impetus for the federal Second Amendment and ignores the inherent significance of the guarantees of the state bills of rights.

In the years 1776 through 1783, four states adopted bills of rights explicitly recognizing "the right of the people to bear arms," and four other states adopted "well regulated militia" guarantees which mandated an armed populace. While none of the other six states adopted bills of rights in that period, the political values expressed in those states were similar to those expressed in states with bills of rights. The federal Second Amendment reflected the experiences of all the original states, even those which adopted no bill of rights in the eighteenth century. These experiences also help explain the impetus for and intent of the guarantees of the right to have arms under the various state constitutions up through the present. The purpose of this work is to address the extent to which the right to keep and bear arms was considered to be a fundamental right explicitly or implicitly guaranteed in the first fourteen states (the thirteen original colonies and Vermont), whether under a bill of rights, constitution, or charter.

This study begins with an analysis of the complaints by the colonists of British infringements on the right to keep and bear arms in Boston during 1768–1775. Taken primarily from original newspaper accounts written in Massachusetts and widely reprinted in the other colonies, this information has been virtually unknown to scholars. The British used many methods of disarming the colonists, from embargoes and "temporary" confiscations to entrapment and direct seizure at gunpoint.

The body of this work is an analysis of the right to have arms as recognized in each of the first states. States are grouped according to those that had bills of rights, including either a "right to bear arms" guarantee (Pennsylvania, North Carolina, Vermont, and Massachusetts) or, if not, a "well regulated militia" guarantee (Virginia, Maryland, Delaware, and New Hampshire). The next category are those states that had a constitution without a bill of rights (New York, New Jersey, South Carolina, and Georgia), and then those that had neither a constitution nor a bill of rights, but continued their colonial charters (Connecticut and Rhode Island).

The extent to which the right to keep and bear arms was considered a fundamental right in each state roughly between the beginning of the Revolution in 1775 and the adoption of the federal Second Amendment in 1791 is analyzed from a variety of sources. Some of these sources include: newspaper reactions to British attempts to disarm the inhabitants of Boston during 1768–1775; the mobilization of the armed people into independent and organized militias; the records of the conventions that adopted declarations of rights, and editorials thereon; the writings of the founding fathers of the individual states; and laws passed concerning firearms. The sources that exemplify these experiences vary depending on each state's history and the extent to which the original records have been preserved and are accessible.

The great debate over the proposed federal Constitution without a bill of rights, demands for an arms guarantee, and the ratification of the Second Amendment have been analyzed by this author in *That Every*

Man Be Armed, and will not be repeated here. Aspects of the federal controversy will be treated only where, as in the case of some of the smaller states, needed to illustrate attitudes at the state level toward the right to keep and bear arms and whether a state bill of rights is necessary.

Nineteenth and twentieth century developments in state constitutional conventions concerning the right to keep and bear arms conclude the study. Several of the original states that had no bill of rights adopted them during the antebellum period. Reconstruction saw the adoption or alteration of state bills of rights, particularly in the Southern States as the price of readmission into the Union. Little further activity occurred until the last two decades, when the passage of firearms prohibitions prompted the adoption of stronger protections for the right to keep and bear arms.

The complete history of the right to keep and bear arms remains hidden in many respects, and interested scholars will find much to uncover in original records. Hopefully, this admittedly incomplete and imperfect study will encourage others to undertake the kind of scholarly endeavors that an explicitly guaranteed constitutional right, no matter how controversial, deserves.

While only he is responsible for the views expressed in and shortcomings of this book, the author expresses his appreciation for the provocative observations of a number of scholars on the general background of the right in question and the hidden history of the state bills of rights. Some of those scholars include David Caplan, Ronald Collins, Lawrence Cress, Robert Dowlut, Richard Gardiner, David Hardy, George Knight, Janet Knoop, Joyce Malcolm, and Robert Shalhope. For his critical comments on this manuscript, the author thanks John P. Kaminski, Director of the Center for the Study of the American Constitution at Madison, Wisconsin.

An earlier draft of Chapter 2 of this book was originally published as *The Right to Bear Arms in the First State Bills of Rights: Pennsylvania, North Carolina, Vermont, and Massachusetts,* 10 VERMONT LAW REVIEW 255–320 (Fall 1985), and the author reiterates his appreciation for the comments of the law review editors. Special thanks for preparation of the manuscript go to Nancy Cammarata and Lisa Halbrook.

CHAPTER 1

The Inhabitants of Boston Disarmed

American resistance to British taxation and various grievances came to a head in 1768, the focal point of the confrontation being Boston. Smuggling, boycotts on tea, resistance to customs agents, riots, and general unrest were rapidly moving British strategists to a military solution. The colonists, particularly those in New England, clearly foreboded the coming occupation.

A meeting of Boston freeholders, moderated by James Otis, and also led by Samuel Adams, John Hancock, and Samuel Cushing, was held at Faneuil Hall on September 12 and 13. Several resolutions were passed deploring standing armies, taxation without representation, and other grievances. Among the measures considered was the following:

Upon a Motion made and seconded, the following vote was passed by a very great Majority, *viz.*

WHEREAS, by an Act of Parliament, of the first of King *William* and Queen *Mary*, it is declared, that the Subjects being Protestants, may have arms for their Defence; It is the Opinion of this town, that the said Declaration is founded in Nature, Reason and sound Policy, and is well adapted for the necessary Defence of the Community.

And Forasmuch, as by a good and wholesome Law of this Province, every listed Soldier and other Householder (except Troopers, who by Law are otherwise to be provided) shall always be provided with a well fix'd Firelock, Musket, Accoutrements and Ammunition, as in said Law particularly mentioned, to the Satisfaction of the Commission Officers of the Company; and as there is at this Time prevailing Apprehension, in the Minds of many, of an approaching War with France: In order that the Inhabitants of this Town may be prepared in Case of Sudden Danger: VOTED, that those of the Inhabitants, who may at present be unprovided, be and hereby are requested duly to observe the said Law at this Time.[1]

The Act of Parliament enacted when William and Mary ascended the throne was the Declaration of Rights of 1689, which stated that James II had subverted "the Laws and Liberties of this kingdom," in part "by causing several good Subjects, being Protestants, to be disarmed, at the same Time when Papists were both armed and employed, contrary to law."[2] The "true ancient and indubitable rights" it declared included "that the Subjects which are Protestants, may have Arms for their Defence suitable to their Condition, and as are allowed by Law."[3] The Bostonians contended that Americans retained all rights of Englishmen.

Boston requested that the other towns in the province consider the resolutions and agree to meet in a convention.[4] Delegates from sixty-six towns met at Faneuil Hall, and on September 26 presented a petition to the governor stating that "it is generally apprehended that a standing army is immediately to be introduced among the people, contrary . . . to the Bill of Rights—a force represented to be sufficient to over-awe and controul the whole civil power of the province; and must render every right & possession dreadfully precarious."[5] The governor refused to receive the petition and declared the convention illegal.

The same day the governor rejected the petition, the press asserted that he was planning to disarm the inhabitants. In a warning which would be reprinted all over the colonies, a patriot "A.B.C."—probably Samuel Adams—wrote:

It is reported that the Governor has said, that he has Three Things in Command from the Ministry, more grievous to the People, than any Thing hitherto made known. It is conjectured 1st, that the Inhabitants of this Province are to be disarmed. 2d. The Province to be governed by Martial Law. And 3d, that a Number of Gentlemen who have exerted themselves in the Cause of their Country, are to be seized and sent to Great-Britain.

Unhappy America! When thy Enemies are rewarded with Honors and Riches; but thy Friends punished and ruined only for asserting thy Rights, and pleading for thy Freedom.[6]

Two days later, the British troops landed in Boston and took over key points, including Faneuil Hall.[7] Pursuant to the Town Committee's previous resolution, the citizens did not resist.[8] "Not the least attempt has been made or even contemplated to oppose the landing of the King's Troops, or their encampment on the Common. . . . It is not doubted that the Posse Comitatus, in aid of the Civil Magistrate, when necessary, will be sufficient to maintain every Individual in the Exercise and Enjoyment of his Rights and Property."[9]

Royalists hotly denied that the troops would disarm and violate the rights of the inhabitants. In response to one such denial, "A.B.C.," who claimed above that the people would be disarmed, martial law declared, and patriots would be taken to England without being charged with any crime, stated:

I observe Mr. Draper [a Tory printer] in his last paper says he is authorized to assure the Publick, that the Reports mentioned in your Paper of September 26, was an infamous Lie. . . . Mr. Draper (as he was about the Town, and these Reports were the subject of much Conversation) must have known he was publishing a Falsehood. . . . When an armed Force is bro't in upon a peaceable Country against their Consent, and in Violation of their Rights as Men and British subjects, we have Reason to believe that soon unheard of Oppressions are coming upon us.[10]

The decision to send troops was made partly in response to disturbances throughout the summer and talk of resistance to occupation. A British merchant seaman who left Boston in late August had reported on arrival in Glasgow, "that at the time of his sailing from thence, upwards of 10,000 men had taken up Arms, and declared themselves resolved to oppose any military Force that should be sent against them."[11]

The Boston resolution's reference to a possible war with France as a reason to arm, which followed other resolutions denouncing standing armies being kept among the people, fooled no one. A proroyalist committee from the Town of Hatfield, Hampshire County, stated:

If your town meant sincerely, we can't see the need they had of interposing in military matters, in an unprecedented way requesting their inhabitants to be provided with arms, &c. (a matter till now always supposed to belong to another department,) especially as they must know such a number of Troops would be a much better defence in case of war, than they had heretofore been favoured with: to suppose what you promise they may be intended for, is to mistrust the King's paternal care and goodness.[12]

A more moderate response came from "A Citizen" of New York, who praised the citizens for not offering armed resistance:

I was led into these Reflections by observing with how much seeming Glee and Triumph, some People amongst us, noted for having always been the greatest Sticklers for prerogative Doctrines and despotic Power,—Endeavour to decry the Behaviour of our oppressed Brethren of Boston, and maliciously and invidiously sneer at their not having opposed the Landi⁃ ⁃ of the Troops, as some evil-minded Persons gave out they intended.—And tho' I blame their having given some Room for so idle a Report, by the ridiculous Puff and Bombast, (for which our Eastern Brethren have always been but too famous) warning every Man to provide himself with a good Firelock, Ammunition, &c. under the disingeneous, canting, Jesuitical Pretence of the Prospect of a French War, fully as absurd and hypocritical as is the Pretence of a Military Establishment in America for *its Protection and Defence.*[13]

The British made efforts to disarm the citizens. One report stated: "That part of the troops had been quartered in the castle and barracks, and the remainder of them in some old empty houses. That the inhabitants had been ordered to bring in their arms, which in general they had complied with; and that those in possession of any after the expiration of a notice given them, were to take the consequences."[14] The report did not disclose where this surrender of arms allegedly took place.

It is difficult to imagine much compliance with such an order, if it really existed, since such reports were neither widespread nor extensively protested. However, disarming the colonists was clearly being contemplated. From London, "it is said orders will soon be given to prevent the exportation of either naval or military stores, gun-powder, &c. to any part of North-America."[15]

With the occupation of Boston there began to be published in colonial newspapers the column "Journal of the Times," which became the most widely circulated pre-Revolutionary writing after Dickinson's *Letters from a Pennsylvania Farmer*. It was written in Boston, sent to New York secretly and published in the *New York Journal*, and then reprinted in newspapers all over the colonies and even in England. Its anonymous authors probably included Samuel Adams, John Adams, Josiah Quincy, and various editors.[16]

In the first of several references to the arms issue, the "Journal" found a hidden irony in the illegal quartering of troops among the populace: "Some of the Consequences of bringing the Troops into this Town, in direct violation of the Act of Parliament, . . . instead of Quartering them in the Barracks on Castle Island, are likely to be the scattering proper Tutors through the Country, to instruct the Inhabitants in the modern Way of handling the Firelock and exercising the Men."[17] However, according to reports coming from London, the colonists needed little instruction: "The total number of the Militia, in the large province of New-England, is upwards of 150,000 men, who all have and can use arms, not only in a regular, but in so particular a manner, as to be capable of shooting a Pimple off a man's nose without hurting him."[18]

Of course, the consequences of occupation were largely negative. "A Number of Robberies have been lately committed by the Soldiers . . . which before was a Crime unknown in this Town."[19] The papers are filled with accounts of soldiers harassing, assaulting, challenging, and stealing from citizens. At the end of 1768, one writer stated: "We have seen the military introduced against a parcel of unarmed people; and we have been told, it was to assist the civil magistrates.... We have seen ... the dependents on gov-nm--t hiring armed ruffians to overturn the foundation of the constitution."[20] Another writer analogized that British tax policy was akin to highway robbery which could be resisted.[21]

Meanwhile, the British Parliament did not take kindly to all the talk about the citizens arming themselves and activities perceived as riots. The House of Lords passed the following on December 15:

5. *Resolved*, That in these Circumstances of the Province of Massachusetts-Bay, and of the Town of Boston, the Preservation of the Public Peace, and the due Execution of the Law became impracticable, and without the Aid of a Military Force to support and protect the Civil Magistrate, and the Officers of his Majesty's Revenue.

6. *Resolved*, That the Declarations, Resolutions and Proceedings in the Town Meetings at Boston, on the 14th June and 12th September, were illegal, unconstitutional, and calculated to execute Sedition and Insurrection in his Majesty's Province of Massachusetts-Bay.[22]

The "Journal" constantly complained that the colonists' motives were being misrepresented to the King and Parliament. The September 1768 assertion of the rights to have arms and to petition was singled out for comment:

It seems that the transactions of the town of Boston in Sept. last, in making mention of a law of this province, that requires all the inhabitants to be provided with arms, and in proposing that the several towns should make choice of persons, there being no Assembly, to join in humble petitions to our gracious sovereign, for the redress of grievances, and to prevent rash and violent measures, at so critical a season, were a principal part of those misrepresentations. It is certain that those transactions were not in any degree contrary to law.... Very few can doubt, that no art has been unemployed, no pains spared by some men among us, to represent those proceedings of the town, not only as illegal, but to the highest degree factious and seditious.[23]

The column described how "one man in particular" spread the misrepresentation that the decision to arm amounted to treason. It concluded: "The vote of the town, respecting being provided with arms, was agreeable to a law of the province, and at a time when a principal officer at Halifax, had wrote up that a war with France was inevitable."[24]

The King's speech at the opening of Parliament, and debate in the House of Commons, prompted the writers of the "Journal" to make an ongoing defense of the Boston vote calling upon each citizen to arm and

of the assembly which adopted it. Samuel Adams, author of the next editorial on the subject, argued:

For it is certainly beyond human art and sophistry, to prove the British subjects, to whom the *privilege* of possessing arms is expressly recognized by the Bill of Rights, and, who live in a province where the law requires them to be equip'd with *arms*, &c. are guilty of an *illegal act*, in calling upon one another to be provided with them, as the *law directs*. . . . One man has as good reason to affirm, that a few, in calling for a military force under *pretence* of supporting civil authority, *secretly* intended to introduce a general massacre, as another has to assert, that a number of loyal subjects, by calling upon one another to be provided with arms, *according to law*, intended to bring on an insurrection.

It will be equally difficult to prove it *illegal*, for a number of British subjects, to invite as many of their fellow subjects as they please, to convene and consult together, on the most prudent and constitutional measures for the redress of their grievances.[25]

In an article he signed "E.A.," Samuel Adams published perhaps the most remarkable analysis of the right to keep and bear arms in the pre-Revolutionary era. He recalled the absolute English monarchs, with their doctrines of nonresistance and divine right, and traced the reigns of "a race of kings, bigotted to the greatest degree to the doctrines of *slavery* and regardless of the *natural, inherent, divinely hereditary* and *indefeasible* rights of their subjects."[26] Quoting freely from Sir William Blackstone, Adams assessed the results of the Glorious Revolution of 1689:

At the revolution, the British constitution was again restor'd to its original principles, declared in the bill of rights; which was afterwards pass'd into a law, and stands as a bulwark to the natural rights of subjects. "To vindicate these rights, says Mr. *Blackstone*, when actually violated or attack'd, the subjects of England are entitled first to the regular administration and *free course of justice* in the courts of law—next to the right of *petitioning the King* and parliament for redress of grievances—and lastly, to the right of *having and using arms for self-preservation and defence.*" These he calls "auxiliary subordinate rights, which serve principally as *barriers* to protect and maintain inviolate the three great and primary rights of *personal security, personal liberty* and *private property*": And that of *having arms for their defense* he tells us is "a public allowance, under due restrictions, of the *natural right of resistance and self-preservation*, when the sanctions of society and laws are found *insufficient* to restrain the *violence of oppression.*"— How little do those persons attend to the rights of the constitution, if they know anything about them, who find fault with a late vote of this town, calling upon the inhabitants to *provide themselves with arms for their defence* at any time; but more especially, when they had reason to fear, there would be a necessity of the means of self preservation against the *violence of oppression.*[27]

Adams' last above remark clearly implied that private citizens could use arms to protect themselves from military oppression. The passage continues even more explicitly as follows:

Everyone knows that the exercise of the military power is forever *dangerous* to civil rights. . . . But there are some persons, who would, if possibly they could, perswade the people *never to make use* of their *constitutional* rights or terrify them from doing it. No wonder that a resolution of this town to *keep arms* for its own defence, should be represented as having at bottom a *secret intention* to oppose the landing of the King's troops: when those very persons, who gave it this colouring, had before represented the peoples petitioning their Sovereign, as proceeding from a *factious* and *rebellious* spirit.[28]

The House of Commons, on February 8, 1769, adopted the resolutions of the Lords which sought to justify the intervention of military forces and to condemn resolutions passed by the Town of Boston.[29] It is unclear when the "Journal" authors first saw Parliament's resolution. However, in a passage which paraphrases Samuel Adams' above comments, they continued to defend the private right to have arms, and implied that military oppression could be rightfully resisted:

Instances of the licentious and outrageous behavior of the *military conservators* of the peace still multiply upon us, some of which are of such a nature, and have been carried to so great lengths, as must serve fully to evince that a late vote of this town, calling upon the inhabitants to provide themselves with arms for their defence, was a measure as *prudent* as it was *legal*: such violences are always to be apprehended from military troops, when quartered in the body of a populous city; but more especially so, when they are led to believe that they are *become necessary to awe a spirit of rebellion*, injuriously said to be existing therein. It is a natural right which the people have reserved to themselves, confirmed by the Bill of Rights, to keep arms for their own defence; and as Mr. Blackstone observes, it is to be made use of when the sanctions of society and law are found insufficient to restrain the violence of oppression.[30]

Through 1769, the papers are filled with protest against standing armies, the quartering of soldiers, and the military execution of the civil law. There had been "an increase of military force, not an increase of militia; they could not so well be relied on for . . . their cruelty to the unarmed and innocent."[31] On June 15, the Massachusetts House of Representatives sent a message, authored by Samuel Adams, to Governor Francis Bernard with the complaint: "The use of the military Power to enforce the Execution of the Laws, is in the Opinion of this House inconsistent with the Spirit of a free Constitution, and the very nature of Government—Nor can there be any necessity for it; for the Body of the People, the Posse Comitatus, will always aid the Magistrate in the Execution of such Laws as ought to be executed."[32]

Among the unjust laws which were thought not worthy of enforcement were those administered by the customs collectors. Of vessels with goods coasting from one province to another, one complaint stated, "sufferance must be obtained at the Customs House before Shot, Powder, Rum, Sugar, Molasses and any triffling Article are taken into a coaster."[33] Other unjust British policies were those based on armed violence, such as impressment of sailors, which the "Journal" thought could justifiably be resisted with deadly force.[34]

The Boston Massacre in early 1770, in which British troops fired into a crowd throwing snowballs, was widely perceived as an act of murder.[35] One town petition characterized it as "the horrid and barbarious action committed last Monday evening, by a party of those troops, by firing with small arms, in the most wanton, cruel and cowardly manner, upon a number of unarmed inhabitants."[36] This proved anew that "Standing Armies have ever proved to be destructive to the Liberties of a People"[37] and constituted "an unlawful assembly" against the English Bill of Rights.[38]

While advertisements for ammunition laced the papers,[39] citizens were exhorted to combine together to protect civil liberty. "A Military Citizen" wrote that

our being able to load and fire and take good Aim, as we do when fowling or firing at Mark, will by no Means qualify us to encounter regular Forces in our open country. . . . We must be able to do it *together* with uniform motions. . . . The manner of loading and firing as explained in the *Manual Exercise* is designed for this very purpose. . . .

This then is the Business and Duty of every Man in the Province, liable to be called forth at an Alarm, . . . to learn the use of the *firelock* and of their *Legs* (that is, to form, march and wheel).[40]

About a month after the Massacre, soldiers chased citizens away from a Liberty Pole, pursuing a Mr. Bicker to his house, where they tried to break in and threatened to shoot anyone who entered. Armed citizens sounded the alarm and chased the soldiers away. "A Number of the Citizens were up all Night, and under Arms, which probably prevented any Mischief being done, as [the soldiers] repeatedly swore they would set fire to the House, and burn or destroy every Person in it."[41]

Despite such incidents, tensions began to cool as the occupation turned from months to years and became more routine. Nonetheless, the philosophical war waged on. Complaints about the standing army quartered among the inhabitants continued, but the clashes subsided.

The last part of 1774 through the first half of 1775 was characterized by systematic British attempts to disarm the Americans and the outbreak of the Revolutionary War. In September 1774, the Crown-appointed counsellors of Boston considered banning possession of arms by the people, leading to widespread protests:

It is said, it was proposed in the Divan last Wednesday, that the inhabitants of this Town should be disarmed, and that some of the new-fangled Counsellors consented thereto, but happily a majority was against it.—The report of this extraordinary measure having been put in Execution by the Soldiery was propagated through the Country, with some other exaggerated stories, and, by what we are told, if these Reports had not been contradicted, we should by this date have had 40 or 50,000 men from the Country (some of whom were on the march) appear'd for our Relief.[42]

After calling upon the inhabitants to arm themselves,[43] the Provincial Congress, presided over by John Hancock, protested to General (and Governor) Gage: "Have not invasions of private property by your Excellency been *repeatedly* made at Boston? . . . Have you not by removing the ammunition of the province, and by all other means in your power endeavoured to put it in a state utterly defenseless?"[44] Gage replied in a proclamation that "A Number of Persons unlawfully assembled . . . calling themselves a *Provincial Congress*, . . . did among other unlawful Proceedings, take it upon themselves to Resolve and direct a new and unconstitutional Regulation of the Militia."[45]

In response to the British seizure of several tons of gunpowder, "several Thousands . . . assembled at Cambridge, mostly in Arms, with a Design to go to Boston, where the Powder had been carried and stored, to demand the same, and, if necessary, to attack the Troops."[46] While this did not materialize, the British reportedly attempted to disarm militiamen in Boston. In one incident, "a party of the militia being at exercise on Boston common, a party of the army surrounded them and took away their fire arms; immediately thereupon a larger party of the militia assembled, pursued the Army, and retook their fire arms. Whereupon the Governor ordered the man of war to fire upon the Town, which was instantly obeyed; several houses were damaged, and only 6 people killed."[47] The date of this alleged event was not reported.

Meanwhile, a royal proclamation imposed an embargo on any arms and ammunition going to America. The same issue as the above reports noted "that some ships fitting out at Liverpool could not have permission to take on board any gun-powder, guns, or swords, . . . which . . . proves the fears of the ministry, respecting America, to be very great."[48] An American sympathizer in England asserted that "the proclamation against sending guns and gun powder out of this kingdom will be of very little use or effect, because the Americans will certainly procure whatever quantity of them they want from Holland, France, and Spain."[49] Despite reported arms seizures by customs officers, "the inhabitants of Boston, and of the province of Massachusetts Bay, are *now in arms.*"[50]

"A Watchman" recalled the lesson of the Carthaginians, who complied with the demand "that they must deliver up all their Arms to the Romans," only to be destroyed.[51] He continued:

Could they [the Ministry] not have given up their Plan for enslaving America without seizing . . . all the Arms and Ammunition? and without soliciting and finally obtaining an Order to prohibit the Importation of warlike Stores in the Colonies? . . . And shall we like the Carthaginians, peaceably surrender our Arms to our Enemies, in Hopes of obtaining in Return the Liberties we have so long been contending for? . . .

I . . . hope that no Person will, at this important Crisis, be unprepared to act in his own Defence, should he by Necessity be driven thereto. And I must here beg Leave to recommend to the Confederation of the People of this Continent, Whether, when we are by an arbitrary Decree prohibited *the having* Arms and Ammunition by Importation, we have not by the Law of Self Preservation, a Right to seize upon all those within our Power, in order to *defend the* LIBERTIES which GOD and Nature have given us?[52]

The year 1775 opened with a meeting of freeholders at Faneuil Hall chaired by Samuel Adams resolving that British oppression "roused the People to think of defending themselves and their Property by Arms, if nothing less could save them from Violence and Rapine."[53] Gage's denial that private property had been seized was refuted as follows: "The next assertion is, that no man's property has been seized or hurt, except the King's. We need not enumerate all the instances of property seized: It is enough to say that a Number of Cannon, the Property of a respectable Merchant in the Town, were seized and carried off by Force."[54]

"A Foreigner" replied that government was entitled to disarm citizens of cannon, and that the colonists were secretly preparing such armaments for insurrectionary purposes:

In support of this charge nothing is offered but general *intimations* of property being *violently* taken away from the owners; except that a number of cannon belonging to a respectable merchant, were seized and carried off *by force*. . . . Has not a government the same right to avail itself of the necessary means of defence against dangerous *internal* insurrections as against *foreign* invasions? . . . Again, who carried cannon off privately in a boat to a mill-pond, and when detected declared it to be nothing but a boat-load of *old iron?*[55]

A patriot conceded the Tory charge that "many of the people had for some time past been arming" by replying that "the people of this province have hitherto acted purely on the defensive."[56] The Tory's denial

that arms had been seized was about as credible as the patriot's claim
that the articles seized were not arms at all: "We are told, that it is
an undoubted act, that the supposed boxes of small arms, lead, & c.
which were lately seized by the custom-house officers at New York, and
caused so much disturbance there, *turns out* to be—What?—Why only
a few boxes of *Printing Types*! Aye, says a wag, and what was the Gun-
Powder?—Why truly, nothing but two cakes of Printing Ink!"[57]

Despite the fundamental rights to the use of arms and the press, the
patriots recognized that these objects could be misused. A pro-American
pamphlet published in London justified the Boston Tea Party with the
following analogy: "When a pawnbroker knowingly puts arms into the
hands of a highwayman or ruffian, does the law insure to him payment
for the same, at the hands of any one who, being assaulted, seized and
destroyed them? Are not all deadly weapons . . . made use of in violation
to the laws of civil society, for injuring any man in limb, life, or property,
a *lawful spoil* to the injured party?"[58]

Similarly, the Committees of Observation in Hartford County chaired
by William Wolcott rejected "any measure that may be construed in any
degree to infringe [the liberties] of the press. . . . "However, of the Tory
press which spreads malicious falsehoods: "A press thus conducted,
ceases to be a blessing to mankind, becomes highly the reverse, and is
not unlike firebrands, arrows and death, in the hands of a madman."[59]

Meanwhile, patriot writers boasted of the superiority of the inhabitants
in the use of firearms. Charles Lee wrote: "The yeomanry of America
besides infinite advantages over the peasantry of other countries, are
accustomed from their infancy to firearms; they are expert in the use of
them. Whereas the lower and middle people of England, are, by the
tyranny of certain laws, almost as ignorant in the use of a musket, as
they are of the ancient Catapulta."[60] Writing as "Novanglus," John Adams agreed, adding that firearms could be manufactured in or smuggled
into America:

We know that all those colonies have a back country which is inhabited by a
hardy, robust people . . . and habituated like multitudes of New-Englandmen,
to carry their fuzees or rifles upon one shoulder to defend themselves against
the indians. . . . But "have you arms and ammunition?" I answer we have; but
if we had not, we could make a sufficient quantity of both;—Who should hinder?
We have many manufacturers of fire-arms now, whose arms are as good as any
in the world. . . . But if we neither had them nor could make them, we could
import them.[61]

Alongside the above are quotations from James Burgh's *Political Dis-
quisitions* (1774), including the following favorite passage: "The confidence, which a standing *army* gives a minister, puts him upon carrying

things with a higher hand, than he would attempt to do, if the people were armed, and the court unarmed, that is, if there were no land-force in the nation, but a militia." Reciting many grievances, Burgh concluded, "there is no end to observations on the difference between the measures likely to be pursued by a minister backed by a standing *army*, and those of a court awed by the fear of an *armed people.*"[62]

The practical nature of the struggle was exemplified by the experience of Thomas Ditson, who was tarred and feathered by British soldiers. In his affidavit, Ditson claimed, "I enquired of some Townsmen who had any Guns to sell; one of whom I did not know, replied he had a very fine Gun to sell."[63] Since the one who offered the gun was a soldier, Ditson continued:

I asked him if he had any right to sell it, he reply'd he had, and that, the Gun was his to dispose of at any time; I then ask'd him whether he tho't the Sentry would not take it from me at the Ferry, as I had heard that some Persons had their Guns taken from them, but never tho't there was any law against trading with a Soldier; . . . I told him I would give four Dollars if there was no risque in carrying it over the Ferry; he said there was not. . . . I was afraid . . . that there was something not right . . . and left the Gun, and coming away he followed me and urg'd the Gun upon me.[64]

When he finally paid money to the soldier, several other soldiers appeared and seized Ditson, who they proceeded to tar and feather. However, instead of entrapment, the soldier swore in his affidavit, it was a case of a rebel trying to obtain arms and urging a soldier to desert. The citizen said "that he would buy more Firelocks of the Deponent, and as many as he could get any other Soldier to sell him."[65]

Meanwhile, one writer urged "the importance of having Cartridges properly made with a ball in each. I would therefore strongly recommend it to my countrymen immediately to be provided each man (able to bear arms) with at least twenty well made Cartridges."[66] He suggested that four rounds could be loaded and fired in one minute (an incredible speed for flintlock muskets) "in defence of our Rights and Liberties."[67]

The British were wise to the American game, and the following ammunition seizure reported from Boston also alleged that soldiers killed people along the road: "The Neck Guard seized 13,425 musket cartridges with ball, (we suppose through the information of some dirty scoundrel, of *which* we have now many among us) and about 300 lb. of ball, which we were carrying into the country—this was *private* property.—The owner applied to the General first, but he absolutely refused to deliver it."[68] Another patriot attacked the illegal basis of this seizure:

It is said that the troops, under your command, have seized a number of cartridges which were carrying out of the town of Boston, into the country; and as you were pleased to deny that you had meddled with private property, to the President of the Continental Congress, I would gladly be informed on what different pretence you now meddled with those cartridges. . . . I cannot conceive you will urge the late ridiculous proclamation [banning export of arms and ammunition to America] in defence of the action. That CREATURE, absurd and strained as it is, can have no reference to the carriage of powder and shot from any one inland place to another. But admitting it had, are Royal Proclamations again to be forced upon us for LAWS? I can, indeed, Sir, account for your conduct in this and many other instances, upon no other footing than that of an actual conspiracy to overthrow the laws and constitution of the country you are sworn to protect.[69]

The Revolutionary War was sparked when militiamen exercising at Lexington refused to give up their arms. The widely published American account of April 19, 1775, began with the order shouted by a British officer: " 'Disperse you Rebels—Damn you, throw down your Arms and disperse.' Upon which the Troops huzz'd, and immediately one or two Officers discharged their Pistols, which were instantaneously followed by the Firing of four or five of the Soldiers, then there seemed to be a general discharge from the whole Body."[70]

Three days after Lexington and Concord, Gage represented to the Selectmen of Boston that "there was a large body of men in arms" hostilely assembled, and that the inhabitants could be injured if the soldiers attacked.[71] The next day a town committee met with Gage, who promised "that upon the inhabitants in general lodging their arms in Faneuil Hall, or any other convenient place, under the care of the selectmen, marked with the names of the respective owners, that all such inhabitants as are inclined, may depart from the town. . . . And that the arms aforesaid at a suitable time would be return'd to the owners."[72]

The committee recommended "that the town accept of his excellency's proposal, and will lodge their arms with the selectmen accordingly."[73] "The town unanimously accepted of the foregoing report, and desired the inhabitants would deliver their arms to the Selectmen as soon as may be."[74]

In his contemporary account, Richard Frothingham noted: "On the 27th of April the people delivered to the selectmen 1778 fire-arms, 634 pistols, 973 bayonets, and 38 blunderbusses; and on the same day it was announced in a town-meeting, that General Gage had given permission to the inhabitants to remove out of town, with their effects, either by land or by water; and applications for passes were to be made to General Robertson."[75] Frothingham explained about the passes: "I have one of the original passes given by General Gage. It shows that everything but arms and ammunition was allowed to pass: _____Boston, April, 1775. Permit _____, together with _____ family, consisting of _____ persons, and ＿＿ effects, to pass ＿＿ between sunrise and sunset. By order of his Excellency the Governor. No arms nor ammunition is allowed to pass."[76]

The committee continued to meet with Gage through April 30, when it reported to the town: "The committee waited on his Excellency General Gage with the papers containing the account of the arms delivered to the selectmen, and the return made to them by the constables of the town relative to the delivery of the arms in their respective wards."[77] On the same date the Provincial Congress resolved:

Whereas, an agreement hath been made, between General Gage and the inhabitants of the town of Boston, for the removal of the persons and effects of the inhabitants of the town of Boston, as may be so disposed, excepting their fire-arms and ammunition, into the county.

Resolved, That any of the inhabitants of this colony, who may incline to go into the town of Boston with their effects, fire-arms and ammunition excepted, have tolleration for that purpose. . . .

P.S. Officers are appointed for the giving permits for the above purposes.[78]

An editorial described the background in more detail and told the predictable result. The Sunday after the battle at Lexington, a town meeting chose a committee of selectmen to meet with Gage. "The General convenanted with them—that if the inhabitants of Boston would give up their arms and ammunition, and not assist against the King's troops, they should immediately be permitted to depart with all their effects, merchandise included; finally, the inhabitants gave up their arms and ammunition—to the care of the Selectmen: the General then set a guard over the arms." Gage was then in a position to, and did, refuse the passage of both merchandise and people.[79] On announcing that no Bostonian could leave, "the same day a town meeting was to be held in Boston, when the inhabitants were determined to demand the arms they had deposited in the hands of the select men, or have liberty to leave town."[80]

An anonymous patriot addressed "the perfidious, the truce-breaking Thomas Gage" as follows:

But the single breach of the capitulation with them [the people of Boston], after they had religiously fulfilled their part, must brand your name and memory with eternal infamy—the proposal came from you to the inhabitants by the medium of one of your officers, through the Selectmen, and was, *that if the inhabitants would deposit their fire-arms in the hands of the Selectmen, to be returned to them after a reasonable time, you would give leave to the inhabitants to remove out of town with all their effects, without any lett or molestation.* The town punctually complied, and you remain an infamous monument of perfidy, for which an Arab, a Wild Tartar or Savage would dispise you!!![81]

On June 12, Gage proclaimed martial law and offered a pardon to all who would lay down their arms except Samuel Adams and John Hancock.[82] A patriot responded by asking, "are you not ashamed to throw out such an insult upon human understanding, as to bid people disarm themselves till you and your butchers murder and plunder them at pleasure! We well know you have orders to disarm us, and what the disposition of the framers of these orders is, if we may judge from the past, can be no secret."[83] A patriot in a more humorous mood offered a poem entitled "Tom Gage's Proclamation," which told how the general had sent an expedition "the men of *Concord* to disarm" and how he afterward reflected:

> Yet e'er I draw the vengeful sword
> I have thought fit to send abroad
> This present gracious Proclamation,
> Of purpose mild the demonstration;
> That whoseoe'er keeps gun or pistol,
> I'll spoil the motion of his systole;
> Or, whip his breech, or cut his weason
> As has the measure of his Treason:—
> But every one that will lay down
> His hanger bright, and musket brown,
> Shall not be beat, nor bruis'd, nor bang'd,
> Much less for past offences, hang'd,
> But on surrendering his toledo,
> Go to and fro unhurt as we do:—
> But then I must, out of this plan, lock
> Both SAMUEL ADAMS and JOHN HANCOCK;
> For those vile traitors (like debentures)
> Must be tuck'd up at all adventures;
> As any proffer of a pardon,
> Would only tend those rogues to harden:—
> But every other mother's son,
> The instant he destroys his gun,
> (For thus doth run the King's command)
> May, if he will, come kiss my hand. . . .
> Meanwhile let all, and every one
> Who loves his life, forsake his gun.[84]

Gage's seizures and attempts to seize the guns, pistols, Brown Bess muskets, and swords known as hangers and Toledos of the individual citizens of Boston who were not even involved in the hostilities sent a message to all of the colonies that the right to keep and bear private arms was in a perilous condition. The final break came when the Continental Congress adopted the Declaration of Causes of Taking Up Arms on July 6, 1775, which had been drafted by Thomas Jefferson and John

Dickinson and which complained: "It was stipulated that the said inhabitants having deposited their arms with their own magistrates, should have liberty to depart.... They accordingly delivered up their arms, but in open violation of honor, in defiance of the obligations of treaties, which even savage nations esteem sacred, the governor ordered the arms deposited as aforesaid, that they might be preserved for the owners, to be seized by a body of soldiers."[85]

Even though it mentioned only the disarming of Boston, by the time the Declaration passed the colonists believed that the Ministry's intention was to disarm all Americans. The Virginia House of Burgesses responded to Governor Dunmore's seizure of gunpowder in that state just after Lexington and Concord as follows:

The inhabitants of this country, my Lord, could not be strangers to the many attempts in the northern colonies to disarm the people, and thereby deprive them of the only means of defending their lives and property. We know, from good authority, that the like measures were generally recommended by the Ministry, and that the export of pow[d]er from Great Britain had been prohibited. Judge then how very alarming a removal of the small stock which remained in the public magazine, for the defence of the country, and the stripping of the guns of their locks, must have been to any people, who had the smallest regard for their security.[86]

Patriot newspapers throughout the colonies published a report from London that in fact all the colonists were to be disarmed: "It is reported, that on the landing of the General Officers, who have sailed for America, a proclamation will be published throughout the provinces inviting the Americans to deliver up their arms by a certain stipulated day; and that such of the colonists as are afterwards proved to carry arms shall be deemed rebels, and be punished accordingly."[87]

Understandably, this policy would be applied to patriots who actively resisted the British, but it was also applied to the inhabitants of whole towns and cities, which were either bombarded if arms were not surrendered, or occupied and then disarmed after a census was taken.[88] By 1777, confident of a British military victory, Colonial Undersecretary William Knox circulated to members of the Ministry a comprehensive policy entitled "What is Fit to be Done with America?" Besides a state church, unlimited tax power, a standing army, and a governing aristocracy, the plan anticipated: "The Militia Laws should be repealed and none suffered to be re-enacted, & the Arms of all the People should be taken away, ... nor should any Foundery or manufactuary of Arms, Gunpowder, or Warlike Stores, be ever suffered in America, nor should any Gunpowder, Lead, Arms or Ordnance be imported into it without Licence."[89]

Meanwhile, as war raged, in 1776 the colonies declared formal independence, and the individual states began to adopt constitutions and bills of rights. Perceived British plans and actual attempts to disarm the Americans would leave a definite imprint on the founding fathers of each state as they engaged in constitution making.

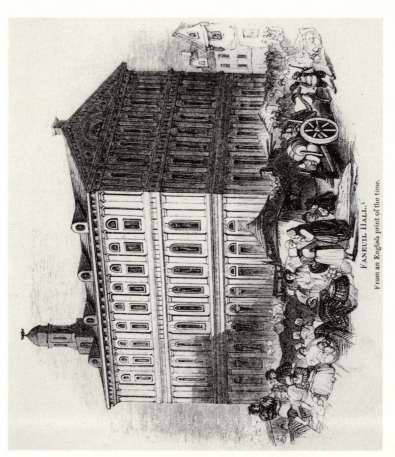

FANEUIL HALL.¹
From an English print of the time.

Faneuil Hall, where in 1768 Boston's freeholders resolved that the subjects "may have Arms for their defense." In 1775, the inhabitants turned in 1778 muskets, 634 pistols, 973 bayonets, and 38 blunderbusses to their selectmen here. The selectmen recorded the owners' names and firearm descriptions, but the guns were seized by Gage and never returned. (Courtesy: Massachusetts Historical Society, Boston)

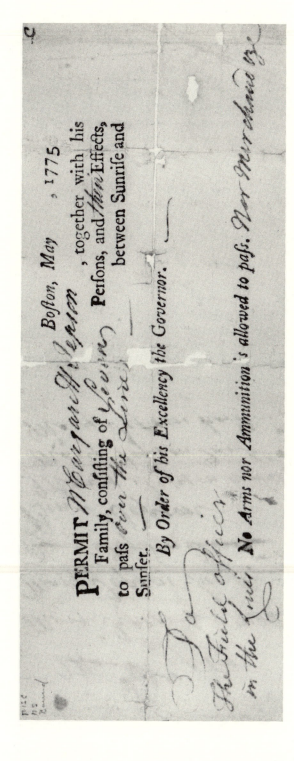

A family of seven managed to obtain this pass from General Gage to leave Boston, provided that "no arms nor ammunition is allowed to pass." Gage promised these passes to all citizens of Boston who surrendered their firearms for "temporary safekeeping." After Gage's troops seized the firearms, the General refused to issue passes as promised. (Courtesy: Massachusetts Historical Society, Boston)

CHAPTER 2

"The Right to Bear Arms" in the State Declarations of Rights

Like other perceived oppressions, the British attempts to disarm the inhabitants of Boston over the period 1768–1775 were widely reported and criticized in the newspapers of the other colonies. When independence was finally declared and the time came to adopt constitutions, eight of the new states adopted formal declarations of rights. Four of these states—Pennsylvania, North Carolina, Vermont, and Massachusetts—explicitly recognized a right to bear arms. The adoption of these declarations of rights and other manifestations of a right to bear arms in those four states are analyzed in this chapter.

PENNSYLVANIA

The Declaration of Rights of 1776

The constitutional convention of Pennsylvania, presided over by Benjamin Franklin, met from July 15 through September 28, 1776, a longer period than most state conventions.[1] The Virginia Declaration of Rights had been published in Philadelphia just over a month before the convention began.[2] From the beginning, a majority in the convention were Associators, members of armed associations.[3]

Initially, eleven persons were appointed to the declaration of rights committee.[4] The session on July 25 approved the Declaration of Independence, and appointed James Cannon and Colonel Timothy Matlack to the committee for bringing in an essay for a frame of government.[5]

Cannon and Matlock were elected to the convention by ultraradicals with the backing of the militia, which originated in extralegal associations of armed men.[6]

Cannon, a militia leader and the state's leading patriot writer next to Thomas Paine, was chief author of the Declaration of Rights, adopted some three weeks later.[7] Cannon was apparently assisted by Judge George Bryan and Colonel Matlack. A contemporary wrote that the Pennsylvania Constitution "was understood to have been principally the work of Mr. George Bryan, in conjunction with Mr. Canon, a schoolmaster."[8] John Adams wrote that the Pennsylvania "Bill of Rights is taken almost verbatim from that of Virginia, which was made and published two or three months before that of Philadelphia was begun. It was by Mr. Mason, as that of Pennsylvania was by Timothy Matlack, James Cannon and Thomas Young and Thomas Paine."[9]

George Bryan, later a Justice of the Pennsylvania Supreme Court, was the most influential member of the convention.[10] Professor James Cannon of the College of Philadelphia contributed most of the phraseology of the document.[11] Cannon, along with Dr. Thomas Young and Thomas Paine, were leaders of the radical Whig Society.[12] Dr. Young, a member of the Continental Congress, would later persuade the Vermont convention to adopt the Pennsylvania Declaration of Rights as a model.[13] Thomas Paine, whose *Common Sense* appeared in early 1776, was already influencing affairs in Pennsylvania and throughout the colonies.[14]

Judge Bryan sought "to identify himself with the people, in opposition to those, who were termed the *well born*."[15] Cannon had a "scholastic predilection for the antique in liberty."[16] Matlack, an Associator, when once asked by a Quaker why he wore a sword, replied: "That is to defend my property and my liberty."[17] It is not surprising that these individuals would frame the Declaration of Rights with the following provision: "That the people have a right to bear arms for the defense of themselves, and the state; and as standing armies in the time of peace, are dangerous to liberty, they ought not to be kept up; and that the military should be kept under strict subordination to, and governed by the civil power."[18]

Pennsylvania was the first state to adopt the explicit language that "the people have a right to bear arms," language which would reappear in the bills of rights of other states and the United States. The term "bear arms," even in the same sentence as a rejection of standing armies, was not limited to the militia. While the declaration of a right to bear arms to defend the state against the established royal government was more radical, the framers did not overlook the less disputed right to bear arms for self-defense.

The declaration of a right to bear arms to defend self and state appears not to have been disputed in the convention or in the press. While some parts of the declaration were highly controversial, no objections were voiced in the newspapers from the time the declaration was first published.[19] Freedom of religion in particular was not deemed as fundamental as other rights. When Benjamin Franklin revised the Declaration of Rights, he suggested no change in the right to bear arms clause, yet unsuccessfully opposed the profession of faith required for assemblymen.[20] Newspaper attacks on the religious guarantees and certain other matters were extreme and persistent, but bearing arms was not questioned.[21]

One writer saw the Declaration of Rights as "equal to any thing of the kind now extant in the various governments that we know in the world."[22] "The Magna Carta or the Great Charter of Britain, and the Bill of Rights exhibited at the Revolution, are not touched, nor allowed to be touched, by their Parliaments, and we at this time blame them, and bear arms against them, because they have deprived us, and still attempt to deprive us, of the privileges of that Constitution."[23] "Casa" wrote "To the Freemen of Pennsylvania": "The Bill of Rights should always include the natural rights of every freeman, and the essential principals of free government. . . . This bill should be UNALTERABLE. The least violation of any part of it, whether by legislature—the courts of law—or the people, should always be punished as high treason against the state."[24]

The article in the Constitution on the militia met with some sarcasm. It provided in part: "The freemen of this commonwealth and their sons shall be trained and armed for its defense, under such regulations, restrictions and exceptions as the general assembly shall by law direct."[25] A satire on the Constitution stated: "In section the *fifth*—the freemen shall be *trained and armed* for their defense, and the militia shall elect their officers, & c. Oh, how I am transported at the velocity of the mental operations of these geniuses! They ought not to be compared to any thing but *leaden* bullets flying from the muzzles of rifles, hot, heavy, rapid, and yet twisting to their marks."[26]

Another section of the Constitution provided: "The inhabitants of this state shall have liberty to fowl and hunt in seasonable times on the lands they hold, and on all other lands not inclosed."[27] This provision was criticized in the most comprehensive attacks on the new constitution, adopted by an assembly of dissidents, which devoted most of its attention to issues such as "the Christian religion is not treated with proper respect."[28] A minor objection was "that several regulations improper to be taken notice of therein, are mentioned in the said Constitution. . . . Fishing, fowling, and hunting."[29]

Much more was at stake than the right to hunt, "Remarks on the

Resolves" replied. Under English law, game belongs to the King, who grants rights to lords of manors. From this privilege stemmed deprivation of the right to keep and carry guns:

In order to prevent poachers, as they are called, from invading this aristocratical prerogative, the possession of *hunting dogs, snares, nets*, and *other* engines by unprivileged persons, has been forbidden, and, under pretence of the last words, *guns* have been seized. And though this was not legal, as guns are not engines appropriated to kill game, yet if a witness can be found to attest before a Justice that a gun has been thus used, the penalty is five pounds, or three months imprisonment fall on the accused.

. . . Thus penal laws, and trials without juries, are multiplied on a trivial subject, and the freeholders of moderate estates deprived of a natural right. Nor is this all; the body of the people kept from the use of guns are utterly ignorant of the arms of modern war, and the kingdom effectually disarmed, except of the standing force. . . . Is any thing like this desired in Pennsylvania?[30]

While modeled on the Virginia Declaration of Rights, the Pennsylvania Declaration made significant improvements. The rights of assembly and petition, and an unprecedented recognition of religious liberty, were included only in the latter.[31] Although Virginia recognized the right of "the Body of the People, [to be] trained to Arms,"[32] Pennsylvania more explicitly provided "that the people have a right to bear arms for the defense of themselves, and the state."[33] As the chief authority on the first Pennsylvania constitution concludes, "the *Declaration of Rights* was the true expression of the ideals of the American Colonists, and the guarantees contained therein were the product of long and severe experience."[34]

Thomas Paine's Influence

John Adams' assertion that Thomas Paine participated in making the Pennsylvania Declaration of Rights[35] was not literally correct in that Paine was not in Philadelphia when the convention met. However, Paine's ideas were influential, and his comments on the Declaration after its adoption further clarify the sentiments of the time, particularly on the meaning of the right to bear arms.

Gun seizures under English game laws which imposed property qualifications were lambasted by Paine in 1775 in a poem written for *Pennsylvania Magazine*. Based on a true story about three judges who hung a farmer's dog, the poem included the following:

> Each knew by instinct when and where
> A farmer caught or killed a hare;
> Could tell if any man had got

One hundred pounds per ann. or not;
Or what was greater could divine
If it was only ninety-nine.
For when the hundred wanted one,
They took away the owner's gun.[36]

When *Common Sense* was published in Philadelphia in early 1776, "taking up arms"[37] was pictured by Paine as both necessary and realistic: "Our small arms [are] equal to any in the world. . . . Saltpeter and gunpowder we are every day producing."[38] The pro-Tory position taken by some Quakers was based on a double standard, "As if all sin was reduced to, and comprehended in, *the act of bearing arms,* and that by the *people only.*" Not condemning the invading soldiers was illogical, *"for they likewise bear* ARMS."[39]

In July 1776, the same month the Pennsylvania constitutional convention began its deliberations, Paine wrote in the *Pennsylvania Magazine:*

The supposed quietude of a good man allures the ruffian; while on the other hand, arms like laws discourage and keep the invader and the plunderer in awe, and preserve order in the world as well as property. The balance of power is the scale of peace. The same balance would be preserved were all the world destitute of arms, for all would be alike; but since some *will not*, others *dare not* lay them aside. . . . Horrid mischief would ensue were one half the world deprived of the use of them; . . . the weak will become a prey to the strong.[40]

In the *American Crisis* (1777), Paine took notice of General Gage's letter "in which he informs his masters, 'That though their idea of his disarming certain counties was a right one, yet it required him to be master of the country, in order to enable him to execute it.' "[41] Even if the American soldiers all went home, Paine addressed British commander-in-chief Howe, "You would be afraid to send your troops in parties over the continent, either to disarm or prevent us from assembling, least they should not return."[42] Conquest of the armed populace was impossible.

Paine held that "a Bill of Rights should be a plain positive declaration of the rights *themselves* . . . it should *retain much natural rights* as are either consistent with, or absolutely necessary toward our happiness in a state of civil government."[43] In later years he wrote:

By this mutual compact, the citizens of a republic put it out of their power, that is, they renounce, as detestable, the power of exercising, at any future time any species of despotism over each other. . . .

This pledge and compact is contained in the declaration of rights prefixed to the constitution (of Pennsylvania), and is as follows [Here Paine quotes the Declaration in full, including]:

XIII. That the people have a right to bear arms in the defense of themselves and the state.[44]

The Lack of Legislative Infringement

The same provincial conference which called for the constitutional convention which adopted the Declaration of Rights, also resolved that a militia be raised, and "that each Private procure his own Musket or Rifle."[45] Similarly, the first General Assembly to meet after adoption of the Constitution declared that it is the duty of all freemen to be at all times prepared to resist the enemy.[46] Another militia act stated: "A well regulated militia is the only safe and constitutional method of defending a free state, as the necessity of keeping up a standing army, especially in times of peace, is thereby superceded."[47]

The Pennsylvania Constitution established a Council of Censors to meet every seven years to determine whether the Constitution had been preserved inviolate. The Council's report for 1784 found several violations of the Bill of Rights, including unjust seizures of property, illegal searches, and lack of jury trial.[48] No violation of the right to bear arms was suggested, and very little legislation existed on the subject of firearms.

Legislation that predated the Revolution imposed a fine on "any person or persons, of what sex, age, degree, or quality soever, [who] shall fire any gun or other fire arms . . . within the city of Philadelphia."[49] Any person who "wantonly, and without reasonable occasion, discharge and fire off any hand-gun, pistol or other firearms" in inhabited areas on New Years' night was subject to fine.[50] A hunting regulation punished any person who "shall presume to carry any gun, or hunt" on the land of others without permission, or who "shall presume to fire a gun on or near any of the king's highways."[51]

In 1779, the General Assembly passed a disarming act aimed at Tories. It declared that "it is very improper and dangerous that persons disaffected to the liberty and independence of this state should possess or have in their own keeping, or elsewhere, any fire arms."[52] The act empowered militia lieutenants:

to disarm any person or persons who shall not have taken any oath or affirmation of allegiance to this or any other state, and against whom information on oath shall be given before any justice of the peace, that such person is suspected to be disaffected to the independence of this state; and shall take from every such person any cannon, mortar, or other piece of ordnance, or any blunderbuss, wall piece, musket, fusee, carbine, or pistols or any other firearms, or any hand gun . . . out of any building, house or place belonging to such persons.[53]

Aside from anti-Tory legislation, no legislation was passed in Pennsylvania from the time of the Revolution for decades afterward which even remotely infringed on the right to bear arms.[54]

The Declaration of Rights of 1790

The Pennsylvania Declaration of Rights of 1790 was a result of the constitutional convention which met from November 24, 1789, through September 2, 1790. That convention unanimously resolved that the Declaration of 1776 "requires alterations and amendments, in such manner as the rights of the people, reserved and excepted out of the general powers of government, may be more accurately defined and secured."[55] A committee of nine was elected to draft proposed changes.[56]

A number of the delegates had participated in the convention which ratified the U.S. Constitution in 1787. Leading characters[57] included James Wilson, who in support of the federal constitution had argued that "however wide and various the firearms of power may appear, they may all be traced to one source, the people."[58] Also included were John Smilie and William Findley, both signers of the Dissent of Minority, which urged adoption of a federal bill of rights, including an amendment "that the people have a right to bear arms for the defense of themselves and their own state, or the United States, or for the purpose of killing game; and no law shall be passed for disarming the people or any of them."[59]

The delegates in the Pennsylvania convention of 1789–1790 were acutely aware of the progress of the proposed federal bill of rights, which Pennsylvania would not ratify until March 10, 1790. The delegates would consider a provision similar to what became the federal Second Amendment as originally drafted by James Madison: "The right of the people to keep and bear arms shall not be infringed; . . . but no person religiously scrupulous of bearing arms shall be compelled to render military service in person."[60]

In its first report, the committee charged with recommending amendments submitted the following:

XIX. That the right of the citizens to bear arms in defense of themselves and the state, and to assemble peaceably together, and apply in a decent manner, to those invested with the powers of government, for redress of grievances or other proper purposes, shall not be questioned.

XX. That those who conscientiously scruple to bear arms shall not be compelled to do so, but shall pay an equivalent for personal service.[61]

This proposal was widely published throughout the country, including in states which had not yet ratified the federal bill of rights.[62] It is interesting that this language, which combined the rights to bear arms and to assemble in the same article, was being considered at the same time as that of the Second Amendment, with its combination of a militia clause and the right to bear arms. Moreover, the rights to assemble and to bear arms were logically connected in the minds of patriots who had assembled in arms before and during the Revolution.

Further committee action separated the assembly and arms clauses. Minutes of the committee of the whole reflect the following:

The twentieth section of the said bill of rights being under consideration, it was moved by Mr. Pickering, seconded by Mr. McKean, to amend the same so as to read as follows, viz.

That the right of the citizens to bear arms in defense of themselves and the state shall not be questioned; but those who conscientiously scruple to bear arms shall not be compellable to do so, but shall pay an equivalent for personal service. Which was carried in the affirmative, and the said section, as amended, adopted.[63]

Timothy Pickering and Chief Justice Thomas McKean,[64] both of whom had served in Pennsylvania's ratification convention, followed Madison's example by combining a right-to-bear-arms guarantee with a conscientious objector exception. While the conscientious objector clause was deleted from what became the Second Amendment, the fact that it was considered there did not imply that the right to bear arms belonged only to militias. The same kind of clause was also considered in the Pennsylvania convention as a qualification of the right to bear arms "in defense of *themselves* and the state."

In addition to the arms guarantee, the committee of the whole agreed to a provision that "the freemen of this commonwealth shall be armed and disciplined for its defense."[65] The convention rejected a proposal to change "shall" to "may,"[66] apparently because the right to bear arms was already provided for elsewhere.

Meanwhile, unsuccessful attempts were made to alter the conscientious objector clause.[67] A memorial from the Quakers protested that the "article materially affects our religious liberties, which proposes that those who conscientiously scruple to bear arms shall pay an equivalent for personal service; such an equivalent it is well known we cannot, consistent with our principles, voluntarily pay."[68] The convention refused to reconsider.[69]

In the final version, the troublesome clause was moved to a more logical place. The Declaration of Rights provision simply stated: "That the right of the citizens to bear arms in defense of themselves and the state shall not be questioned."[70] The militia clause in the body of the Constitution read: "The freemen of this commonwealth shall be armed and disciplined for its defense: Those who conscientiously scruple to bear arms, shall not be compelled to do so, but shall pay an equivalent for personal service."[71]

NORTH CAROLINA

"The Right of Every English Subject to Be Prepared with Weapons for His Defense"

In 1771, a young lawyer named James Iredell wrote a letter to his mother which included the following lines:

Be not afraid of the Pistols you have sent me. They may be necessary Implements of self Defense, tho' I dare say I shall never have Occasion to use them. . . . It is a Satisfaction to have the means of Security at hand if we are in no danger, as I never expect to be. Confide in my prudence and self regard for a proper use of them, and you need have no Apprehension.[72]

James Iredell would go on to become a Justice of the U.S. Supreme Court. In the years between the time of the above letter and when he became Justice Iredell, he played prominent roles in the constitutional development of both North Carolina and the United States. Iredell's letter captures the sentiments of his generation about a right which went unquestioned.

To be sure, royalists would become increasingly fearful of what they described as the "inhabitants in arms" who protested the stamp tax.[73] In 1774, North Carolina's future first governor Richard Caswell urged upon his neighbors that "it is indispensably necessary for them to arm and form into a company or companies of independents."[74] Willie Jones, the distinguished radical leader, led the Halifax Committee of Safety, which provided arms to the people.[75] Caswell and Jones were to play leading roles in North Carolina constitutional development.

Lexington sparked the seizure of public arms and arms smuggling by the colonists. Colonial Governor Martin proclaimed against those "endeavouring to engage the People to subscribe papers obliging themselves to be prepared with Arms, to array themselves in companies, and to submit to the illegal and usurped authorities of Committees."[76] "The Inhabitants of this County on the Sea Coast," he wrote in mid–1775, "are . . . arming men, electing officers and so forth. In this little town [Newburn] they are now actually endeavouring to form what they call independent Companies under my nose."[77]

In a widely published message to the committees of safety, Richard Caswell, William Hooper, and Joseph Hewes, North Carolina's members of the Continental Congress, stated:

It is the Right of every *English* Subject to be prepared with Weapons for his Defense. We conjure you . . . to form yourselves into a Militia. . . .
Carefully preserve the small quantity of Gunpowder which you have amongst

you, it will be the last Resource when every other Means of Safety fails you; Great-Britain has cut you off from further supplies. . . .

We cannot conclude without urging again to you the necessity of arming and instructing yourselves, to be in Readiness to defend yourselves against any Violence that may be exerted against your Persons and Properties.[78]

The above address provoked Governor Martin to issue his "Fiery Proclamation," which deplored the message by Hooper, Hewes, and Caswell, "the preposterous enormity of which cannot be adequately described and abhor'd. . . . [I]t proceeds upon these false and infamous assertions and forgeries to excite the people of North Carolina to usurp the prerogative of the Crown by forming a Militia and appointing officers thereto and finally to take up arms against the King and His Government."[79]

Governor Martin warned that all "persons who hath or have presumed to array the Militia and to assemble men in Arms within this Province without my Commission or Authority have invaded His Majesty's just and Royal Prerogative and violated the Laws of their Country to which they will be answerable for the same."[80]

The governor's threats failed to deter the North Carolinians. Beginning with their individual right to have weapons for defense, they asserted a right to associate in militia companies independent of the government and to use those arms against despotism. A typical committee of safety resolution of the time referred to "the painful necessity of having recourse to Arms for the preservation of those rights and Liberties which the principles of our Constitution and the Laws of God, Nature, and Nations have made it our duty to defend."[81]

Toward the end of 1775, Joseph Hewes wrote from Philadelphia that arms and ammunition "are very scarce throughout all the Colonies, I find on enquiry that neither can be got here, all the Gunsmiths in the Province are engaged and cannot make Arms near so fast as they are wanted."[82] Hewes reported that "I have furnished myself with a good musket and Bayonet."[83] Yet arms remained scarce, due to the British embargo. "Americans ought to become industrious in making those articles at home, every Family should make saltpetre, every Province have powder Mills and every colony encourage the making of Arms."[84]

The right of the English subject to have weapons would become a duty in 1776. The Provincial Congress of North Carolina resolved "that each Militia Soldier shall be furnished with a good Gun, Bayonet, Cartouch Box, Shot Bay and Powder Horn, a Cutlass or Tomahawk; and where any person shall appear to the Field Officers not possessed of sufficient Property to afford such Arms and Accoutrements, the same shall be provided at Public Expense."[85]

The Declaration of Rights of 1776

The delegates at the North Carolina constitutional convention which met in November and December, 1776, had been instructed by their constituents to adopt a declaration of rights. The inhabitants of Mecklenburg directed "that you shall endeavor that the form of Government shall set forth a bill of rights containing the rights of the people and of individuals which shall never be infringed in any future time by the law-making power or other derived powers in the State."[86] The delegates were urged to acknowledge certain maxims, including that "the principal supreme power is possessed by the people at large, the derived and inferior power by the servants which they employ."[87]

The North Carolina convention had two guides for a declaration of rights. Virginia rested a free state on "the body of the people, trained to arms,"[88] while Pennsylvania declared "that the people have a right to bear arms for the defense of themselves, and the state."[89] The committee appointed to frame a bill of rights and constitution included convention President Richard Caswell and Joseph Hewes,[90] both of whom had asserted "the Right of every *English* Subject to be prepared with Weapons for his Defense."[91]

The committee reported the Bill of Rights a month later. It was debated, paragraph by paragraph, for three days, and then adopted.[92] Willie Jones appears to have been its draftsman, and Richard Caswell its inspiration. In the constitutional convention of 1835, one delegate relied on the tradition that Caswell "dictated the principles, if not the terms" of the Constitution.[93] Another delegate averred: "The existing Constitution is thought to have been as much or more the work (the 32d section [a religious test oath] excepted) of WILLIE JONES, than any other one individual, yet under that very charter was he [as a deist] proscribed by the bigotry of the framer of the 32d section. Shall a clause be retained in our Constitution which would exclude from office a JONES, the Champion of the Whigs in the Convention of 1776, that formed our State Constitution?"[94]

Little debate appears to have been raised by proposals to declare such rights as bearing arms and free assembly. But the above reference to bigotry exemplifies the lack of agreement over whether the free exercise of religion was a fundamental right. The convention would adopt a guarantee of religious freedom. The watering down of this guarantee in Article 32 was described by convention delegate Samuel Johnston as follows: "Unfortunately one of the Members from the back Country introduced a Test by which every person before he should be asked to share in the Legislature should swear that he believed in the holy Trinity and that the Scripture of the Old Testament was written by divine inspiration. This was carried after a very warm debate and has blown up such a flame that every thing is in danger of being thrown into confusion."[95]

The above version was changed in the final document, which retained at Article 32 a sectarian test for office holding. Its purpose was to exclude Catholics, Jews, and atheists from public office.

As adopted, the Declaration of Rights asserted the following interconnected propositions:

I. That all political power is vested in, and derived from, the People only.

XVII. That the People have a Right to bear Arms for the Defense of the State; and as standing Armies in Time of Peace are dangerous to Liberty, they ought not to be kept up. . . .

XVIII. That the People have a Right to assemble together.[96]

Having assembled in arms against the royal army since the days of the Regulators, these propositions were unquestionable to North Carolinians now engaged in armed revolt. "The right of every *English* Subject to be prepared with Weapons for this Defense" was thus expanded to include explicit recognition of arms bearing "for the Defense of the State" and against the royal government, a more radical proposition. The framers intended to guarantee individual rights when they used the term "the People," as in the right to bear arms and assembly provisions respectively. The militia is not mentioned, and when a collective right was intended, it was explicitly declared: "The Property of the Soil in a free Government being one of the essential Rights of the collective Body of the People, it is necessary . . . that the Limits of the State should be ascertained with Precision."[97]

An Attribute of Free Citizenship

The statutes in force in North Carolina during the last quarter of the eighteenth century reflect the recognition of the right to have arms. An enactment of 1787 declared "that all Freemen and indentured Servants within this State, from 15 to 50 years of age, shall compose the militia thereof."[98] Privates furnished their own muskets and rifles, while horsemen had pistols.[99] No man could go or ride armed to the terror of the people,[100] but each was required to pursue felons and follow the hue and cry.[101]

A statute passed during the royalist period imposed a property qualification for hunting deer, violation of which included forfeiture of the gun.[102] After independence, game legislation included only deer seasons and prohibition of hunting in the woods with a gun at night by fire light.[103] For the first half century after independence, there were no laws at all which prohibited possession of guns and pistols by freemen in North Carolina.[104]

Disarming laws were, however, aimed at slaves. A mid-eighteenth-century enactment provided that "no slave shall go armed with Gun, Sword, Club, or other Weapon," unless he had a certificate to carry a gun to hunt, issued on the owner's permission.[105] Another act required the master to post bond for a certificate "allowing any Slave to carry a Gun and hunt in the Woods."[106] The justice of the peace was to appoint a "Searcher for Guns, Swords, and other Weapons" among slaves.[107]

Thus, under the Constitution and laws of North Carolina, the right to keep and carry arms went unquestioned. The only exception related to slaves, and even some of them were allowed guns for hunting. Having arms was manifestly an attribute of free citizenship.

The idea of the armed citizen expanded westward with the settlers. In 1786, people in the western part of North Carolina, an area to become Tennessee, declared themselves independent. Calling their state "Franklin," these pioneers adopted a Declaration of Rights modeled on that of North Carolina, including the provision "that the People have a Right to bear Arms for the Defense of the State."[108] The people of Franklin complained of many injustices committed by the state of North Carolina, but did not allege violations of the bill of rights.

Willie Jones, the draftsman of North Carolina's Declaration of Rights of 1776, would lead the antifederalist majority in the North Carolina ratifying convention of 1788 to demand a bill of rights to the proposed federal Constitution.[109] A chief objection to the Constitution in that state was exemplified in a federalist's account of a sermon which mentioned the proposed federal capitol: " 'This, my friends,' said the preacher, 'will be walled in or fortified. Here an army of 50,000, or perhaps 100,000, will be finally embodied, and will sally forth and enslave the people, who will be gradually disarmed.' This absurd assumption set our blood in fermentation strongly excited already in party feeling."[110]

This scenario repeated itself in the ratifying convention, where delegates quarrelled over the need of a bill of rights. James Iredell, the federalist leader who earlier had expressed a fondness for pistols, urged:

A bill of rights, as I conceive, would not only be incongruous, but dangerous. No man, let his ingenuity be what it will, could enumerate all the individual rights not relinquished by this Constitution. Suppose, therefore, an enumeration of a great many, but an omission of some, and that, long after all traces of our present disputes were at an end, any of the omitted rights should be invaded, and the invasion be complained of; what would be the plausible answer of the government to such a complaint? Would they not naturally say, " . . . So long as the rights enumerated in the bill of rights remain unviolated, you have no reason to complain. This is not one of them."[111]

An armed populace, not a paper bill of rights, would prevent the invasion of rights by government, Iredell argued: "The only resource against usurpation is the inherent right of the people to prevent its exercise. . . . The people will resist if the government usurp powers not delegated to it."[112]

Willie Jones then rose with a resolution in his hand "stipulating for certain amendments to be made previous to the adoption by this state."[113] Jones persuasively argued that the Constitution should not be adopted until a bill of rights was certain.[114] Over objections by federalists, the convention passed a Declaration of Rights which included: "That the people have a right to keep and bear arms; that well regulated militia, composed of the body of the people, trained to arms, is the proper, natural, and safe defense of a free state."[115]

The above propositions declared the individual right to have arms, and the protection of freedom through a popular militia. The state right to maintain a militia was the subject of a separate proposed amendment: "That each state respectively shall have the power to provide for organizing, arming, and disciplining its own militia, whensoever Congress shall omit or neglect to provide for the same."[116]

North Carolina did not adopt the federal Constitution until the adoption of a bill of rights appeared imminent.[117] In both its state constitution and the federal Constitution, North Carolina insisted on explicit recognition of the right of the people to bear arms.

VERMONT

Pistols for Their Defense: The Green Mountain Boys

Keeping and bearing arms was not only an abstract right, but also a constant practice of Vermont's founding fathers. Led by Ethan and Ira Allen, the Green Mountain Boys sought independence first from New York and later from Great Britain. In his detailed accounts of their exploits, Ira Allen vividly exposited the role of firearms in the hands of the people for purposes of defending the person and the incipient state.

Ira Allen chronicled a series of incidents initiated in 1772 when New York Governor Tryon, assisted by British troops, sought to dispossess Vermont's settlers of their lands. In one of the first confrontations, Ira Allen and two friends were accosted by a group of Yorkers with Indian allies. "Capt. Baker had a cutlass, I. Vanornam a gun and I a case of pistols. These were all the arms we had; nevertheless, we determined to defend the ground." The Green Mountain Boys were able to force the surrender of the larger group. Allen told the captured leader that he would have shot him if necessary to prevent "being a prisoner and tryed by the Supreme Court of New York by the acts of outlawry & c."

Allen then demonstrated his marksmanship by shooting a small mark some distance away.[118]

Firearms were regularly carried for hunting game, survival, and self-defense. On a typical outing, Allen recalled that "I took six days provisions in my pack, a small pocket pistol, little horn of powder, and a hatchet of a small size."[119] The Allens sought to survey, purchase, and develop wilderness land, which conflicted with the plans of New York's governor and land jobbers. Before setting out to purchase land near the New York border, "Col. Ethan Allen, Capt. Remember Baker and myself armed with holsters and pistols, a good case of pistols each in our pockets, with each a good hanger [sword]."[120] Lodging with a Quaker during that journey, Ira Allen recalled: "We took our pistols out of our holsters and carried them in with us. He looked at the pistols saying 'What doth thee do with those things?' He was answered 'Nothing amongst our friends,' but we were Green Mountain Boys, and meant to protect our persons and property, and that of our friends on the New Hampshire Grants against the unjust claims of the land jobbers & c. of New York."[121]

In early 1774, Col. Ethan Allen and Lt. Ira Allen learned of a Yorker plot to capture them, take them to the Poughkeepsie jail, and collect the reward. "The Colonel and Lieutenant armed, however for their defense, but they were not disturbed."[122] New York then passed an act, described by Ira Allen as "the most mandatory and despotic of anything which ever appeared in the British colonies," sentencing Green Mountain Boys who refused to surrender to death.[123] In response, Vermont town committees resolved that "our inhabitants hold themselves in readiness, at a minute's warning, to aid and defend such friends of ours, who, for their merit and attachment to the great and general cause, are falsely denominated rioters."[124]

While the Vermonters' friction with New York escalated, a broader conflict broke out when the armed colonists fought British troops at Lexington and Concord in April 1775. Ethan Allen promptly led the Green Mountain Boys to capture Fort Ticondaroga. Ira Allen described this feat of armed citizens as follows:

Thus, in a few days, at the commencement of hostilities between the British and the Americans, two hundred undisciplined men, with small arms, without a single bayonet, made themselves masters of the garrisons of Ticondaroga, Crown Point, and St. Johns . . . *to the honour of the Green Mountain Boys.* It is to be remembered, that this was the first offensive part taken against Great Britain in the American revolution.[125]

The Declaration of Rights of 1777

As had been the practice for years, throughout 1776 conventions and committees met in Vermont to plan resistance to the British and to secure land titles against New York claims. Petitioning the Continental Congress, Vermonters argued that they had the same right of independence from New York as America had from Britain.[126]

At a convention in September 1776, Ira Allen and six others formed a committee which reported rudimentary objectives for Vermont, including the following: "To regulate the Militia; To furnish troops according to our ability, for the defence of the Liberties of the United States of America."[127] The convention resolved "that each non-commissioned officer and soldier immediately furnish himself with a good gun with a Bayonet, sword or tomahawk."[128] As his biographer stated, at this and other conventions Ira Allen and his friends "were assigned to all important committees and generally constituted a majority. No paper was drawn that Ira Allen did not have opportunity to review. Indeed for ten years few if any state papers of Vermont were issued that he did not prepare or assist in preparing."[129]

In January 1777, representatives of the towns decided that Vermont should be a free and independent state. The convention declared that the rights of all Vermont inhabitants "shall be considered to be such privileges and immunities to the free citizens and denizens, as are, or, at any time hereafter, may be allowed, to any such inhabitants of any of the free and independent states of America: And that such privileges and immunities shall be regulated in a bill of rights, and by a form of government, to be established at the next adjourned session of this convention."[130]

The constitutional convention which met July 2–8, 1777, had several models to choose from, but was predisposed toward that of Pennsylvania.[131] For several months, the address "To the Inhabitants of Vermont" by Dr. Thomas Young of Philadelphia had circulated, urging the Pennsylvania Constitution "as a model, which, with a very little alteration, will, in my opinion, come as near perfection as anything yet concocted by mankind."[132] A friend of Ethan Allen, Young had influenced the Pennsylvania Declaration of Rights.[133]

Among the provisions included in the Declaration of Rights adopted by the Vermont convention taken verbatim from that of Pennsylvania was the following: "That the people have a right to bear arms for the defence of themselves and the State; and, as standing armies, in the time of peace, are dangerous to liberty, they ought not to be kept up."[134] Vermont also copied Pennsylvania in declaring "that the inhabitants of this State, shall have liberty to hunt and fowl, in seasonable times, on the lands they hold, and on other lands (not enclosed)."[135]

Although no convention journals were preserved, the above language clarifies the fundamental character of the right to carry arms to Vermont's founding fathers. To "bear arms" meant to possess guns, pistols, and swords for defense of self and state or for hunting. Indeed, the framers of this provision carried a gun and a brace of pistols on their persons as a common practice. Recognition of bearing arms to defend the state was more radical than self-defense, since it justified action by armed private citizens to defend an incipient state from the constituted authorities of both New York and Great Britain.

Vermont's first constitution was framed in just six days, but it was not finally ratified until the convention reconvened on Christmas Eve of 1777. Ira Allen traveled over a hundred miles through winter snows to attend, and then retraced his steps after the convention appointed him to have the Constitution printed and distributed so that elections could be held.[136]

Vermont adopted new constitutions twice more in the next two decades, but the right-to-arms provision remained unaltered. The usage of the term "bear arms" as an individual right for defense of self and state remained the same in the constitution of 1787,[137] which became binding just before the federal constitutional convention met, and the constitution of 1796.[138]

Vermont reenacted right-to-bear-arms provisions both before and after the proposal and ratification of the federal Second Amendment. Further, Vermont was admitted by Congress into the Union on February 18, 1791, and thereby ratified the federal Bill of Rights before Virginia's ratification at that year's end made it binding. Vermonters probably understood the Second Amendment to protect bearing arms, as the state Declaration specified, "for the defence of themselves and the State."

Houses into Arsenals: The Voyage of the Olive Branch

As in Pennsylvania, in Vermont the Council of Censors which met periodically to determine whether violations of the Constitution had occurred made no mention of infringement on the right to bear arms.[139] The only law on the books passed in the years 1779–1786 concerning firearms mandated rather than restricted arms. An act "Regulating the Militia" required that all males aged sixteen to fifty "shall bear arms, and duly attend all musters," and that "every listed soldier and other householder, shall always be provided with, and have in constant readiness, a well fixed firelock . . . or other good fire-arms."[140] Another act reiterated that every male shall "provide himself, at his own expense, with a good musket or firelock,"[141] and that horsemen "shall always be provided with . . . holsters with bear-skin caps, a case of good pistols, a sword or cutlass."[142]

The understanding in Vermont of the right to keep and bear arms may be gleaned from the founders' personal accounts, the Declaration of Rights provision, and the militia laws. Unfortunately, the boundary disputes with New York and the state's claim to legitimacy dominate

Vermont's political literature from the 1770s through the next two decades. Commentaries on such matters as the Declaration of Rights are virtually nonexistent, partly because the rights enumerated were taken for granted. Fortunately, Ira Allen, early Vermont's most prolific political writer, was involved in and recorded a series of events at the end of the century which further exemplify the perceived nature of the personal right to bear arms.

In 1796, as a Major General of the Vermont militia, Ira Allen traveled to Europe to acquire arms. In Paris, he contracted with the French Directory to purchase 20,000 muskets and 24 fieldpieces. En route to New York, the vessel known as the *Olive Branch* laden with the arms was seized and claimed by a British ship of war as a lawful prize. France and England being at war, Allen was accused in the Court of Admiralty of seeking to foment a Jacobin revolt against the British in Canada.[143]

Allen published numerous documents from the *Olive Branch* litigation which exposed the nature of the right to distribute, acquire, and possess arms in America. Allen declared that his purpose had been "to purchase arms in Europe for the use of the Vermont Militia, as a sufficient number of muskets for that purpose could not be procured in the United States. By the laws of Vermont, every male, from the age of sixteen to forty-five, is obliged to bear arms at their own expense."[144]

The prosecutor accused Allen of acquiring far more arms than necessary for the militia. Allen replied: "As each Militia man pays for his own musket, the deponent is convinced that he could have disposed to advantage of a much greater number than that by him contracted for."[145] Besides 30,000 men "able to bear arms" in Vermont alone, "each militiaman belonging to the said [United] States is bound to find his own musket or firelocks . . . and that by the laws of the States aforesaid . . . individuals are permitted to buy arms, and convey them into the United States."[146]

While conceding that a gunsmith who trades in arms may legitimately have a large quantity in his house, the prosecution disputed the right of an individual to possess arms for 20,000 men.[147] Creation of an independent army was said to be inconsistent with modern government.[148]

Private citizens are entitled to acquire and keep unlimited quantities of arms, counsel for Allen countered, because an armed populace is the sure foundation of a free state. "Government have nothing to fear from its Militia. . . . Arms and military stores are free merchandise, so that any who have property and choose to sport with it, may turn their gardens into parks of artillery, and their houses into arsenals, without danger to Government."[149]

The British courts eventually ordered the restoration of the arms to Allen. The arms were sold through distributors in New York who then went bankrupt, leaving Allen with no proceeds. Curiously, the end result was that the arms were indeed distributed to the American public, as Allen had planned.[150]

The legacy of Ira Allen, founding father of Vermont, symbolizes the understanding of the right to keep and bear arms in the early republic. This legacy included the exercise of this right by carrying pistols for self-protection, explicit recognition thereof in the Declaration of Rights, and the distribution of thousands of muskets to the populace. Pistols in the pocket and an arsenal at home were options available to every citizen of the Green Mountain state.

MASSACHUSETTS

The Common Law Exposited

The rights to keep and use arms to defend the home, every man's "castle," and to carry arms for self-defense when outside the home, were repeatedly expostulated in the Massachusetts courts on the eve of the revolution. Arising from conflicts between colonists and the British, these doctrines were set forth by the leading trial lawyers of the time, including James Otis, Josiah Quincy, and John Adams. The courtroom dramas in which these figures acted are preserved in the papers of John Adams, who generalized their scripts in the Massachusetts Declaration of Rights of 1780.

The arguments of James Otis against writs of assistance influenced colonial opposition against British regulation, and contributed to bills of rights rejecting general warrants and unreasonable searches and seizures.[151] As of 1761, general standing warrants entitled holders to enter any house by day and search for smuggled goods.[152] In the famous Lechmere case Otis argued: "This Writ is against the fundamental Principles of Law. . . . A Man, who is quiet, is as secure in his House, as a Prince in his Castle."[153]

According to Otis, a single legislative precedent existed for general warrants: "No more than one instance can be found of it in all our law books, and that was in the zenith of arbitrary power, viz. In the reign of [Charles] II when Star-chamber powers were pushed in the extremity."[154] In 1662, in the reign of Charles II, the following interconnected acts were passed: a customs measure which allowed a writ of assistance to search for and seize contraband;[155] a militia act providing for general warrants to search homes for arms;[156] and an act which allowed such warrants to search for unlicensed printed matter.[157] The colonists' revolt against similar measures would be reflected in the state and federal bills of rights.

In a 1769 prosecution, Otis and Adams defended a seaman named Corbet for killing with a fish gig a British impressment officer who fired on the Americans. Not only was impressment illegal, but also the law provided for self-defense: "Self Preservation is first Law of Nature. . . . This Right and Duty, are both confirmed by the municipal Laws of every civilized Society."[158]

The impressers being rioters, and the deceased having first fired a pistol in the face of Corbet, the latter "had an undoubted Right . . . to have darted a Harpoon, a dagger thro the Heart of every Man in the whole Gang."[159] Counsel argued: "The Killing of Lt. Panton was justifiable Homicide. Homicide se defendendo. I. Hawkins [PLEAS OF THE CROWN] 71. . . . 'the killing of dangerous Rioters, by any private Persons, who cannot otherwise suppress them, or defend themselves from Them, inasmuch as *every private Person seems to be authorized by the Law to arm himself* for the Purposes aforesaid.' "[160]

It befell John Adams and Josiah Quincy to defend British soldiers in the Boston Massacre trials of 1770, and the former began his argument with the famous words: "I am for the prisoners at the bar, and shall apologize for it only in the words of the Marquis *Beccaria*: 'If I can but be the instrument of preserving one life, his blessings and tears of transport, shall be sufficient consolation to me, for the contempt of all mankind.' "[161] Both prosecution and defense attorneys stipulated that the Bostonians had the right to arm themselves for self defense. The issue was whether the inhabitants or the soldiers were the aggressors.[162]

Samuel Quincy's argument for the prosecution assumed the right of the populace to carry arms in public places when endangered by soldiers. When the soldiers sallied out "with clubs, cutlasses, and other weapons of death; this occasioned a general alarm; every man therefore had a right, and very prudent it was to endeavor to defend himself if attacked; this accounts for the reason of Dr. *Young* or any one inhabitant of the town having a sword that evening."[163]

As to the soldiers, John Adams upheld the right of "Self Defence, the primary Canon of the Law of Nature." As to the populace, Adams conceded on the authority of Hawkins: "Here every private person is authorized to arm himself, and on the strength of this authority, I do not deny the inhabitants had a right to arm themselves at that time, for their defence, not for offence, that distinction is materiel and must be attended to."[164]

The court's charge to the jury asserted the duty of private persons to have arms: "It is the duty of all persons (except women, decrepid persons, and infants under fifteen) to aid and assist the peace officers to suppress riots, & c. when called upon to do it. They may take with them such weapons as are necessary to enable them effectually to do it."[165] The jury acquitted the soldiers of the murder charges.

In a 1771 assault case defended by Otis, Quincy, and Adams, the first relied on "Orat[ion] pro Milone beginning."[166] The editor of Adams' papers notes: "When in 52 B.C. Titus Annius Milo stood trial for Clodius' murder, Cicero defended him. . . . The passage cited by Otis seems to be: " 'When arms speak, the laws are silent; they bid none to await their word. . . . And yet most wisely, and, in a way, tacitly, the law authorizes self-defense. . . . The man who had employed a weapon in self-defence was not held to have carried that weapon with a view to homicide.' "[167]

Similarly, in a 1774 case, Adams wrote: "An Englishmans dwelling House is his Castle. . . . [E]very Member of Society has entered into a solemn Covenant with every other that he shall enjoy in his own dwelling House as compleat a security, safety and Peace and Tranquility as if it was . . . defended with a Garrison and Artillery."[168] This philosophical basis of the right to protect the home and life with arms would find its way through Adams' pen in the Massachusetts Declaration of Rights of 1780.

The Declaration of Rights of 1780

Following rejection by the populace of a constitution with no bill of rights in 1778, a convention met the following year to frame a more acceptable constitution. The subcommittee charged with drafting the constitution included James Bowdoin, Samuel Adams, and John Adams.[169] While John Adams alone drafted the constitution and declaration of rights, presumably the three discussed the general concept. Bowdoin had chaired the 1768 Boston town meeting which declared the right to have arms, an action Sam Adams frequently defended.

Other state bills of rights explicitly recognized the right to "bear" arms, but none used the term "keep" arms. In early 1775, Samuel Adams had mentioned "that we may all be soon under the necessity of keeping *Shooting Irons*."[170] Given the "home-as-castle" doctrine, John Adams needed no prompting to add "to keep and" to the phrase "bear arms." He also added "for the common defense" after these words, presumably because it was to stifle that purpose (rather than to prevent hunting or self-defense against robbers) that the British had seized arms from both individuals and town arsenals.

As proposed by Adams, the arms guarantee read: "The people have a right to keep and bear arms for the common defence. And as, in time of peace standing armies are dangerous to liberty, they ought not to be maintained without the consent of the legislature; and the military power shall always be held in an exact subordination to the civil authority, and be governed by it."[171] While no provision caused as much controversy as the freedom-of-religion guarantee, some questions were raised about this article. "The Convention went into the consideration of the 18th article, (the subject military power,) and after considerable debate, and expunging the word "standing' before the word "armies,' accepted the same."[172] Perhaps some controversy revolved around "the common defence" as a possible restriction on the right to keep and bear arms. If so, proponents of the clause probably pointed to Article I of the Declaration, which includes among the unalienable rights "defending their lives and liberties; . . . and protecting property." Also, the right to keep and bear arms remained in "the people," who would be able to use their arms for lawful purposes besides the common defense.

Even so, due to their having felt the impact of British disarming measures more than the other colonies, at least two towns objected to the clause as too narrow. The town of Northhampton resolved:

We also judge that the people's right to keep and bear arms, declared in the seventeenth article of the same declaration is not expressed with that ample and manly openness and latitude which the importance of the right merits; and therefore propose that it should run in this or some like manner, to wit, The people have a right to keep and bear arms as well for their own as the common defence. Which mode of expression we are of opinion would harmonize much better with the first article than the form of expression used in the said seventeenth article.[173]

Similarly, the town of Williamsburg proposed the following alteration:

Upon reading the 17th Article in the Bill of Rights. Voted that these words their Own be inserted which makes it read thus; that the people have a right to keep and to bear Arms for their Own and the Common defence.

Voted Nemine Contradic. _____ Our reasons gentlemen for making this Addition Are these. 1st that we esteem it an essential privilege to keep Arms in Our houses for Our Own Defense and while we Continue honest and Lawful subjects of Government we Ought Never to be deprived of them.

Reas. 2 That the legislature in some future period may Confine all the fire Arms to some publick Magazine and thereby deprive the people of the benefit of the use of them.[174]

The Northhampton resolution would have made the arms provision specifically recognize that arms could be kept and borne for individual self-defense. John Adams, draftsman of the Declaration, perhaps deemed this unnecessary in view of the recognition accorded this common-law right when Articles 1 and 17 were read together. The fear expressed in the Williamsburg resolution about not being able to keep firearms in the home should they be relegated to a public magazine glossed over the fact that the Declaration guaranteed the right "to keep," and not just to "bear" arms. If "the people" could "keep" their firearms in the home or "bear" them abroad for "the common defense," the same arms would be available for "defending their lives and liberties; . . . and protecting property."[175]

A review of the Boston *Independent Chronicle* for 1780 reveals no controversy over the arms or press guarantees, but bitter dispute on freedom of religion.[176] That paper's only references to firearms just before adoption of the Constitution was an advertisement for "100 Pair Horseman's Pistols, neatly mounted with Steel. Inquire of the Printer."[177]

The intent of the draftsman of the Declaration of Rights concerning the right to keep and bear arms is further evident from his philosophical influences. After the convention ended, Adams sailed to Paris. One of his purchases there was a 1780 edition of Beccaria's *Crimes and Punishments*. In trials a decade before, Adams had relied on the English translation of 1770.[178] He was fond of quoting Beccaria's adage that if he could but save but one life, it would be worth the contempt of mankind.[179] Another favorite quote was: "Every Act of Authority, of one Man over another for which there is not an absolute Necessity, is tyrannical."[180] Consistent with these two precepts, Adams may well have agreed further with Beccaria's concept of "false ideas of utility": "The laws of this nature, are those which forbid to wear arms, disarming those only who are not disposed to commit the crime which the laws mean to prevent. . . . Does not the execution of this law deprive the subject of that personal liberty, so dear to mankind . . . ? It certainly makes the situation of the assaulted worse, and of the assailants better, and rather encourages than prevents murder."[181]

The English philosophers also influenced the views of Adams in regard to individual rights. Adams wrote: "I had read Harrington, Sydney, Hobbes, Nedham and Locke, but with very little Application to any particular Views: till these Debates in Congress and these Interrogations in public and private, turned my thoughts to those Researches, which produced . . . the Constitution of Massachusetts."[182]

Each of the five political theorists cited by Adams as sources of the Massachusetts Constitution upheld the citizen's right to keep, bear, and use arms. In his *Defence of the Constitutions of Government of the United States* (1787–1788), Adams endorsed the words of James Harrington: "The public sword, without a hand to hold it, is but cold iron. The hand which holds this sword is the militia of a nation."[183] "[A] government of citizens, where the commonwealth is equal, is hardest to be conquered [because] . . . such citizens, being all soldiers, or trained up to their arms, which they use not for the defence of slavery, but of liberty, [are] . . . the vastest body of a well-disciplined militia, that is possible in nature."[184]

For Algernon Sidney, popular government meant that "the body of the People is the public defense, and every man is armed and disciplined."[185] The "summe of the Right of Nature," Thomas Hobbes postulated, is "by all means we can, to defend our selves."[186] This is why, "when taking a journey, [a man] arms himself . . . and this when he knows there bee Laws . . . to revenge all injuries shall bee done him . . .

he rides armed."[187] John Locke agreed that private persons "have a right to defend themselves and recover by force what by unlawful force is taken from them."[188] The people never gave absolute power to the legislator, for they would not "have disarmed themselves, and armed him, to make prey of them when he pleases."[189]

While Adams refused to countenance the use of arms without popular support to dissolve government, he upheld the right of "arms in the hands of citizens, to be used at individual discretion, . . . in private self-defence, or by partial orders of towns."[190] In the following quotations from Marchamont Nedham's *Right Constitution of a Commonwealth* (1656), Adams expressed his agreement with each proposition except the suggestion that the defeated monarchists may be disarmed:

"That the people be continually trained up in the exercise of arms, and the militia lodged only in the people's hands, or that part of them which are most firm to the interest of liberty, that so the power may rest fully in the disposition of their supreme assemblies." The limitation to "That part most firm to the interest of liberty," was inserted here, no doubt, to reserve the right of disarming all the friends of Charles Stuart, the nobles and bishops. Without stopping to enquire into the justice, policy, or necessity of this, the rule in general is excellent. . . . One consequence was, according to [Nedham], "that nothing could at any time be imposed upon the people but by their consent. . . . " "As Aristotle tells us, in his fourth book of Politics, the Grecian states ever had special care to place the use and exercise of arms in the people, because the commonwealth is theirs who hold the arms: the sword and sovereignty ever walk hand in hand together." This is perfectly just. "Rome and the territories about it, were trained up perpetually in arms, and the whole commonwealth, by this means, became one formal militia."[191]

In sum, each of the philosophical forebears of the Massachusetts Declaration of Rights—Harrington, Sidney, Hobbes, Locke, and Nedham—upheld the right of the people at large to have and use arms. While Hobbes rejected any right of armed commoners to revolt against a monarch unless required for self-preservation, the other four were inspirations for such revolts in 1689 and 1776. The use of arms for private self-defense was unquestioned by all five. Given these influences, the broad language of the Massachusetts Declaration was probably intended to embody the right to keep and bear arms for both individual "safety" and "common defense."[192]

The Perpetual Laws and the Federal Amendments

In the two decades which followed the adoption of the Declaration of Rights in 1780, no laws were passed to prohibit the individual possession of firearms for lawful purposes. The use of "any offensive weapon" in a robbery was the first prohibition enacted in that period which specifically mentioned arms.[193] Shays' Rebellion in September 1786 led to two arms-related acts. The first provided that "if any persons to the number of twelve, or more, being armed with clubs, or other weapons" gather, a justice of the peace could order them to disperse within an hour. The official could then "require the aid of a sufficient number of persons in arms, if any of the persons assembled as aforesaid shall appear armed."[194] The second such act declared:

Whereas in a free government, where the *people have a right to bear arms for the common defence*, and the military power is held in subordination to the civil authority, it is necessary for the safety of the State that *the virtuous citizens thereof should hold themselves in readiness*, and when called upon, should exert their efforts to support the civil government, and oppose the attempts of factious and wicked men who may wish to subvert the laws and Constitution of Their country.[195]

Shays' Rebellion also prompted the federal constitutional convention in Philadelphia in 1787. When the federal Constitution was debated in the Massachusetts ratifying convention, Theodore Sedgwick queried concerning standing armies: "If raised, whether they could subdue a nation of freemen, who know how to prize liberty, and who have arms in their hands?"[196] The understanding in that convention that no peaceable citizens could rightfully be disarmed, and of the perception in Massachusetts a year and half later that the proposed federal Bill of Rights reflected this ideal, would be expressed as follows:

It may be well remembered, that the following "amendments" to the new constitution for these United States, were introduced to the convention of this commonwealth by its present Lieutenant-Governor, that venerable patriot, SAMUEL ADAMS. . . . Every one of the intended alterations, but one, have been already reported by the committee of the House of Representatives in Congress, and most probably will be adopted by the federal legislature. In justice therefore to that long tried Republican, and his numerous friends, you gentlemen, are requested to republish his intended alterations, in the same paper, that exhibits to the public, the amendments which the committee have adopted, in order that they may be compared together. . . .

"And that the said constitution be never construed to authorize Congress to infringe the just liberty of the Press, or the rights of Conscience; or *to prevent the people of the United States who are peaceable citizens, from keeping their own arms*; or to raise standing armies, unless when necessary for the defence of the United States, or of some one of them; or to prevent the people from petitioning in a peaceable and orderly manner, the federal Legislature, and for a redress of grievances; or to subject the people to unreasonable searches and seizures of their persons, papers, or possessions."[197]

The understanding in Massachusetts of the federal Second Amendment is further clarified by the front page of the special July 4, 1789, issue of the Boston *Massachusetts Centinel*, which explained that to prevent tyranny, "the people are confirmed by the next article in their right to keep and bear their private arms."[198] The Massachusetts Declaration of Rights of 1780 was the first such state document to refer to the right to "keep" arms, a term now incorporated in the proposed federal Bill of Rights. On the other hand, the U.S. Senate rejected a proposal to add, after "to keep and bear arms," the words "for the common defense,"[199] which appeared in the Massachusetts Declaration. This rejection may have resulted from the possibility that these words could be construed to restrict the right.

A review of statutes enacted through the remainder of the century reveals two pertinent items. The enrollment of "each and every free able bodied white male citizen" of ages eighteen to forty-five was required by the militia act,[200] which provided: "Each horseman shall furnish himself with . . . a pair of pistols,"[201] and each infantryman "shall constantly keep himself provided with a good musket . . . or with a good rifle."[202] By contrast, "each company of artillery shall be provided with two good field pieces."[203] Thus, individuals furnished themselves with the kinds of "arms" that they could "keep and bear," that is, pistols, muskets, and rifles, while the commonwealth apparently provided heavier armament.

While the peaceable keeping or carrying of arms for lawful purposes was unrestricted, the legislature reenacted the ancient Statute of Northhampton[204] in the following form: "That every Justice of the Peace . . . may cause to be staid and arrested, all affrayers, rioters, disturbers, or breakers of the peace, and such as *ride or go armed offensively, to the fear or terror of the good citizens of this Commonwealth*, or such others as may utter any menaces or threatening speeches, and . . . shall require of the offender to find surities for his keeping the Peace, and being of good behavior."[205]

This enactment reflects the common-law interpretation of the ancient statute that going about in public armed with pistols, absent "*malo animo* [bad purpose]" or a specific intent "to terrify the King's subjects," was justifiable in view of the "general connivance to gentlemen to ride armed for their security."[206] The enactment vindicated a person to "ride or go armed" defensively, with no intent to cause fear or terror to the citizens.[207]

Arms in Every Hand: The Legacy of the Adamses

As governor of Massachusetts at the end of the century, Samuel Adams sent a message to the legislature on the need to maintain a militia of the whole people. "In our Declaration of Rights, which expresses the sentiments of the people, the people have a right to keep and bear arms for the common defense."[208] Adams warned the legislature never to rely on either a standing army or "a select militia, a small body to be disciplined in a camp with all the pomp & splendor of a regular army."[209] "Where there are no invidious exemptions, partial distinctions or privileged bands, every Man, it is presumed, would pride himself in the right of bearing arms."[210]

In 1823, William H. Sumner published a lengthy letter to John Adams entitled *The Importance of the Militia to a Free Commonwealth*. While this was over four decades after the adoption of the Massachusetts Declaration of Rights, the work was endorsed by Adams, the framer of that declaration, and is a clear exposition of the concept of a militia to that generation. It also shows the relation between private keeping of arms and a free commonwealth as viewed in Massachusetts.

The militia is, simply put, "essential to the preservation of our civil rights."[211] Begun by the pilgrims who provided their own arms, it alone had provided security for religious freedom. "The militia is intended for defence only; standing armies for aggression, as well as defence. The history of all ages proves that large armies are dangerous to civil liberty. Militia, however large, never can be, for it is composed of citizens only, armed for the preservation of their own privileges."[212]

According to Sumner, the country's terrain and arms in every household made militia operations favorable. Combining the centuries-old "castle" doctrine with the right to "keep" arms, Sumner observed:

An enemy would be always unwilling to invade such a territory; but notwithstanding, if its population, like that of Europe, chiefly consisted of an unarmed peasantry, and its whole reliance was on its regular army, one pitched battle would decide its fate. But a country of well trained militia-men is not conquered when its army is beaten. . . . Here, every house is a castle, and every man is a soldier. Arms are in every hand.[213]

Sumner contended that the need of the people to "keep" arms precluded the storage of the arms in a public arsenal. Moreover, growing urbanization meant that the arms kept would not be used as often for hunting, and thus that militia training was even more necessary:

It is true, that it is better that the arms should be kept by the men themselves, at their own dwellings, than in the public arsenals. They thus learn to take care of them, at least; and as opportunities for hunting and practical shooting offer, they improve as marksmen. But few boys would learn their catechisms, if the books which contained them, were to be found in the public libraries, only; and but few men would be familiar with the use of arms, which were not kept in their own possessions.

. . . But where the country is settled, the general use of arms is given up; and, as the forests are cleared, drilling becomes necessary as a substitute for that habitual exercise of shooting at game, which has obtained for Americans the reputation of being the best riflemen in the world. If this be not required in the populous parts of the country, the backwoodsmen alone will be able to defend themselves as none others will be accustomed to the use of the arms with which they are to be furnished.[214]

In his answer to Sumner's letter, John Adams wrote:

Your manuscript dissertation concerning the militia . . . is so conformable to all my opinions concerning it from my cradle, that it seemed to be living my life over again. . . .
   . . . The American states have owed their existence to the militia for more than two hundred years. Neither schools, nor colleges, nor town meetings have been more essential to the formation and character of the nation than the militia. . . . Impose its constitution by every prudent means, but never destroy its univer- sality. A select militia will soon become a standing army. . . . Whenever the militia comes to an end, or is despised or neglected, I shall consider this union dissolved, and the liberties of North America lost forever.[215]

John Adams' reflections symbolize the political philosophy that a bal- anced republic is best maintained where every individual keeps arms. This world view had been expressed in the Boston resolutions of 1768, and again in the Declaration of Rights of 1780. As will be seen, it was shared equally in those states which adopted bills of rights which rec- ognized a well-regulated militia.

Thomas B Adams. From his Father
1800

A N

E S S A Y

O N

C R I M E S

A N D

P U N I S H M E N T S,

TRANSLATED FROM THE ITALIAN;

W I T H A

C O M M E N T A R Y,

A T T R I B U T E D T O

Monf. De V O L T A I R E,

TRANSLATED FROM THE FRENCH.

THE FOURTH EDITION.

In rebus quibuſcumque difficilioribus non expectandum,
ut quis ſimul, & ferat, & metat, ſed præparatione opus
eſt, ut per gradus matureſcant.

BACON.

L O N D O N:
Printed for F. NEWBERY, at the Corner of
St. Paul's Church-Yard.

M DCC LXXV.

The Italian philosopher Beccaria influenced the Founding Fathers on the subjects of criminal justice and the right to carry arms. John Adams gave this copy of the 1775 English translation of Beccaria's essay to his son, Thomas B. Adams. (Courtesy: Rare Books Division, Boston Public Library)

i vantaggi sono il prevenire delitti importanti, e che, essendone palesi gli effetti ed occulti gli autori, intimoriscono il popolo; di più si contribuisce a mostrare che chi manca di fede alle leggi, cioè al pub- lico è probabile che manchi al privato. sembrerebbemi che una legge generale, che promettesse l'impunità al complice palesatore di qualun- que delitto fosse preferibile ad una speciale dichiarazione in un caso particolare, perché così preverrebbe le unioni col reciproco timore. una tal legge però dovrebbe accompagnare l'impunità col bando del delatore........ ma invano tormento me stesso per distruggere il rimor- so che sento autorizzando le sacrosante leggi, la base della morale umana, al tradimento, ed alla dissimulazione. Beccaria. §.37

328. falsa idea di utilità è quella, che sacrifica mille vantaggi reali, per un inconveniente o immaginario, o di poca conseguenza, che toglierebbe agli uomini il fuoco perché incendia, e l'acqua per- chè annega; che non ripara ai mali, che col distruggere. le leggi che proibiscono di portar le armi, sono leggi di tal natura; esse non disarmano che i non inclinati, né determinati ai delitti, mentre coloro che hanno il coraggio di poter violare le leggi più sacre della umanità è le più importante del Codice, come rispetteranno le mi- nori, e le puramente arbitrarie? queste peggiorano la condizione degli assaliti, migliorando quella degli assalitori, non iscemano gli omicidi, ma gli accrescono, perché è maggiore la confidenza nell'assalire i disarmati, che gli armati: queste si chiaman leggi, non prevenitrici, ma paurose dei delitti, che nascono dalla tumultuosa impressione di alcuni fatti particolari, non dalla ragionata medita- zione degl'inconvenienti, ed avantaggi di un decreto universale. ib. §. 40.

329. e meglio prevenire i delitti, che punirli: questo è il fine prin- cipale d'ogni buona legislazione, che è l'arte di condurre gli uomi- ni al massimo di felicità, o al minimo d'infelicità possibile. il proibire una moltitudine di azioni indifferenti non è prevenire i de- litti, che non possono nascere, ma egli è un crearne dei nuovi, egli è un definire a piacere la virtù ed il vizio, che ci vengono predi-

Falsa idea d'utilità.

Prevenire i delitti.

"False ideas of utility . . . the laws that forbid the carrying of arms. . . ." Jefferson copied in his Commonplace Book kept in 1774–1776 the entire passage from Beccaria, in Italian, which concludes that such laws "serve rather to encourage than to prevent homicides, for an unarmed man may be attacked with greater confidence than an armed man." The Common- place Book has been called "the source-book and repertory of Jefferson's ideas on government." (Courtesy: Jefferson Papers, Manuscript Division, Library of Congress)

CHAPTER 3

"A Well Regulated Militia" in the State Declarations of Rights

Four of the states which adopted declarations of rights—Virginia, Maryland, Delaware and New Hampshire—did not explicitly use the words "a right to bear arms." However, the declarations of these states did uphold "a well regulated militia," meaning that that body of the people would be trained to arms to counter the real or potential oppression of a standing army. Moreover, recognition of a right to bear arms was manifested in these states in sources other than the declarations of rights. In fact, the conventions of Virginia and New Hampshire insisted that a federal bill of rights be adopted and that it recognize the right to bear arms. The following analyzes the perceived nature of a well regulated militia and the right to bear arms in the above four states.

VIRGINIA

The Declaration of Rights

Virginia was the first of all the colonies to adopt a bill of rights, which became the prototype for those of other colonies. The Virginia Declaration of Rights, adopted in convention on June 12, 1776, included the following interconnected propositions:

I. That all Men are by Nature equally free and independent, and have certain inherent Rights . . . ; namely, the Enjoyment of Life and Liberty, with the Means of . . . pursuing and obtaining . . . Safety.

II. That all Power is vested in, and consequently derived from, the People. . . .

XIII. That a well regulated Militia, composed of the Body of the People, trained to Arms, is the proper, natural, and safe Defense of a free State; that standing Armies, in Time of Peace, should be avoided, as dangerous to Liberty.

The author of the Declaration was George Mason, who had employed similar phraseology during the previous two years in his writings on the Fairfax Independent Militia Company. As Mason insisted in 1775, "a well regulated Militia, composed of the Gentlemen, Freeholders, and other Freemen," would preserve liberty, and thus "we do each of us, for ourselves respectively, promise and engage to keep a good Firelock."[1] In the same year, comparable language was proposed by Patrick Henry and adopted by the Virginia convention: "That a well regulated Militia, composed of Gentlemen and Yeomen, is the natural Strength, and only Security, of a free Government."[2]

Pursuant to its resolution, the 1775 convention appointed Henry, Jefferson, Richard Henry Lee, and others to a committee to plan the "embodying, arming, and disciplining such a Number of Men as may be sufficient for that purpose."[3] The convention also recommended "that every Man be provided with a good Rifle" and "that every Horseman be provided . . . with Pistols and Holsters, a Carbine, or other Firelock."[4] This background clarifies the meaning of the Declaration of Rights adopted a year later. Every freeman would have "the means" of obtaining "safety," "all power" would remain in "the people," and "a free state" would be defended where the citizens kept and trained with "arms" (rifles, firelocks, carbines, and pistols) and associated themselves into "militia."[5]

Having adopted the Declaration of Rights, the 1776 convention proceeded to consider various proposals for a constitution. Thomas Jefferson prepared a draft which consisted of three parts. The first part contained the grievances and charges against George III which Congress would adopt less than a month later on July 4, in the Declaration of Independence. Next followed a proposed political system which would have altered the existing aristocratic structure. A third portion included a bill of rights which stated: "All persons shall have full & free liberty of religious opinion. . . . No freeman shall ever be debarred the use of arms. . . . There shall be no standing army but in time of . . . actual war. Printing presses shall be free, except . . . where by commission of private injury they shall give cause of private action."[6]

Jefferson's proposals contain matters which thirteen years later would find expression in the First and Second Amendments—the freedoms of religion, arms, and the press. In a second draft, Jefferson added a prohibition on the holding of newcomers to the state in slavery, and a tentative bracketed item to the arms guarantee: "No freeman shall be debarred the use of arms [within his own lands or tenements]."[7] Jefferson used brackets to indicate that the contents thereof were optional or open to question.[8] The reference to use of arms on one's own lands and tenements may have been a rebuke to English game laws which prohibited commoners from hunting on their own land. It also would have allowed legislation to establish a deer hunting season and thus to prevent taking of deer off of one's property, which Jefferson proposed to the Virginia assembly not long after.[9] A third draft of the constitution listed the above and other matters under the title "Rights Private and Public."[10]

On June 29, 1776, the Virginia convention adopted a constitution. The preface incorporated Jefferson's strictures against George III, while the text was based on proposals submitted by George Mason and others.[11] It contained no additional bill of rights since the Declaration of Rights had been adopted just over two weeks before. The postulate that "no freeman shall be debarred the use of arms" had been expressed in other words in that declaration—"the Body of the People, trained to Arms"— and indeed was fundamental to the American world view at that time.[12]

Jefferson's Commonplace Book

The proposition expressed by Jefferson above that "no freeman shall ever be debarred the use of arms" was fundamental to the world view of the American patriots. "The elementary books of public right," on which the Declaration of Independence and Jefferson's above related drafts were based, upheld the right to use arms for defense of self and the commonwealth.[13] However, more immediate sources influenced Jefferson and his contemporaries at this time in respect to the adoption of a basic political system and the ensuing revision of Virginia's statutory law. Jefferson kept a Commonplace Book during the years 1774–1776 which "may well be considered as the source-book and repertory of Jefferson's ideas on government."[14] Indeed, the authorities relied on in the Commonplace Book were highly regarded by many of the state constitution makers of the day.

The Commonplace Book consists of quotations from traditional legal authorities and penal reformers along with brief comments by Jefferson. It reveals what Jefferson deemed worthy of copying and what he was reading at the time. Thus, among the quotations from Coke's *Institutes* copied by Jefferson was the following: "If a man be present when one is murdered or robbed, and doth not endeavor to attack the offender, nor levy hue and cry, he shall be fined and imprisoned."[15] Jefferson read, but did not copy, Coke's related dictum that "a man may not only use force and arms, but assemble company also," for "*Armaque in armatos sumere jura sinut* [the laws permit the taking up of arms against armed persons]."[16]

Perhaps the most significant figures detailed by Jefferson were the penal reformers Montesquieu, Beccaria, and Eden. Beside reading Montesquieu's vindication of the right of armed self-defense and his denunciation of Venice's death penalty for bearing firearms,[17] Jefferson copied this passage: "In republics, it would be extremely dangerous to make the profession of arms a particular state, distinct from that of civil functions. . . . In republics a person takes up arms only with a view to defend his country and its laws; it is because he is a citizen he makes himself for a while a soldier."[18]

Writing *"False idee di utilità* ("false ideas of utility") in the margin, Jefferson copied in full the following passage from Beccaria:

False is the idea of utility that sacrifices a thousand real advantages for one imaginary or trifling inconvenience; that would take fire from men because it burns, and water because one may drown in it; that has no remedy for evils, except destruction. The laws that forbid the carrying of arms are laws of such a nature. They disarm those only who are neither inclined nor determined to commit crimes. Can it be supposed that those who have the courage to violate the most sacred laws of humanity, the most important of the code, will respect the less important and arbitrary ones, which can be violated with ease and impunity, and which, if strictly obeyed, would put an end to personal liberty— so dear to men, so dear to the enlightened legislator—and subject innocent persons to all the vexations that the guilty alone ought to suffer? Such laws make things worse for the assaulted and better for the assailants; they serve rather to encourage than to prevent homicides, for an unarmed man may be attacked with greater confidence than an armed man. They ought to be designated as laws not preventive but fearful of crimes, produced by the tumultuous impression of a few isolated facts, and not by thoughtful consideration of the inconveniences and advantages of a universal decree.[19]

Jefferson read similar sentiments in William Eden, who combined observations of Montesquieu and Beccaria as follows: "It is a Law at Venice, that those, who carry fire-arms about their persons, shall suffer death. This law is founded in apparent utility; nevertheless it is contrary to the nature of things, to make the bare possession of the means of mischief equally penal with the most criminal use of those means."[20] By contrast, under English law "homicide is justifiable . . . in the case of any woman, who kills a ravisher in defence of her chastity; or of any traveller, who, in the immediate defence of his property, shoots a highwayman."[21] Further, homicide is excusable, "first, *per infortunium* . . . if (for instance) it should consist in shooting at game . . . Secondly, by self-defence."[22]

In sum, the sources Jefferson consulted in preparation of his Commonplace Book reveal the premises for his proposal that "no freeman shall ever be debarred the use of arms." The armed citizen would protect himself and the community from both the private criminal and tyrannical government. These same premises would be reflected in the revision of Virginia's statutes.

The Revisal of the Laws

In 1776, the General Assembly appointed a Committee of Revisors to draft a restatement of statutory law for Virginia. The committee included Jefferson, Mason, Lee, Wythe, and Pendleton, but Jefferson played the leading role, with Mason and Lee not participating at all. Jefferson's researches expressed in his Commonplace Book found practical application, and Montesquieu, Beccaria and Eden influenced what the then Governor Jefferson and George Wythe eventually reported to the General Assembly in 1779.[23] Jefferson's proposals for statutory reform clarify in depth the extent to which the individual keeping and bearing of firearms was considered fundamental in Virginia at that time.

The Committee of Revisors set for itself the following method of procedure, as described by Jefferson:

We concluded not to meddle with the common law, i.e., the law preceding the existence of the statutes, further than to accommodate it to our new principles and circumstances; but to take up the whole body of what was wanting, and reduce the whole within as moderate a compass as it would bear, and to the plain language of common sense, divested of the verbiage, the barbarous tautologies and redundancies which render the British statutes unintelligible. From this, however, were excepted the ancient statutes, particularly those commented on by Lord Coke, the language of which is simple, and the meaning of every word so well settled by decisions, as to make it safest not to change words where the sense was to be retained.[24]

The work of the committee would have immediate application. The armed revolution against the British was proceeding in earnest, and Jefferson was appointed to a committee to bring in a bill for regulating and disciplining the militia. Jefferson reported, and the General Assembly passed, a bill which provided that the militia would consist of all free males, hired servants and apprentices, between the ages of sixteen and fifty years.[25] Every private was required to equip himself "with a rifle and tomahawk, or common firelock and bayonet," and to "constantly keep one pound of powder and four pounds of ball." If any "be so poor that he cannot purchase such arms, the said court shall cause them to be procured at the expence of the public."[26]

Jefferson's militia bill deleted the restriction in a previous act that free mulattoes, negroes, and Indians "shall appear without arms" at muster.[27] In the mid-1780s, after the experiences of the Revolution, the General Assembly reaffirmed that "the defence and safety of the commonwealth depend upon having its citizens properly armed and taught the knowledge of military duty."[28]

The General Assembly took little action on the revisal of the laws until 1785–1786. The Bill for Preservation of Deer was never enacted, but is significant as to common linguistic usage of the term to "bear" arms. The bill was presented to the whole House in 1785 by James Madison, just four years before he drafted the federal Second Amendment's wording about the right to "bear" arms.[29] The bill provided for deer hunting seasons outside one's enclosed land with punishment as follows:

Whosoever shall offend against this act, shall forfeit and pay, for every deer by him unlawfully killed, twenty shillings, one half thereof to the use of the commonwealth, and the other half to the informer; and moreover, shall be bound to their good behavior; and, if within twelve months after the date of the recognizance *he shall bear a gun out of his inclosed ground, unless whilst performing military duty*, shall be deemed a breach of the recognizance, and be good cause to bind him anew, and *every such bearing of a gun* shall be a breach of the new recognizance and cause to bind him again.[30]

The bill followed legislation earlier in the century which sought to halt the alarming depopulation of deer. While it deleted as a penalty the "twenty lashes, on his or their back, well laid on" of the previous act,[31] it added that a violator who, within a year, "shall bear a gun out of his inclosed ground, unless whilst performing military duty" would be bound to his good behavior. Binding one to his good behavior each time he carried a gun perhaps was intended to cause a stern reminder from a judge not to hunt deer or the posting of a bond.

There are two interesting aspects about this proposal as it relates to the right of an individual to carry arms. First, the bill would have prohibited the bearing only of "a gun," not of "arms" in general. In the linguistic usage of the time, "guns" were distinguishable from "pistols."[32] Given its purpose to protect deer, the bill would not have prohibited violators from bearing pistols, which were unsuitable for hunting deer but which, following Beccaria, enabled potential victims of crime to defend themselves. Even so, the House was apparently unwilling to restrict the places where game violators bore their guns, and no further action was taken after the bill was read twice.[33]

Second, the bill would have put a game violator on his good behavior not to "bear a gun out of his inclosed ground, unless whilst performing military duty," and bind him to his good behavior anew for "every such bearing of a gun."[34] To Jefferson, Madison (the draftsman of the federal Second Amendment) and their contemporaries, to "bear" a firearm meant broadly to carry it in one's hands or on one's person, as for instance a deer hunter would do. The terms "bear arms" were not restricted to militia service in that the bill specifically addressed the "bearing of a gun" by "any person" when *not* "performing military duty."

A bill on crime and capital punishment reflects the influences which Jefferson relied on in his Commonplace Book. The preamble paraphrases Beccaria,[35] whose sentiments against capital punishment were incorporated into the bill to cover all crimes but treason and murder. The bill was defeated in the House by one vote because, as Madison wrote Jefferson: "The rage against Horse stealers had a great influence on the fate of the Bill."[36]

Jefferson would have removed any penalties for homicides which did not constitute murder or manslaughter.[37] His marginal note evidences the influence of Beccaria and Eden:

Beccaria. . . . Homicides are 1. Justifiable. 2. Excusable. 3. Felonious. . . . The 1st are held to be totally without guilt, or rather commendable. The 2d is in some cases not quite unblamable. . . . The killing a man in defence of one's person, which is a species of excusable homicide; because altho' cases may happen where these also are commendable, yet most frequently they are done on too slight appearance of danger. . . . Excusable homicides are by Misadventure, or in self-defense.[38]

Just as the law clearly distinguished between felonious and lawful homicides, and hence the right to use arms in the latter instance, so too it created a line of demarcation between the reckless brandishing of arms and the peaceful bearing of arms for lawful purposes. Jefferson's bill to punish affrays, introduced by Madison and enacted in 1786, provided:

That no man great nor small, of what condition soever he be, . . . be so hardy to come before the Justices of any court, or other of their ministers of justice doing their office, with force and arms on pain to forfeit their armour to the commonwealth and their bodies to prison at the pleasure of a court, nor *go nor ride armed* by night nor by day, in fairs or markets or in other places *in terror of the country,* upon pain of being arrested and committed to prison by any Justice on his own view, or proof by others, there to abide for so long a time as a jury, to be sworn for that purpose by the said Justice, shall direct, and in like manner to forfeit his armour to the commonwealth.

But no person shall be imprisoned for such offence by a longer space of time one month.[39]

This was a reenactment of the Statute of Northampton,[40] one of what Jefferson called "the ancient statutes . . . commented on by Lord Coke, the language of which is simple, and the meaning of every word so well settled by decisions," as to warrant few changes.[41] Jefferson would have

been aware of Coke's explanation that this statute was intended to reduce the random deeds of chivalry, but that "the laws permit the taking
up of arms against armed persons."[42] Coke's discussion of the meaning
of "affray" as real or threatened combat a few pages later was copied
by Jefferson in his Commonplace Book.[43]

Thus, the prohibition on going or riding "armed . . . in terror of the
country" was intended to punish affrays occasioned by the brandishing
of and fighting with weapons in public places.[44] Jefferson was undoubtedly aware that the meaning of this ancient statute commented on by
Coke was well settled in *Rex* v. *Knight* (1686), which held that going
about in public armed with pistols, in view of the "general connivance
to gentlemen to ride armed for their security," did not constitute "going
or riding armed in affray of peace."[45] "The meaning of the statute . . .
was to punish people who go armed to terrify the King's subjects," that
is, with "*malo animo* [bad purpose]."[46]

The restatement of the law proposed by the Committee of Revisors
went so far as not to prohibit *any* of the inhabitants from owning and
carrying common firearms. This would have been a radical departure
for a colony which prohibited the possession of firearms to slaves.[47]
Perhaps the deletion stemmed from Jefferson's opposition to slavery
and recognition of the right of all persons to armed self-defense. The
General Assembly did not accept this and in 1785, reenacted the slave
code provisions, on which Jefferson made the following notes:

<no slave to be witness>

<not to go from tenements or dwelling of master

overseer or employer without pass or token>

<not to keep arms>

<not to pass with arms.>

<riots, routs, unlawful assemblies, trespasses & seditious speeches.>[48]

Only three years later, free Virginians demanded that these same
rights to speak, assemble, and keep arms be expressly recognized in the
proposed federal compact.[49] The Virginia Declaration of Rights of 1776,
authored by George Mason, had been the first written bill of rights
adopted by any of the independent states. It contained the phrase that
"a well-regulated militia, composed of the body of the people trained
to arms, is the proper, natural, and safe defense of a free state."[50] Virginia's declaration was reflected almost clause by clause in the bills of
rights of other states, which to some extent amplified or improved that
of Virginia. One such addition was the explicit assertion by four states
that "the people have a right to bear arms."[51]

In 1788, at the Virginia convention which considered ratification of the proposed federal Constitution, it was George Mason's turn to learn from those who had learned from him. Mason drafted a new clause which he placed before the militia clause: "that the people have a right to keep and bear arms."[52] This bill of rights was reported out of the committee on proposed amendments to the Constitution by George Wythe,[53] a member of the Committee of Revisors whose members understood the term "to bear" a firearm simply to signify its carrying by a member of the public. Another member of the bill of rights committee was James Madison,[54] who had introduced the Committee of Revisors' game bill which included this definition of bearing arms, and who was soon to author the Second Amendment to the federal Constitution.

By the time Virginia's ratification in 1791 made the federal Bill of Rights effective, the Founding Fathers of that state had become the Founding Fathers of the United States. For decades after the Second Amendment was adopted, Madison had no further occasion to comment on the right to bear arms, since that right went unquestioned.

Madison's career came full circle as he served as a delegate to the Virginia constitutional convention of 1829. Reflecting on the danger to a republic of limited suffrage as had been advocated at the convention, Madison's comment best sums up the philosophy of the Revolutionary generation as follows: "A Government resting on a minority, is an aristocracy not a Republic, and could not be safe with a numerical physical force against it, without a standing Army, an enslaved press, and a disarmed populace."[55]

MARYLAND

That Catholics and Protestants May Have Arms

Unlike that of Virginia, the body politic in Maryland was historically divided between Catholics and Protestants. Each group sought political domination, which often entailed disarming the members of the group not in power. The nature of a well regulated militia and the right to bear arms as understood in Maryland was rooted in Catholic-Protestant political conflicts dating back to 1689.

Under the Colonial Charter, Lord Baltimore's settlers were English subjects with "all privileges, franchises and liberties of this our kingdom of England."[56] When these freedoms had diminished to the breaking point in England, in 1689 the Protestant majority replaced King James II with William and Mary. The Glorious Revolution reached Maryland's shores and led to replacement of Baltimore's government by one more sympathetic to the rights of Englishmen.

Like those of James II, Baltimore's ministers were accused of seeking to destroy "the English Liberties by disarming the Protestants."[57] The trouble began when the royal government confiscated all public arms normally kept by individuals, and redistributed them only "into such hands as shall faithfully serve the King."[58] Marylanders armed themselves and associated together to overthrow the tyranny quickly and bloodlessly.[59] John Coode, leader of the republicans, explained that "the attempts to disarm the Protestants in this Province . . . gave us just case to fly to arms."[60]

The above language is similar to the English Declaration of Rights, which alleged that James II sought to subvert liberty "by causing several good Subjects, being Protestants, to be disarmed, at the same time when Papists were both armed and employed, contrary to law."[61] Among the "true, ancient and indubitable rights" declared was "that the Subjects which are Protestants, may have Arms for their Defence suitable to their Condition, and as are allowed by law."[62]

The arms of some Catholics in Maryland were confiscated as a result of the Glorious Revolution. In 1695, the Maryland Council "Ordered that all persons who took any private Arms from Roman Catholicks or others in the time of the late Revolution that they bring and deliver all such Arms up into the hands of the Colonel of the County where taken, who is hereby Obliged & Required to Cause the same to be restored to the Right Owners."[63] Moreover, the assembly passed legislation guaranteeing the right of all persons, regardless of religion, to have arms. Press masters were authorized to seize various goods from the inhabitants, but no person "shall presume at any time to Seize Press or Carry away from the Inhabitant Resident in this Province, any Arms or Ammunition of any kind whatsoever upon any Duty or Service, or upon any Account whatsoever."[64]

The right of Catholics to keep and bear arms does not appear to have been disputed again until the middle of the next century. Maryland hardly participated in the French and Indian War, but the colony's Catholic population was under suspicion of French sympathies. In 1756 the Assembly passed a draconian law providing that "all Arms Gunpowder and Ammunition of what kind soever any Papist or reputed Papist within this Province hath or shall have in his House or Houses or elsewhere shall be taken from Such Papist or reputed Papist by Warrant under the hand of one Justice of the Peace for the County wherein such Papist or reputed Papist shall be Resident and that the said Arms and Ammunition so taken Shall be kept in the Such Place as the Said Justice shall appoint."[65] Any Catholic who refused to turn over his arms would forfeit them and be imprisoned. No exception existed for Catholics willing to take a loyalty oath, although the law was self-repealing one year from its enactment.

By the 1760s, when most colonists were complaining about losing their liberties guaranteed in the English Bill of Rights, leaders of Maryland's sizable Catholic population began viewing independence as a way to regain liberties lost by the Revolution of 1689. Charles Carroll of Carrollton and other Catholics who were to shape Maryland's constitution aimed to recover the English liberties from which they had been disinherited almost a century before.[66]

Carroll must have taken offense at the only provision in the Bill of Rights to limit its guarantee to persons of one religion—"that the Subjects which are Protestants, may have Arms for their Defence." However, Catholics in Maryland were no longer deprived of arms.[67] A work on penal laws against Catholics in England and the colonies which impressed Carroll[68] did not include deprivation of arms among the rights of Englishmen which Catholics were being denied as of 1764.[69] Although he denounced duelling, Carroll readily provided himself with belt pistols, pocket pistols being scarce, when threatened by a Protestant challenger.[70]

In 1768, the *Maryland Gazette* published Boston's resolution that all householders should keep arms and ammunition, based on the Bill of Rights provision that "Protestants may have Arms for their Defence."[71] A few days later came the report that martial law would be declared in Boston, and "that the Inhabitants of this Province are to be disarmed."[72]

As revolution approached, patriots upheld the ideal that all the people, Protestant and Catholic alike, should keep and bear arms. In late 1774, the meeting of deputies appointed by the counties resolved, without reference to religion:

That a well regulated militia, composed of the gentlemen, freeholders, and other freemen, is the natural strength and only stable security of a free government . . . ; will . . . render it unnecessary to keep any standing army (ever dangerous to liberty) in this province; and therefore it is recommended . . . that each man be provided with a good firelock . . . and be in readiness to act on any emergency.[73]

A contemporary noted that "large sums have likewise been collected for the purchase of arms and ammunition, and *persons of all denominations* are required to associate under military regulations."[74] By summer of 1775, "in every district of this province the majority of the people are actually under arms."[75] In regard to armed resistance to the British, Maryland's Catholics and Protestants had buried the hatchet.

Armed resistance was justified in the 1775 resolution of the Maryland convention as follows: "We, therefore, inhabitants of the province of Maryland, firmly persuaded that it is necessary and justifiable to repel force by force, do approve of the opposition by arms, to the British troops employed . . . for destroying the essential securities for the lives, liberties, and properties of the subjects."[76] Having and using arms was not merely a right of personal defense, but more broadly a right to associate for common defense.

The above preparations were in response to General Gage's attempt to disarm the people of Boston and a fear that the British were planning to seize the private arms of all Americans. The *Maryland Gazette* reported that 60,000 colonists had assembled at Boston but that most had left, "leaving an army of 15,000 to watch General Gage's motions, who, we are told, has given the inhabitants of Boston permission to leave the town on condition they leave their arms behind them."[77] The British proclamation imposing an embargo on the export of arms and ammunition to the colonies was announced,[78] as was the expected proclamation that all Americans would be required to turn in their arms by a certain date.[79]

Local patriots began taking direct action against area Tories. A typical item notes that "a great body of people came into the town, with loaded arms, and expressed a resolution to tar and feather him, whatever might be the determination of the committee."[80] The Association of the Freemen of Maryland found Gage's actions "sufficient causes to arm a free people in defence of their liberty" and directed that "the minute men exercise with their own firelocks."[81] When the constitutional convention met a year later, the stage was thus set for recognition of a well regulated militia composed of the armed populace.

The Declaration of Rights of 1776

On June 27, 1776, the militia of Ann Arundel County adopted resolves directed to their delegates in the upcoming constitutional convention. These delegates included Charles Carroll of Carrollton, his cousin Charles Carroll the Barrister, Samuel Chase, Thomas Johnson, and William Paca.[82] The Militia Resolves were an important political development in Maryland colonial literature.[83]

In proposing a constitution for Maryland, the Resolves sought guarantees for jury trial and habeas corpus.[84] Declaring against standing armies, it added: "That a well regulated militia be established in this province, as being the best security for the preservation of the lives, liberties and properties of the people."[85] Militiamen should choose their own officers, and "guns for such unarmed men who are not able to purchase the same" would "be provided at the public expense."[86]

The above resulted from the participation in the election of all taxpayers who bore arms.[87] Contrary to the usual property qualifications, Rezin Hammond told protesters in Anne Arundel County "that every man that bore arms in defense of his country had a right to vote, and if they were allowed no vote they had no right to bear arms."[88] Election officials reciting property qualifications were interrupted with shouts of "let every free man vote that carries arms."[89]

In mid-August 1776, the Maryland constitutional convention began its deliberations. The Militia Resolves were repeated as instructions to the delegates from Anne Arundel County.[90] While the Whig-dominated convention would reject the democratic constitution proposed in the Resolves,[91] both Whigs and Democrats were in accord with a militia composed of the whole people. The Democrats were inspired by Dr. Richard Price, the English philosopher, Thomas Paine, and the radicals of the Pennsylvania constitutional convention which was proceeding at the same time.[92] John Adams and Carroll of Carrollton inspired the Whigs.[93]

The committee appointed to draft a declaration of rights and constitution included Matthew Tilghman, Charles Carroll of Carrollton, Thomas Johnson, George Plater, William Paca, Samuel Chase, Robert Goldsborough, Robert T. Hooe, and, until he lost his convention seat, Charles Carrollton the Barrister. Each of the committee members were Whigs, assuring defeat for the Democratic faction.[94]

A declaration of rights was soon reported, but not debated for some time. At the end of September, William Fitzhugh moved as follows: "As the establishing a bill of rights and formation of a new government on the authority of the people only, are matters of the utmost importance to the good people of this state," that the proposals be printed for the people to consider.[95] The motion passed. There were constant interruptions to convention business, so that by mid-October John Parnham moved "that this Convention will enter on no new business (except from evident necessity) until they have finished the consideration of the declaration of rights and form of government."[96] The convention proceeded to do so, but by the end of the month Fitzhugh unsuccessfully moved, "as the bill of rights formerly printed . . . has been materially altered by a committee of the whole house," that it be printed before further consideration for the people at large to read.[97]

Little else is known about the drafting of the Declaration of Rights. It was reported, considered, slightly amended, and adopted by November 3.[98] The rights it recognized were limited. Freedom of speech was guaranteed only in the legislature.[99] The clause "all persons, professing the Christian religion, are equally entitled to protection in their religious liberty," limited freedom of religion to Catholics and Protestants.[100]

While explicitly recognizing few individual rights, the right of the people at large to be armed was implicit in the following provision: "That a well-regulated militia is the proper and natural defence of a free government."[101] The Declaration also rejected standing armies.[102] Since previous usage defined a well-regulated militia as composed of all the freemen of the state, the militia clause guaranteed the right of the people at large to keep and bear arms.

The Rights of a Freeman

The perception of a right to bear arms in Maryland was further reflected in sources other than the Declaration of Rights. The statutory law of the state reveals no infringements on this right. That fact, together with the assurances of the federalists, perhaps explains why the Maryland ratifying convention would adopt the federal Constitution without any demand for recognition of that right or a bill of rights at all.

A review of Maryland statutes dating back to 1692 which were still on the books in 1794 reveals no laws which interfered with the freeman's right to own and possess arms. Only one firearms restriction existed, and it applied to slaves.

Originally passed in 1715, the statute provided:

That no negro or other slave within this province shall be permitted to carry any gun, or any other offensive weapon, from off their master's land, without license from their said master; and if any negro or other slave shall presume to do, he shall be carried before a justice of peace, and be whipped, and his gun or other offensive weapon shall be forfeited to him that shall seize the same and carry such negro so offending before a justice of peace.[103]

Harsh as it was, this statute allowed slaves to carry guns on the master's land without a permit, and abroad with a permit, rather than imposing an absolute prohibition. The same act promoted the arming of freemen by forfeiting the weapon to the person who turned the slave in rather than to the state.

Since the free citizens of Maryland were not deprived of arms, they apparently recognized no need for an explicit guarantee in their state constitution other than the militia clause. When the federal constitution was proposed, however, the fear arose that congressional power over the militia could result in the disarming of the people.

Luther Martin's "Letter on the Constitution," an initial version of which was delivered to the Maryland legislature in early 1788, became a major Anti-Federalist tract. Among Martin's many objections was that the proposed government was given power "to increase and keep up a standing army as numerous as it would wish, and, by placing the militia under its power, enable it to leave the militia totally unorganized, undisciplined, and even to disarm them."[104] This was contrary to the principle that the armed citizenry should be able to check oppression. "By the principles of the American revolution, arbitrary power may, and ought to, be resisted even by arms, if necessary."[105]

Despite these objections, a majority in the Maryland constitutional convention would, without answering any arguments from the Anti-Federalists, ratify the Constitution. After doing so, a committee was appointed to consider possible amendments. Three of the committee members had been members of the committee which had drafted the Maryland Declaration of Rights of 1776.[106] The committee adopted several amendments, first of which was "that Congress shall exercise no power but what is expressly delegated by this Constitution."[107] This was intended to moderate congressional power over the state bills of rights.[108]

The committee also proposed that the militia shall not be subject to martial law in peacetime, "for all other provisions in favor of the rights of men would be vain and nugatory, if the power of subjecting all men, able to bear arms, to martial law at any moment should remain vested in Congress."[109] However, the committee rejected proposals against standing armies and a national religion.[110] Ironically, the committee later determined not to report any amendments.[111]

Maryland adopted the federal Constitution without proposing any amendments.[112] However, Maryland was the second state to ratify the proposed federal Bill of Rights, including what became the Second Amendment right of the people to keep and bear arms.[113] Maryland's action would be paralleled by that of its small neighbor, the state of Delaware.

DELAWARE

The Declaration of Rights of 1776

Before 1776, Delaware was part of Pennsylvania. Although most of its people supported independence from Pennsylvania, they were divided on the question of independence from Britain. In the Continental Congress, two of Delaware's delegates—Thomas McKean and Caesar Rodney—voted for independence.[114] George Read voted against, and John Dickinson left the Congress rather than sign the Declaration of Independence.[115]

The split vote over independence foretold political divisions in Delaware for the following two decades. McKean and Rodney would lead the Whigs, otherwise known as the country or democratic party. The Tories, the court or aristocratic party, would be led by Read and Dickinson. In their first test of strength, the election of a convention of delegates to frame a state constitution, the Tories predominated.[116]

The constitutional convention began on August 27, 1776, with George Read presiding. On September 2, Read and nine other delegates were appointed to "be a Committee to prepare a Declaration of Rights and

Fundamental Rules of this State."[117] Three days later, the committee reported having made progress.[118]

On September 6, Thomas McKean was appointed to the committee to draft a declaration of rights.[119] A resident of Pennsylvania, McKean was a follower of Judge George Bryan,[120] the most influential member of the Pennsylvania convention, which had recently adopted a declaration of rights.[121]

According to one source, McKean authored the Delaware constitution.[122] However, the Pennsylvania Declaration of Rights (and later the rest of the Pennsylvania constitution) had been published in August in Pennsylvania newspapers,[123] which circulated in Delaware. Further, a declaration of rights had been reported, but not adopted, in the Maryland convention by late August.[124] By September 11, the Delaware Declaration of Rights was reported to the convention and read "by Paragraphs, and being debated and amended was agreed to."[125] George Read, convention president and chairman of the committee, wrote Caesar Rodney that the declaration "is made out of the Pennsylvania and Maryland Draughts."[126]

As adopted, the Delaware declaration provided for an armed populace as follows: "That a well regulated Militia is the proper, natural and safe Defense of a free Government."[127] Similar language appeared in the Maryland[128] and Virginia declarations,[129] but not that of Pennsylvania. However, both Delaware and Pennsylvania declarations included provisions that standing armies are dangerous to liberty, and that the military should be kept subordinate to the civil power.[130]

Unlike Pennsylvania, Delaware did not specifically declare that the people may bear arms for defense of self and state.[131] However, much of the Delaware convention concerned the arming of the people and the encouragement of independent militia companies. Just after the Declaration was approved, Thomas McKean was appointed to a committee to evaluate a gunsmith's proposals for erecting a gunlock manufactory in the state.[132]

The delegates considered a petition of persons who apologized for their involvement in a recent insurrection. Since they promised to conduct themselves peaceably, the convention resolved "that they be again restored to the Favour of their Country, and that their Arms be redelivered to them."[133] As for the people at large, the convention resolved that militia members were required to provide their own arms.[134]

Not all rights were taken for granted. The Declaration of Rights failed explicitly to protect freedom of speech. Only "Persons professing the Christian Religion ought forever to enjoy equal Rights and Privileges in this State."[135] A critic commented that "there are some good things in the Delaware constitution, which are evidently borrowed from the Pennsylvanian, but mangled like a school-boy's abridgement of a Spectator's paper. Some of their bill of rights, explained by tories, might prevent all American defence."[136]

Whigs, Tories, and Loyalists

Like the other colonies, Delaware traditionally recognized keeping and bearing arms as both a right and a duty. Prerevolutionary militia acts required each male to "provide himself" with a firearm and "to keep such Arms and Ammunition by him."[137] "Being persuaded that a well regulated militia is the most effectual Guard and Security to every Country," the colonial assembly provided "that the Inhabitants may be armed, trained and disciplined in the Art of War . . . to defend themselves, their Lives and Properties."[138]

For security against pirates, "all the Inhabitants and Freemen" of the seaport of Lewes were obliged to meet armed on the sound of the alarm.[139] The only restriction on possession of firearms in Delaware was "that no bought Servant, or Negro or Mulatto Slave, shall, upon any Pretence whatever, be allowed to bear Arms, or to be mustered in any of the Companies of the Militia within this Government."[140]

On the eve of the Revolution, whigs formed an armed association. Commanded by Caesar Rodney, its members promised to "defend the liberties and privileges of America, as well natural as constitutional, against all invaders of such as may attempt the least violation or infringement of them."[141] However, a large portion of Delawareans were Tories or loyalists who opposed independence. In May 1776, just after Congress recommended that the colonies form new governments, John Haslet wrote Caesar Rodney: "But [I] fear Congress must either disarm a large part of Kent and Sussex [counties] or see their Recommendation treated with contempt."[142]

In June 1776, Tory insurrections in opposition to independence broke out in Dover and Sussex. The diary of a Lewes resident described the events as follows: "Col. [Caesar] Rodney came to try Tories with 1000 men. . . . also a Fair Representation of Riflemen to Reduce a Tory Insurrection here . . . Tories ordered to bring in their arms and ammunition."[143] But when Tory leader William Polk protested, the Council of Safety replied: "We . . . are totally strangers with respect to your complaint of a number of guns being taken from you."[144]

A majority of delegates elected to the Delaware constitutional convention of 1776 were Tories.[145] Richard Basset, a leader of the June insurrection, was elected to the convention, where he served on the committee which framed the Declaration of Rights.[146] As noted, the convention voted to return the arms to those who participated in the recent insurrection.[147]

In October, hundreds of armed Tories swarmed on Lewes to guarantee that only friends of the King voted for the new legislature. At least one person who had been disarmed in the June insurrection was elected to office.[148] William Polk, who complained of seizure of Tories' arms but who allegedly disarmed Whigs, was appointed as a judge.[149]

Continued Tory attacks on Whigs through 1778 led Sussex assemblymen to propose to President George Read "that no method will so effectively beat down and curb the spirit of disaffection as the taking up a few of their principals and disarming the rest in general."[150] When Read refused to act, a legislative committee warned that "many have taken up arms and assembled together to the terror of the good people," intending to join the British.[151] The assembly recommended that the disaffected be disarmed.[152]

Further disturbances occurred in 1780 when loyalists, sparked in part by rumors that they would be disarmed, themselves roamed Sussex County, disarming Whigs. Participants in what became known as the Black Camp Rebellion, John Collins wrote Caesar Rodney, "began to rob the inhabitants of their arms and the accutrements."[153]

Professor Harold Hancock, author of the leading study on the subject, concluded that the struggle in Delaware, "especially in Sussex County, was like a special kind of Civil War in which the inhabitants tried to disarm one another," albeit with little actual violence.[154] Delaware loyalists "resented the confiscation of arms by whig militia."[155] "Rumors concerning the seizures of weapons . . . stirred up disturbances time and again."[156]

After the war, Whigs refused to recognize rights to suffrage by the loyalists or "Black Camp men." Interference in elections by armed bodies continued unabated in Delaware for another decade. Disturbances reached a peak in October 1787, just as the states began to consider the proposed federal Constitution. In Delaware, the Constitution raised little controversy, both Tories and Whigs favoring the new system.[157] While the other states debated the proposal, Delaware debated the Sussex election.

Charles Polk and Rhoads Shankland were among the Tories elected in a tumultuous situation at the Sussex polls.[158] Protests were lodged with the legislature that militia companies entered Lewes and, "furnished with pistols, clubs, cutlasses, etc. to the great terror of the peaceable inhabitants," beat and prevented people from voting.[159] The Sheriff admitted that "a number of men armed with muskets" marched into Lewes, but "they offered no violence . . . to any person." They were led by revolutionary war veterans determined to prevent Black Camp men from voting.[160] The Tory-dominated legislature then voided the election and, when the election took place again in November, Tories prevented Whigs from voting through threats of violence.[161]

In early 1788, Whigs petitioned the General Assembly that "Charles

Polk, Esquire, one of the elected members, on the Saturday preceding the election, in a public company was heard to advise his friends to carry their firearms; and that Rhoads Shankland, Esquire, another of the elected members, on the next day being Sunday was seen at the head of a party armed with muskets going towards the place."[162] "Those of your petitioners who attended the election observed a number of men armed with clubs, swords, and pistols at the place, and some hundreds of men armed with muskets paraded near, a party of whom made prisoners of some of your petitioners."[163]

Tories in the legislature responded "that the people had a right to assemble as they did in defense of their rights and privileges; nor did the election laws forbid whole armies from assembling, in military array, if they only kept a mile off from the place of election; that the indiscreet expressions of individuals, a few clubs, pistols and swords, and even boxing and fighting about indifferent matters, were no impediments to the freedom of voting."[164] The General Assembly upheld the validity of the election.

Dr. James Tilton, a Whig leader, alleged that the legislative action on the two disputed elections was dictated by Tory leader George Read.[165] In an anonymous pamphlet entitled *The Biographical History of Dionysius, Tyrant of Delaware*, Tilton recalled the bitter divisions of 1776. After the June 1776 insurrection, "the commissioners ordered all those who were convicted from overt acts of an intention of joining the enemy, to be disarmed. With the utmost humility, and apparent gratitude for the lenity of their judges, they hastened to obey the mandate, brought in and delivered up their arms."[166] However, the constitutional convention of 1776 "restored to the Sussex insurgents their arms, and even their respective commands in the militia; and it was not long afterwards, before several of the Sussex deputies, who had served in the convention, took up their residence with the enemy."[167] The pamphlet also denounced a Sussex judge, William Polk, who "plundered his whig neighbor of his arms and ammunition, and . . . joined the insurgents."[168]

The above pamphlet circulated during 1787 when the proposed federal Constitution was being hotly debated. The disputed elections which preceded it indicate the political context in which Delaware ratified the Constitution. Electorial disturbances continued in Sussex County for years. In early 1790, the General Assembly repealed an act which disenfranchised loyalists.[169] However, events at the Delaware constitutional convention the following year would reveal that arms and suffrage were still being debated by the same Whigs and Tories.

Arms Proposals at the Convention of 1791

The Delaware constitutional convention which began at the end of 1791 was dominated by many of the same personalities who had been prominent from the events of 1776 through the recent Sussex election disputes. The committee to consider alterations of the constitution, chaired by John Dickinson, included six members of the constitutional convention of 1776: Nicholas Ridgely, Richard Bassett, John Clayton, Kensey Johns, and Rhoads Shankland. Other committee members were Charles Polk, Thomas Montgomery, Edward Roche, James Sykes, Peter Robinson, and Isaac Cooper.[170]

As the above select committee met, the committee of the whole determined "that the *Declaration of Rights* should be amended in such manner, as more particularly to enumerate, and more precisely define, the rights reserved out of the general powers of government."[171] The need for a more detailed bill of rights was prompted by the greater refinement in bills of rights in America, most recently the still pending amendments to the U.S. Constitution. Delaware ratified the federal Bill of Rights on January 28, 1790, but a sufficient number of states had not yet done so.

On December 15, 1791, Virginia, the eleventh of the fourteen states, finally ratified the federal Bill of Rights, making it effective for all the states. Two days later, the select committee in the Delaware convention reported a detailed declaration of rights, which included the following: "The right of the citizens to bear arms in defence of themselves, and the state, shall not be questioned."[172] This was substituted for the now deleted militia clause of the 1776 Declaration.[173]

The select committee proposal on the right to bear arms was copied verbatim from the Pennsylvania Declaration of Rights of 1790.[174] The proposal was also perhaps prompted by the recently enacted federal Second Amendment. Further, introduction of an arms guarantee reflected an insecurity stemming from the disarming of Whigs by Tories and vice versa dating at least from 1776. Richard Bassett, a member of the committee and a Tory, complained about gun seizures and was himself disarmed in 1776,[175] but went on to serve in the 1776 convention and the federal constitutional convention of 1787. Two other members, Charles Polk and Rhoads Shankland, allegedly encouraged their followers to carry guns at the Sussex election in 1787.[176]

When the right-to-arms proposal reached the committee of the whole, the delegates could not agree on proposed language to qualify the right. The minutes reflect the following:

> The eighteenth Section of the first Article being under Consideration, viz.
> 18. The Right of *the Citizens to bear Arms* in defence of themselves and the State, shall not be questioned.
> It was moved by Mr. Batson, seconded by Mr. Polk, to add to the Section the Words *while acting in strict subordination to the Civil Power:*
> *Which passed in the Negative.*
> A motion was made by Mr. Ridgely, seconded by Mr. Johns, to strike out the Words, the *Citizen to bear Arms,* and, in Lieu thereof, insert the Words, *bearing Arms by Citizens qualified to vote for Representatives.*

It was then moved by Mr. Johnson, seconded by Mr. Clayton, to postpone the last Motion in order to introduce the following:

That there be added to the Section the Words *unless under such Pretensions, any Person disturb the Peace and Happiness, or Safety of Society.*

On the Question for Postponement,

It was determined in the Affirmative.

A Motion was then made by Mr. Bassett, seconded by Mr. Batson, to strike out the said Section,

Which was determined in the Affirmative; And the Section expunged.[177]

Although the delegates did not fear a guarantee of an individual right to bear arms for self-defense, they were apprehensive about groups of armed citizens taking it upon themselves to act in defense of the state, such as during elections. The first proposed amendment, that citizens bearing arms must act "in strict subordination to the Civil Power," clearly sought to restrict militia interference at the polls. Interestingly, Charles Polk, who seconded the motion, won both disputed elections in Sussex in 1787. He apparently resented the interference by Whig militiamen at the first election, and advised his followers to carry firearms at the second.[178]

The second proposed qualification sought to restrict bearing arms to "Citizens qualified to vote for Representatives." In some states, this could have meant that only property owners were guaranteed the rights of citizenship. In Delaware, however, this was clearly an attempt to extend the policy dating from the Revolution of denying suffrage and arms to Black Camp men. While loyalists had been enfranchised in 1790, Whigs in the convention undoubtedly relished an opportunity again to disarm the perceived traitors. The failure of this proposed amendment was probably due to Tory insistence that their loyalist allies not be deprived of arms or the ballot.

The third amended version sought to qualify arms-bearing with the proviso that it not "disturb the Peace and Happiness, or Safety of Society." This again was likely directed against interference by armed bodies with elections.

The delegates being unable to agree on specific language, the whole section was stricken. The movants were Richard Bassett, whose complaint about gun seizures during the Revolution is noted above, and Mr. Batson, who had proposed that the right to bear arms be exercised in subordination to the civil power. Nonetheless, the convention members did recognize the right of the citizens to bear arms. Many had served the year before in the legislature which adopted the federal Second Amendment. Their own select committee had recommended the arms guarantee. The delegates apparently preferred to leave the right unenumerated when they could not agree on restrictive language.

In its final version, adopted in mid–1792, the Delaware Declaration of

Rights included neither a militia clause nor an arms guarantee. The preference against standing armies, and for subordination of the military to the civil power, remained.[179]

Even though the de facto right of the citizen to bear arms went unquestioned, the noncitizen enjoyed no such right. In a message to the constitutional convention of 1791, Warner Mifflin denounced slavery, proposing constitutional recognition of the right of every human born in Delaware to be free.[180] The select committee recommendation that the Declaration of Rights include the phrase all men "are by Birth free and equal" was deleted on motion of John Dickinson.[181] The only legislative infringement on the individual right to bear arms in Delaware was the following: "That if any Negro or Mulatto slave shall presume to carry any guns, swords, pistols, fowling-pieces, clubs, or other arms and weapons whatsoever, without his master's special licence for the same, he shall be whipt with twenty-one lashes, upon his bare back."[182]

The militia act of 1793 provided at "each and every free able bodied white male citizen," ages eighteen through forty-four, must "provide himself with the arms" of either a footman, including a musket or firelock, or a horseman, including a sword and pair of pistols.[183] While the constitutional convention had failed to agree on specific language for a right to bear arms, that right remained a legal duty.

NEW HAMPSHIRE

The Declaration of Rights of 1784 and the Perpetual Laws

New Hampshire was the last state to adopt a declaration of rights in the epoch of the American Revolution. Like Virginia, the first state to do so, New Hampshire explicitly recognized a well-regulated militia, that is, an armed populace. Further, New Hampshire would offer unique language when the states sought protection for the right to bear arms in a federal bill of rights.

On December 14–15, 1774, lawyer and militia chief John Sullivan led New Hampshire citizens to break open His Majesty's Castle William and Mary at Portsmouth Harbor, seizing one hundred barrels of gunpowder and sixty stand of small arms.[184] "A Watchman" apologized by asking, "Whether, when we are by an arbitrary Decree prohibited *the having* Arms and Ammunition by Importation, we have not by the Law of Self Preservation, a Right to seize upon all those within our Power, in order to *defend* the LIBERTIES which GOD and Nature have given us . . . ?"[185] "Amicus Patriae" noted that "they surely meant only to seize the Ammunition belonging to every Town, and private Property, which we have been led to suspect would have been seized upon by Administration, to enforce Obedience to their cruel measures."[186]

The citizens were arming themselves from all possible sources. It was reported from Newport in early 1775 that "POWDER bears a very good Price in this Town; the People from all parts of the Country, the Fall past, having bought up almost all there was, to defend themselves against *Wolves, and other Beasts* of PREY."[187] The attitudes implicit in such statements would be reflected in the constitutional features of the state for the next decade and a half.

New Hampshire was the last of the eight states that adopted a bill of rights in the Revolutionary period. Its brief Constitution of 1776 complained that the British were "depriving us of our national and constitutional rights and privileges."[188] A constitution proposed and rejected by the town meetings in 1779 included a short Declaration of Rights which stated: "We the people of this State, are entitled to life, liberty, and property; and all other immunities and privileges which we heretofore enjoyed."[189]

Several drafts of constitutions were developed in a series of conventions and town meetings during 1781–1783. A convention address to the people held that "the strength and safety of this State will greatly depend on the keeping up a well regulated militia"[190] and that "the Bill of Rights . . . is the foundation on which the whole political fabric is reared."[191] One of the convention leaders was John Sullivan, then attorney general and soon to be president of the state.[192]

A constitution was finally ratified by the towns and made effective in 1784. Its Bill of Rights included the following interrelated articles:

II. All men have certain natural, essential, and inherent rights; among which are—the enjoying and defending life and liberty—acquiring, possessing and protecting property—and in a word, of seeking and obtaining happiness. . . .

X. The doctrine of non-resistance against arbitrary power, and oppression, is absurd, slavish, and destructive of the good and happiness of mankind. . . .

XXIV. A well regulated militia is the proper, natural, and sure defence of a state.

XXV. Standing armies are dangerous to liberty, and ought not to be raised or kept up without the consent of the legislature.

The right to be protected and the duty of each "to contribute his share in the expense of such protection, and to yield his personal service when necessary" was proclaimed.[193] Even so, the right of a pacifist *not* to bear arms was recognized too: "No person who is conscientiously scrupulous about the lawfulness of bearing arms, shall be compelled thereto, provided he will pay an equivalent."[194]

To be sure, the Bill of Rights was limited in certain respects. The Protestant religion was state supported, and the Bill of Rights said that only Christians "shall be equally under the protection of the law."[195] Freedom of speech was recognized only in the legislature.[196]

The Perpetual Laws of the State of New Hampshire, a book of statutes enacted from 1776 to 1788, contains no restriction on the right to keep and bear arms. The Act for the Establishment and Regulation of the Militia of 1786 provided that "the training band . . . shall consist of all the able-bodied male persons within the state, from sixteen years old to forty,"[197] and that all exempt males "shall constitute an alarm list . . . and shall, in all respects, be equipped with arms and accoutrements, as is by this act directed for those of the training band."[198]

The act required that all persons "both in the alarm list and training band, shall be provided, and have constantly in readiness, a good musket, and a bayonet fitted thereto" with ammunition and supplies.[199] Persons unable to furnish themselves with arms would be issued arms by the towns.[200] Once every six months, the commanding officer of each alarm company would "call his company together, and examine their arms and accoutrements," and punish any deficiency of arms.[201] While not a requirement that all firearms be reported to authorities, this mandated that each citizen show a militia official that he owned one musket.

The fire code of Portsmouth included a regulation on large amounts of gunpowder. A 1786 act found that "the keeping of large quantities of gun-powder in private houses in Portsmouth . . . would greatly endanger the lives and properties of the inhabitants thereof, in case of fire; which danger might be prevented, by obliging the owners of such powder, to deposit the same in the magazine provided by said town for that purpose."[202] The act provided:

That if any person or persons, shall keep in any dwelling-house, store or other building, on land, within the limits of said Portsmouth, except the magazine aforesaid, more than ten pounds of gun-powder at any one time, which ten pounds shall be kept in a tin cannister properly secured for that purpose, such person or persons shall forfeit the powder so kept, to the firewards of said Portsmouth, to be laid out by them in purchasing such utensils as they may judge proper for the extinguishing of fire. . . .

That there shall be chosen annually, or oftener if necessity require, by the inhabitants of said Portsmouth, being legal voters, a keeper of said magazine, whose duty it shall be, to receive into, and deliver out of said magazine, all the powder so deposited, and to account therefore.[203]

This was a rare instance in which the early states restricted the keeping at home of ammunition. The purpose of the law was not to control the populace, but to prevent explosions in an urban area caused by large amounts of black powder, a volatile substance. The law also illustrates use of the word "keep," as in "the right to keep arms," to indicate arms or ammunition kept at home, and "deposit" to indicate items stored in a town facility. The owners of the powder were protected by being able to elect the keeper of the magazine and to retrieve their powder on request. As they proved in 1774, the citizens of Portsmouth knew how to withdraw their deposits if the keepers were reluctant.

"Never Disarm Any Citizen": New Hampshire's Contribution to the Federal Bill of Rights

In the period leading to the adoption of the federal Constitution, New Hampshire was an armed society. The ratio of militia to the adult male population was about one to one and a half.[204] Since there was at least one militiaman in each New Hampshire family,[205] each family had at least one firearm. One scholar notes of militia chief John Sullivan: "From the close of the Revolutionary war, Sullivan had been interested in the militia of the state. Arms were in abundance and in 1783 some twenty or thirty regiments of militia were organized embracing about 80,000 men. These were drilled and disciplined by Sullivan, who was elected the Commander-in-chief of the State's military forces."[206]

In September 1786, in the midst of agitation for abolition of debts and after the legislature passed an act allowing former Tories to return to their estates, two hundred "rioters" with fifty muskets engaged in an armed demonstration at the General Court in Exeter.[207] Two thousand militiamen turned out to disperse them.[208] Shays' Rebellion followed immediately in Massachusetts.[209]

Shays' Rebellion produced the federal Constitution, but anti-federalists in New Hampshire insisted that it not be adopted without a bill of rights. The first New Hampshire convention called to consider the proposed constitution contained an anti-federalist majority, and the federalists maneuvered an adjournment so the convention would not reject the constitution.[210]

At the second session of the ratifying convention, a committee of fifteen was appointed to consider amendments. The eight federalists on this committee were led by convention president John Sullivan; the seven anti-federalists were led by Joshua Atherton.[211] The committee's charge was to consider possible amendments to the proposed constitution.[212]

The amendments were apparently already drafted, because they were reported back to the convention the same day. The following are the recommended amendments which concerned individual rights, and these amendments would be reflected in the first three articles of the federal Bill of Rights:

X. That no standing army shall be kept up in time of peace, unless with the consent of three fourths of the members of each branch of Congress; nor shall soldiers in a time of peace, be quartered upon private houses without the consent of the owners.

XI. Congress shall make no laws touching religion or to infringe the rights of conscience.

XII. Congress shall never disarm any citizen, unless such as are or have been in actual rebellion.[213]

While the anti-federalists stressed the need for such written guarantees, the federalists agreed to the substance but did not think it necessary to put them in writing. Both held that "Congress shall never disarm any citizen," although the federalists, with the 1786 disorders in New Hampshire and Massachusetts fresh in mind, would have insisted on the qualification "unless such as are or have been in actual rebellion."

The phrase "never disarm" would apply to keeping, bearing, and lawfully using arms. The right was recognized to lodge in every citizen, and not just in the able-bodied male population which constituted the militia. The provision against standing armies may have been supported by both sides; indeed, the federalists were led by the state militia chief John Sullivan.

Possession of arms, religion and conscience, and no peacetime quartering of soldiers in private houses were the only substantive rights mentioned. Speech, press, and assembly were not mentioned, but the recommended amendments began: "That it be explicitly declared that all powers not expressly and particularly delegated by the aforesaid Constitution are reserved to the several states, to be by them exercised."[214]

Anti-federalist leader Atherton moved that the convention ratify the Constitution subject to the condition that it not be operable in New Hampshire without ratification of the amendments.[215] The federalists moved to ratify the Constitution and to recommend the amendments to Congress.[216] The convention then voted fifty-seven to forty-seven to ratify.[217] The ninth state to ratify, New Hampshire made the Constitution effective.

The following year, the federalists won the Congressional elections in New Hampshire, in part by championing adoption of a federal bill of rights which had been demanded by several states. Anti-federalist Joshua Atherton wrote: "To carry on the farce the Federalists have taken the liberty to step onto the ground of their opponents, and, clothing themselves with their armor, talk high of amendments. . . . New York, Virginia, and other states having gone so fully into the detail of amendments, the strokes of abler hands ha[ve] rendered the lines of my feeble pen unnecessary."[218]

This suggests that Atherton may have authored the bill of rights proposals adopted by the New Hampshire convention, including the guarantee that "Congress shall never disarm any citizen." Among the declarations of rights demanded by Virginia and New York, to which

Atherton referred, was the clause, "that the people have a right to keep and bear arms."[219] These demands led to the proposal of what became the Second Amendment, which New Hampshire ratified with the rest of the federal Bill of Rights on January 25, 1790.

The state constitutional convention of 1791–1792 readopted the previous state bill of rights. The guarantee of a well regulated militia and most other provisions "were read and no debate ensued."[220] No attempt on the floor was made to add an arms guarantee similar to what New Hampshire demanded for the federal Bill of Rights. There was apparently no fear that the state, unlike Congress, would ever "disarm any citizen."

So ends the saga of the first American states to adopt bills of rights. But why did the other six states adopt no declaration of rights during the Revolutionary period? Were the rights to the press or to keep arms not considered fundamental in these other states? As the following chapters suggest, the view was equally prevalent that a freeman had no need of a written list of rights.

CHAPTER 4

Constitutions Without Bills of Rights

Four of the original states adopted written constitutions once independence was declared, but adopted no bill of rights. These states were New York, New Jersey, South Carolina, and Georgia. British war measures left the conventions of these states with little leisure to declare abstract rights. Further, the philosophical views would be expressed that a free people had little use for a written list, and that the existence of such a list could be misconstrued by future despots to deny the existence of any rights not mentioned. The following traces the constitutional conventions and the various manifestations of attitudes toward the right to bear arms in these four states.

NEW YORK

Swords in Defense of Their Liberties

Ever since the British began to threaten the right to have arms in 1768, New York's newspapers were in the forefront of patriotic endeavors to arouse sympathy for Bostonians throughout the colonies. Not surprisingly, in revolutionary New York, keeping and bearing arms was an unquestioned fact. This reality is exemplified by newspapers of New York City in 1776, before its occupation that fall by the British under General Howe.

Detailed instructions for the home manufacture of gunpowder and advertisements for sword canes were published in the *New York Pack-*

et's first issue for 1776.[1] That summer, the New York convention passed a resolution supporting the private manufacture of gunpowder, which that body called "the Means of Defense and Self-preservation."[2]

The following advertisement appeared regularly in the *Packet* and the *Gazette* until the City was occupied by the British: "Those Gentlemen who are forming themselves into Companies in Defense of their Liberties; and others who are not provided with SWORDS may be suited therewith by applying to Charles Oliver Bruff."[3] Various sword designs inscribed with one's favorite patriot slogan could be had.

Discussion ensued in the press about how the armed people could defeat standing armies. "An English American" proposed: "For our security against the introduction of British troops to enslave us in times of tranquility, when we had forgot the use of arms, a perpetual standing militia bill should form part of the compact, by which means the people of the colonies would keep up their martial spirit, and always be prepared against the attack of arbitrary power."[4] The writer proposed that the King could retain a limited force to prevent sudden invasion. "Whoever asserts that 10 or 12,000 soldiers would be sufficient to control the militia of this Continent, consisting of 500,000 brave men, pays but a despicable compliment to the spirit and ability of Americans."[5]

In reply, "An Independent Whig" agreed with a militia composed of the whole people, but rejected a limited standing army: "The Praetorian guards at Rome, were, I believe, not a larger body, if so large; yet they kept the whole world in slavery for many years, raised any one to be Emperor whom they pleased, and cut him off if he happened to disoblige them. . . . A standing army have great power to do mischief, and enslave countries, because they are already raised."[6]

Ineffective at resisting invasion, the writer continued, "the soldiers are the dregs of every nation."[7] "They ought not to be named with the Provincials and Militia, who are freemen, sons of liberty, property, and bravery." A militia trained to be expert at arms would defeat any invader.[8]

As of September 1776, with the British conquest of New York City, newspapers no longer carried editorials supporting an armed populace, formulas for making gunpowder, or advertisements for the sale of arms. The occupation lasted through November 1783, months after the surrender at Yorktown. However, the editorials, formulas, and advertisements apparently had effect. Beginning with the occupation, New York City newspapers included a Proclamation of General Howe at the top of page one of every issue which decried that "several Bodies of armed Men . . . do still continue their Opposition to the Establishment of legal Government and Peace."[9]

The Constitution of 1777

Due to the British invasion, the constitutional convention of New York was one of the most erratic of all the newly independent states. Its place of assembly was repeatedly pushed around the state by British troop movements.[10] In a biography of one of its leaders, Theodore Roosevelt noted that "the members were obliged to go armed, so as to protect themselves from stray marauding parties. "[11]

The convention began its deliberations on August 1, 1776, and unanimously resolved that a committee draft a plan for a new form of government. The committee would "report at the same time a bill of rights; ascertaining and declaring the essential rights and privileges of the good people of this State, as the foundation for such form of government."[12] Thirteen members were elected to this committee.[13]

The committee was ordered to report the constitution and bill of rights on August 26, but the journal includes no mention of the subject on that day. For the next six months, the convention functioned mainly as a committee of safety. Its members were dispersed throughout the state fulfilling various duties. Some fought the invaders while others procured arms and ammunition.[14]

Finally, at the end of March 1777, a draft of a constitution in John Jay's handwriting was reported from committee. Jay played the leading role in framing the instrument, with Gouverneur Morris and Robert R. Livingston as his chief advisors.[15] Contrary to the charge resolved by the convention, the committee reported no bill of rights. Yet no record exists of any objection by the convention members, even those of radical persuasions.[16]

To be sure, the text of the constitution guaranteed jury trial where already practiced and religious toleration. Yet a proposal for complete freedom of religion was staunchly opposed and led to the longest debate of the session. Jay's biographer notes:

> The power of the Church of Rome he knew and feared; he urged, accordingly, amendment after amendment to except Roman Catholics till they should abjure the authority of the pope to absolve citizens from their allegiance and to grant spiritual absolution. The result of his objections was the adoption of a proviso "that the liberty of conscience hereby granted shall not be so construed as to excuse acts of licentiousness or justify practices inconsistent with the safety of the State."[17]

There appears to have been little controversy over other provisions of the constitution, or its lack of a bill of rights. No one questioned the right of the people to keep and bear arms. Many of the convention members (including John Jay) had also participated in the body which assumed the government when the old Colonial Assembly dissolved in April 1775. This body, known as the Committee of Observation, "called on the citizens to arm."[18]

The framers of New York's Constitution of 1777 would not have doubted the fundamental character of the right to carry arms for self protection, for they themselves constantly exercised this right. They considered bearing arms as a civic duty, and included the following in the constitution:

[I]t is the duty of every man who enjoys the protection of society to be prepared and willing to defend it; this convention therefore . . . doth ordain, determine, and declare that the militia of this State, at all times hereafter, as well in peace as in war, shall be armed and disciplined, and in readiness for service. That all such of the inhabitants of this State being of the people called Quakers as, from scruples of conscience, may be adverse to the bearing of arms, be therefrom excused by the legislature.[19]

Under the perilous circumstances, the framers of the New York Constitution sought to outline a plan of government and define certain essential duties of citizens, such as bearing arms. Little time existed to formulate and debate a declaration of rights. The convention journal reflects the following entry for April 20, 1777: "The constitution, or plan of government of this State, as amended, was read throughout, and such amendments as being proposed were unanimously agreed to without debate by every member present; and the general question being put thereon, it was agreed to by every member present, except Colo. Peter R. Livingston, who desired that his dissent thereto be entered on the minutes."[20]

It took nine months for the convention to frame and adopt a constitution. The chaos over a state swarming with redcoats rendered the lack of a written bill of rights a moot issue.

Why New York Demanded a Federal Bill of Rights

Lack of a written bill of rights did not lead to any oppressive legislation in New York, at least not in regard to the right to have arms. Exercise of that right was encouraged to suppress invaders and criminals. But when the federal Constitution was proposed a decade after the adoption of the state constitution, New Yorkers demanded explicit written guarantees for arms bearing and other rights.

After becoming the first chief justice of the New York Supreme Court, John Jay wrote in 1778 that criminals "multiply exceedingly. Robberies become frequent. . . . Punishment must of course become certain, and mercy dormant."[21] Certain and speedy punishment,[22] not deprivation of the right to have arms, was seen as the solution to crime. In fact, the armed citizen played a vital role in suppression of crime. Justice Jay and other penal reformers were influenced by Beccaria's *Essay on Crimes and Punishments*, the only American edition of which was published in New York in 1773.[23] Perhaps Beccaria influenced New York's reformers as much on the right to carry arms for self-defense as on the right against cruel and unusual punishment.[24]

A compilation of New York legislation from 1776 through 1792 contains only three laws concerning firearms ownership and use in situations not involving criminal aggression. Reflecting the traditional hue and cry, one act required "that all men generally be ready, and armed and accoutered, . . . and at the cry of the country, to pursue and arrest felons."[25] The Act to Regulate the Militia, passed in 1786, required every able-bodied male ages sixteen to forty-four to "provide himself, at his own expense, a good musket or firelock," and each horseman was "to furnish himself with . . . a pair of pistols."[26]

The only restrictive legislation concerned dangerous discharge of firearms on the New Year's holidays. A 1785 enactment declared that "great dangers have arisen, and mischief been done by the pernicious practice of firing guns, pistols, rockets, squibs and other fire-works on the eve of the last day of December, and the first and second days of January."[27] The act imposed a fine on any person to "fire or discharge any gun, pistol, rocket, squib or other fire-work, within a quarter of a mile of any building" at those times.[28]

While the New York Constitution to date contains no formal bill of rights, an act in early 1787 declared "that no authority shall, on any pretense whatsoever, be exercised over the citizens of this state, but such as is or shall be derived from and granted by the people of this state."[29] Containing provisions for the rights of petition and speech, and against excessive bail and the quartering of soldiers, the act declared: "that no citizen of this state shall be constrained to arm himself, or to go out of this state, . . . if it be not by assent and grant of the people of this state, by their representatives in senate and assembly."[30] This limited, statutory bill of rights could have been repealed by a simple legislative majority.

The federal constitution as proposed in 1787 likewise contained no bill of rights, but New York would be quick to demand one. Abraham Yates, Jr., who had been chairman of the committee that drafted the state constitution in 1777 without a bill of rights, explained:

The omission of a bill of rights in this state, has given occasion to an inference, that the omission was equally warrantable in the constitution for the United States. . . . While the constitution of this state was in agitation, there appeared doubts upon the propriety of the measure, from the peculiar situation in which the country then was; our connection with Britain dissolved, and her government formally renounced—no substitute devised—all the powers of government avowedly temporary, and solely calculated for defence: it was urged by those who were in favor of a bill of rights, that the power of the rulers ought to be circumscribed, the better to protect the people at large from the oppression and usurpation of the rulers. The English petition of rights, in the reign of Charles the first, and the bill of rights in the reign of King William, were mentioned as examples to support their opinions. Those in opposition admitted, that in established governments, which had an implied constitution, a declaration of rights might be necessary to prevent the usurpation of ambitious men, but that ... our situation resembled a people in a state of nature, ... and as such the constitution to be formed would operate as a bill of rights.

These and the like considerations operated to induce the convention of New York to dismiss the idea of a bill of rights. ... But these reasons will not apply to the general government.[31]

Under the pseudonym "Sydney," Yates published this explanation in the *New York Journal* in 1788, just four days before the New York convention met to consider ratification of the federal constitution. Antifederalist demands for a bill of rights were at high tide.

At least five members of the 1788 convention had been members of the committee which framed the New York Constitution of 1777: John Jay, John S. Hobart, Robert R. Livingston, Robert Yates, and Henry Wisner, Sr.[32] The federalists were led by John Jay and Alexander Hamilton, who had been arguing military establishments would never be a danger "while there is a large body of citizens, little if at all inferior to them in discipline and the use of arms, who stand ready to defend their rights and those of their fellow citizens."[33] The anti-federalists included John DeWitt, who had warned that Congress "at their pleasure may arm or disarm all or any part of the freeman of the United States."[34]

In the convention, Thomas Tredwell expressed a major objection to the Constitution in these words: "Here we find no security for the rights of individuals. ... ; here is no bill of rights, no proper restriction of power."[35] Accordingly, the New York convention ratified the federal Constitution subject to the understanding that certain rights cannot be violated. Among the proposed amendments was the following: "That the people have a right to keep and bear arms; that a well-regulated militia, including the body of the people capable of bearing arms, is the proper, natural, and safe defense of a free state."[36] The amendments were prefaced with the comment that "we, the delegates of the people of the state of New York ... do declare and make known," and ended with the admonition "that the rights aforesaid cannot be abridged or violated."[37]

Two weeks after James Madison proposed the federal bill of rights to Congress in June 1789, the *New York Packet* reprinted an explanation of the proposals. Of what became the Second Amendment, the writer explained "that the people are confirmed by the next article in their right to keep and bear their private arms."[38] Tench Coxe, the anonymous writer, wrote a letter enclosing the article to James Madison, who was then in New York.[39] Madison responded, endorsing Coxe's explanation of the amendment and adding "that the printed remarks . . . are already I find in the Gazettes here."[40] Subsequent issues of the *Packet* reveal no disagreement with Coxe's explanation.

The individual right to keep and bear private arms was deemed fundamental at the founding of the state of New York. While its Constitution of 1777 contained no bill of rights, the common understanding of the time was that freedoms of speech, press, and arms could not be violated. Jealous of an abusive federal power, New York strongly recommended that these freedoms be explicitly guaranteed in the federal Constitution.

NEW JERSEY

Rights in Fact Without a Bill of Rights: The Constitution of 1776

On July 2, 1776 the New Jersey Provincial Congress, assembled as a convention, adopted a constitution. It contained no bill of rights, although it did provide "no Protestant inhabitant of this Colony shall be denied the enjoyment of any civil right, merely on account of his religious principles."[41] The common law of England, and the statute law which had been in effect in the colony to the extent not "repugnant to the rights and privileges contained in this Charter," was declared to remain in force, together with trial by jury.[42]

Professor Charles Erdman's study of this constitution shows that it was framed by a committee of ten chaired by Jacob Green, a Presbyterian minister.[43] The committee spent less than two days finalizing the draft, which was adopted by the committee of the whole in less than two-and-a-half days and by the state Congress in less than one day.[44] The chief draftsman appears to have been Jonathan D. Sergeant, a young attorney who was a friend of John Adams and an advocate of independence.[45]

Why was no bill of rights included in New Jersey's first constitution? First, "the New Jersey lawyers may have considered these fundamental rights were protected by the principles of the common law."[46] Second, the British fleet was anchored off the coast of the colony, and there was no time for theoretical discussions.[47] Just over two decades later, Judge William Griffith wrote that "public sentiment in New Jersey in 1776 dwelt with slight regard upon the *forms* of constitution. Engaged in a desperate conflict for freedom itself, it was thought of more consequence to exert courage in repelling foreign tyranny, than to sit canvassing the comparative merits of *theories*, which were to secure internal liberty, not yet won from our oppressors."[48]

Concerning the first state constitutions to be adopted without bills of rights, Professor Erdman states:

Of the four constitutions which were adopted prior to the Declaration of Independence, three contained clauses which intimated that the instruments of government were of a temporary nature. . . . These were the documents of New Hampshire, South Carolina and New Jersey. No one of these contained a Bill of Rights, whereas Virginia's charter, which was a virtual declaration of independence in itself, did include a statement of fundamental principles.

This fact might be of significance rather than a mere coincidence had all the other Colonies adopted Bills of Rights. But New York and Georgia, adopting constitutions subsequent to July 4, 1776, were lax in this particular.[49]

Still, the New York convention was being chased around the state while its members (who went armed) tried to write a constitution,[50] although conditions were more stable in Georgia, where the convention was part of the state Congress which engaged in ordinary legislation.[51] The conventions of the states which adopted the most elaborate declarations of rights—Virginia and Pennsylvania—were not under military threat as they deliberated. In the time period when it adopted its constitution, the New Jersey Congress was mostly concerned with organizing the militia for immediate defense and sending Tories to jail.[52]

Even though no bill of rights was adopted in New Jersey, several rights were recognized as fundamental. The right to petition and the right of Protestants to have arms were both recognized at common law and in the English Declaration of Rights of 1689.[53] As noted, the New Jersey Constitution guaranteed civil rights only to Protestants. The following directive, passed by the convention one day before it adopted the Constitution, suggests that the right to keep arms was recognized for those willing to bear arms against the British invaders, but not for pacifists and Tories:

Whereas by a regulation of the late Congress, the several committees in this colony, were authorized and directed to disarm all the non-associators and persons notoriously disaffected, within their bounds: and whereas it appears that the said regulation hath not been carried into effect in some parts of the colony; and it being absolutely necessary, in this present dangerous state of public affairs, where arms are much wanted for the public defence, that it should be instantly executed: It is therefore directed and resolved, that the several colonels in this colony do, without delay, proceed to disarm all such persons within their districts, whose religious principles will not permit them to bear arms; and likewise all such as hitherto have refused and still do refuse to bear arms; that the arms so taken be appraised by some indifferent person or persons;

... and that the appraisement and receipt be left in the hands of the person disarmed.[54]

Like tarring and feathering them, disarming and even killing Tories became a habit of patriots. However, the above exhortation to confiscate the arms of pacifists and other nonparticipants in the war, while motivated by the need to acquire scarce arms, was akin to the disarming of nonparticipants by Gage in Boston in 1775, which sparked the Revolution. In the same vein, New York's royal Governor Tyron, reported the Newark-based *New York Gazette*, circulated the following after the fall of New York City: "The Governor of the province recommends to the inhabitants of Suffolk county, the following measures, as the best means for those who have been active in the rebellion to preserve their lives and save their estates, viz. That all offensive arms, indiscriminately, be forthwith collected, in each respective manor, township, and precinct, as soon as possible, to deliver them up at headquarters, to the Commander in Chief of the King's troops."[55]

No Laws on the Books

In fall of 1776, Governor William Livingston recommended to the Council and Assembly of New Jersey "some further regulations respecting the better ordering the Militia,"[56] and the assembly agreed with "the necessity of a well-regulated militia for the defence of a free State."[57] George Washington addressed the county militia of New Jersey a year later as follows: "I therefore call upon you, by all you hold dear, to rise up as one Man, and rid your Country of its cruel invaders. . . . [T]his can be done by a general appearance of all its Freemen armed and ready to give them opposition. . . . I am convinced every Man who can bear a Musket, will take it up."[58]

A typical militia law of the time was the 1781 Act for the regulating, training, and arraying of the Militia, and for providing more effectually for the Defense and Security of the State.[59] The militia included "all effective Men between the Ages of sixteen and fifty Years."[60] "Every person enrolled as aforesaid, shall constantly keep himself furnished with a good Musket . . . [or] a good Rifle-Gun,"[61] while each horseman "shall at all Time keep himself provided with a good Horse, a Saddle properly furnished with a Pair of Pistols and Holsters."[62]

There were virtually no laws on the books restricting the nonaggressive possession or use of weapons. The state code with statutes passed between 1702–1776 reflects only a prohibition on shooting matches for gambling.[63] The code published in 1800 contained certain hunting regulations and a prohibition on setting a loaded gun.[64] While slaves could not hunt on Sundays and needed a pass, they were not disarmed by law.[65]

Aside from an antiduelling law passed in reaction to the affair between Alexander Hamilton and Aaron Burr in 1804,[66] New Jersey passed no law forbidding the possession and nonaggressive use of pistols, even allowing concealed weapons, until the twentieth century.

Lack of a bill of rights tradition in New Jersey explains in part why there was little opposition to a federal constitution without one in that state, which quickly ratified the Constitution with minimal debate.[67] This did not indicate a lack of belief in such rights as bearing arms; the people of New Jersey had responded to Lexington and Concord by arming and associating, and the first Provincial Congress created a militia system in May 1775.[68] In order to retain all of the rights of a freeman, a New Jersey writer argued in 1787 against George Mason's objections to the Constitution, these rights must not be restricted by putting them in a written straightjacket:

The people, or the sovereign power, cannot be affected by any such declaration of rights, they being the source of all power in the government; whatever they have not given away still remains inherent in them. . . . In England the king claims the sovereignty and supports an interest in opposition to the people. It becomes, therefore, both their interest and their duty, at every proper opportunity, to obtain a declaration and acknowledgment of those rights they should hold against their sovereign. But in America (thanks to the interposing providence of GOD!) the people hold all power, not by them expressly delegated to individuals, for the good of the whole.[69]

Despite the above, New Jersey was the first state to ratify the federal Bill of Rights, including the Second Amendment, having done so on November 20, 1789. Lack of any real opposition or debate indicates that the rights enumerated therein were accepted in New Jersey with little question.

SOUTH CAROLINA

The Constitution of 1776

The American Revolution in South Carolina was waged more by armed partisans than by a regular army.[70] In the words of South Carolina patriot John Drayton, "a spirit of independence, which their fathers had brought with them from England, gave to the inhabitants of those Colonies a knowledge of arms, and a spirit intolerant of oppression."[71]

In response to Britain's 1774 embargo on shipments of arms to the colonies, the General Committee, South Carolina's patriotic governing body, resolved " 'that whereas by the late prohibition of exporting arms and ammunition from England, it too clearly appears a design of disarming the people of America, in order the more speedily to dragoon and enslave them;' it was therefore recommended, to all persons, to provide themselves immediately, with at least twelve and a half pounds of powder, with a proportionate quantity of bullets."[72]

The Committee, which was reconstituted as the Provincial Congress, declared in 1775 "that solely for the Preservation and Defense of our Lives, Liberties, and Properties, we have been impelled to associate, to take up Arms."[73] It required "that every person liable to bear arms, shall appear completely armed, once in every fortnight" for militia exercises.[74] Drayton recalled that "in pursuance of the late recommendation of the Provincial Congress, [the mass of citizens] were diligently learning the use of arms; and were forming themselves into volunteer companies."[75] The Congress also adopted measures to encourage a "regiment of Rangers . . . composed of *expert* Rifle-men . . . ; each man, at his own expense, to be constantly provided with a good horse, rifle, shot-pouch and powder-horn, together with a tomahawk or hatchet."[76]

On February 11, 1776, the Provincial Congress elected an eleven man committee to prepare a form of government.[77] In early March, committee member Charles Cotesworth Pinckney, who twelve years later would lead South Carolina's proponents of the U.S. Constitution, delivered a report on the proposed constitution.[78] Deliberations ensued, and on March 26 the assembly adopted a constitution for the state of South Carolina. Although it contained no bill of rights, the right to arms was expressed in its preamble as follows:

Hostilities having been commenced in the Massachusetts Bay, by the troops under command of General Gage, whereby a number of peaceable, helpless, and unarmed people were wantonly robbed and murdered, and there being just reason to apprehend that like hostilities would be committed in all the other colonies, the colonists were therefore driven to the necessity of taking up arms, to repel force by force, and to defend themselves and their properties against lawless invasions and depredations."[79]

The above assumes the existence of a right not only to keep and bear arms, but also to use arms in defense of life, liberty, and property. When the Provincial Congress adopted the Constitution, it also elected William Henry Drayton, who had acted as its president, as the chief justice of the Supreme Court. Drayton was also a member of the Continental Congress. His son wrote: "Mr. Drayton always had about his person, a dirk and a pair of pocket pistols; for the defense of his life."[80]

Chief Justice Drayton soon delivered the first charge to the grand jury of Charleston District. In the course of this patriotic oration he warned that the King of England "will effectually disarm the Colony."[81] Drayton accused George III of "the violation of the fundamental laws" in the same manner as James II had done.[82] The grand jurors were then reminded of the charges against James in the English Bill of Rights of 1689, including: "By causing several good subjects, being Protestants, to be disarmed, at the same time when Papists were both armed and employed contrary to law."[83]

The framers of South Carolina's constitution perhaps deemed a bill of rights as unnecessary because the English Bill of Rights remained in force. A compilation of South Carolina laws published in 1790 noted "all the following Statutes of force here," including the English Bill of Rights, which "declares the Rights of the Citizens."[84] Under the category "Subjects Arms" the editor cited this provision: "That the Subjects which are Protestants may have arms for their Defense suitable to their Conditions, and as allowed by Law."[85]

Disarming Tories and Slaves

The citizens of South Carolina enjoyed an absolute right to keep and bear arms, but militant Tories and black slaves did not. A temporary war measure of disarming Tories who actively opposed independence was passed only days before the adoption of the state Constitution. The Provincial Congress resolved "that all persons who shall hereafter bear arms against, or shall be active in opposing, the measures of the Continental or Colony Congress . . . shall be disarmed, and, at the discretion of the said Committee, taken into custody."[86] This policy was alleviated by the further provision "that if any person who has been disarmed, shall convince the Committee aforesaid, that he sincerely desires to join in support of the American cause, his arms shall be restored to him."[87]

An anecdote concerning the above is revealed in a petition to the patriotic Secret Committee. Someone told the petitioner, a Mr. Hubart, that "a number of arms was sent over to be distributed amongst the Negroes, Roman Catholics, and Indians." Hubart replied, "it was very bad news, that Roman Catholics and Savages should be permitted to join and massacre Christians."[88] A Mr. Martin replied: " 'So, Mr. Hubart, you'll not allow Roman Catholics to carry guns.' Your petitioner answered, that his circumstances were too small, to forbid any party or sect to carry arms."[89] Martin then assaulted Hubart, threatening to kill him with a blade, and cursed the patriotic committee. The committee's sentence: "tar and feather him."[90]

Of more permanent duration was legislation disarming slaves. Two such acts were passed in the 1740s and reenacted in 1783. The first punished the teaching of slaves to write,[91] prohibited their free assembly and travel,[92] and provided: *It shall not be lawful for any slave, unless in the presence of some white person, to carry or make use of fire-arms, or any offensive weapon whatsoever, unless such negro or slave shall have a ticket or license in writing from his master, mistress or overseer.*[93]

Nor did a slave "have liberty to carry any gun, cutlass, pistol or other weapon, abroad from home" on Sundays, even with a license.[94] Slaves could shoot birds on the plantation without a license, "lodging the same gun at night within the dwelling-house of his master, mistress or white overseer."[95]

The second slave code subjected militiamen to patrol duty to guard against a slave insurrection.[96] Patrols were required to search for and whip slaves outside their plantation without permission.[97] "And the said patrols shall have full power to search and examine all negro-houses for offensive weapons and ammunition."[98]

The Constitutions of 1778 and 1790

In 1778, the South Carolina legislature adopted a new constitution.[99] While containing no bill of rights, it mandated due process of law, subordination of the civil to the military, and liberty of the press.[100] The rights to free speech and to bear arms, and prohibition of unreasonable search and seizure, while not specifically mentioned, were not questioned. Freedom of religion was definitely not considered a fundamental right. The longest article in the Constitution concerned such matters as the following: "The Christian Protestant religion shall be deemed, and is hereby constituted and declared to be, the established religion of this State. That all denominations of Christian Protestants in this State, demeaning themselves peaceably and faithfully, shall enjoy equal religious and civil privileges."[101]

The federal Constitution was proposed to the states for ratification in 1787. In January 1788, the South Carolina legislature debated whether to call a convention to consider its ratification. Charles Cotesworth Pinckney, one of South Carolina's delegates to the federal constitutional convention, led the federalists who supported adoption. His explanation of why it included no bill of rights is significant, because Pinckney played a leading role in framing the South Carolina Constitution of 1776, which likewise had no bill of rights. Pinckney stated: "We had no bill of rights inserted in our Constitution; for, as we might perhaps have omitted the enumeration of some of our rights, it might hereafter be said we had delegated to the general government a power to take away such of our rights as we had not enumerated; but by delegating express powers, we certainly reserve to ourselves every power and right not mentioned in the Constitution."[102]

Of the eleven members of the committee which framed the South Carolina Constitution of 1776, three represented South Carolina at the federal constitutional convention of 1787,[103] and seven were delegates at the convention of 1788 which ratified the federal Constitution.[104] They probably all agreed with Pinckney's argument, for they all voted for ratification. For the framers of South Carolina's Constitution of 1776, and the federalists of 1788, lack of a bill of rights did not imply that such rights as free press and bearing arms were not protected rights.

One third of the delegates voted against the federal Constitution.[105] They concurred with Patrick Dollard's remarks that the people were "opposed to this new Constitution, because, they say, they have omitted to insert a bill of rights therein, ascertaining and fundamentally establishing, the unalienable rights of men."[106] In its ratification, the South Carolina convention did not declare the necessity of a bill of rights, as did some states. However, South Carolina would ratify the federal Bill of Rights on January 19, 1790.

On June 3, 1790, South Carolina again adopted a new state constitution. The convention delegates who framed it included Charles Cotesworth Pinckney and several others who framed South Carolina's previous constitutions.[107] No bill of rights proposals were made in the convention, and the constitution was unanimously adopted without a formal bill of rights.[108] However, it protected limited free exercise of religion, jury trial, and liberty of the press.[109] While the rights of freedom of speech and keeping and bearing arms were not specifically mentioned, there were no laws on the books which even remotely infringed on these rights, other than slave codes.[110]

GEORGIA

The Constitution of 1777

At the coming of the American Revolution, Georgia had the smallest population of all the colonies.[111] Even though the agricultural colony produced no well known declarations of rights like those of Virginia or North Carolina, its settlers took for granted such rights as keeping and bearing arms.

As of April 1776, Georgia was governed by temporary Rules and Regulations which reflected the Whig doctrine that governmental power originated with the people.[112] When a convention assembled early the next year to frame a permanent constitution, it was led by radical Whigs,[113] whose political creed emphasized the role of the armed citizen in a republic.

Convention records reflect that on January 24, 1777, a committee of seven was elected to draft a constitution.[114] Its chairman and perhaps most active member was Button Gwinnett,[115] President of Georgia under the old Rules and Regulations. Five days later, Gwinnett reported a proposed constitution to the convention, where it was amended and then unanimously adopted on February 5.[116]

The preamble recites that British oppression "hath obliged the Americans, as freemen, to oppose such oppressive measures, and to assert the rights and privileges they are entitled to, by the laws of nature and reason."[117] The text contained no bill of rights, although it declared against excessive fines and bail and guaranteed habeas corpus, free press, and jury trial.[118] The rights to free speech, religion, and bearing arms were not specifically recognized but were assumed as fundamental by the Whigs who wrote the Constitution. Arms bearing was more than a right, it was mandatory: "Every County in this State that has, or hereafter may have, two hundred and fifty men upwards, liable to bear arms, shall be formed into a battalion."[119]

Lack of a bill of rights in the Georgia Constitution of 1777 may be explained by two reasons. First, under the prevailing Whig philosophy, the people retained all powers not delegated. Second, little time existed for theoretical discussions when the existence of the state was in doubt—Florida was held by the British, who soon captured Savannah.

The Whigs were split between the radical, popular, or country party and the conservative, city, or merchant party.[120] The former, led by Button Gwinnett, favored civilian control over the military while the latter, led by Brigadier General Lachlan McIntosh, held Georgia's new constitution as too democratic.[121] Gwinnett and McIntosh clashed over leadership of an expedition against St. Augustine, Florida. When the legislature approved Gwinnett's conduct, the two faced each other in a duel. Both were wounded, and Gwinnett died in three days.[122]

The British held Savannah and most of the settled areas of Georgia from 1778 through the end of the Revolution. Patriot guerrilla bands, composed of self armed and independent citizens, harassed the invaders without end. British expeditions burned homes and destroyed property as they marched, sparing only those who surrendered their arms on demand.[123]

Georgia's delegates at the Continental Congress in 1778 sought to deny citizenship rights to those who refused to pick up the gun in defense of the Revolution. Article IV of the Articles of Confederation excepted paupers, vagabonds, and fugitives from the guarantee that "the free inhabitants of each of those states . . . shall be entitled to all privileges and immunities of free citizens in the several states." Georgia proposed that "all persons who refuse to bear Arms in defense of the State to which they belong," and persons convicted of treason, should also be excepted from the privileges and immunities of free citizens.[124] Congress declined to add the provision.

Georgia's Firearms Laws

Under the laws of Georgia passed during the years 1755–1800 and still in force in the latter year, having arms was the duty of the free man, while deprivation of arms was the mark of the slave.

The only item in the Georgia code for that period under the topic "Fire Arms" was the act of 1770, passed "for the security and defense of this province from internal dangers and insurrections."[125] This act required that "every male white inhabitant of this province, (the inhabitants of the sea port towns only excepted who shall not be obliged to carry any other than side arms) who is or shall be liable to bear arms in the militia . . . and resorting . . . to any church . . . shall carry with him a gun, or a pair of pistols."[126] Each man was required to "take the said gun or pistols with him to the pew or seat," and these arms were to "be fit for immediate use and service."[127] Indian attacks and fear of slave uprisings prompted this act.

During the period of the ratification of the U.S. Constitution, Georgia passed a number of statutes to suppress "Indian Violences." An act passed in 1789 for discharging troops and "for collecting and securing the public arms" provided that on a certain date "the troops shall deposit their arms in the public storehouse."[128] This followed common linguistic usage of the day in referring to the *depositing* of public arms in an arsenal, in contrast with the *keeping* of private arms by the people, such as had been proposed a few months before in what became the federal Second Amendment.

While public arms were provided for special expeditions, citizens were expected to provide their own arms for militia duty. The act of 1792 required every free white inhabitant to "provide himself . . . with a musket or firelock . . . or with a good rifle."[129]

Legislation concerning "Slaves and Patrols" encompassed the only prohibitions on keeping and bearing arms in Georgia at the end of the eighteenth century. The Council Chamber passed these acts in the years 1765–1770. Every white liable to patrol duty "shall provide for himself, and keep always in readiness, and carry with him on patrol service one good gun or pistol" and was fined "for want of any such arms."[130] "And the said patrols shall have full power to search and examine all negro houses for offensive weapons and ammunition."[131]

Another act declared it unlawful "for any slave, unless in the presence of some white person, to carry and make use of fire arms, or any offensive weapon whatsoever."[132] An exception was made where the slave had a written license from his master or overseer to hunt and kill animals, albeit "lodging the same gun at night within the dwelling house of his master, mistress or white overseer."[133]

Still another act deleted the requirement of a license where the slave used a gun to kill birds and beasts of prey on the plantation,[134] but also established the death penalty "if any slave shall presume to strike any white person" a second time.[135] Any person finding a slave off the plantation without permission, "if he be armed with such offensive weapons aforesaid, him or them to disarm, take up, and whip."[136]

The Constitution of 1789

The date set for the opening of the Georgia convention to consider ratification of the federal constitution in 1787 passed without a quorum being reached. A newspaper item explained: "Our lower country members are tardy, and our upper ones are generally engaged in defending their families and property on the frontiers."[137] When the convention met and adopted the federal Constitution unanimously without proposing a bill of rights, there was obviously one right the delegates would have deemed basic. A settler's family without firearms in an Indian war would have been a massacre waiting to happen.

The federalist argument that the Constitution needed no bill of rights was at home in Georgia, whose state constitution contained no enumeration of rights. In response to the proposal that the federal Constitution declare a free press and jury trial inviolate, one Georgian replied: "What control had the federal government upon sacred palladium of national freedom? . . . The very declaration would have been deemed nugatory, and an implication that some degree of power was given. In short, everything that is not reserved is given."[138] The last sentence, an embarrassing slip of the pen, was corrected in the next issue of the newspaper as follows: "Everything is reserved that is not given."[139]

On November 24, 1788, a convention proposed a new constitution for the state of Georgia, modeled after the federal Constitution. Few records were kept other than a list of the convention delegates, none of whom had served on the seven-member committee which drafted the Constitution of 1777.[140]

No evidence exists that any delegate proposed a specific bill of rights. Like the Constitution of 1777, the text of the Constitution guaranteed free press, jury trial, and habeas corpus.[141] It added free exercise of religion,[142] but deleted the prohibition on excessive fines and bail.

The proposed state constitution sparked minimal debate in the press, but articles in the *Georgia State Gazette* reveal public perceptions of both the proposed state constitution and the recently adopted federal Constitution. A critic averred that the proposal "wears on its very face the detestable stamp of slavery and oppression," and warned: "Be then not surprised if a free and independent people should absolutely refuse to bend their necks to the servile yoke—my sword hangs restless in its scabbard, and shudders at the impending event."[143] Another writer asserted that "the Federal Constitution is universally approved of, and . . . the proposed Constitution of the state of Georgia is as near a copy thereof as the interests of the state will admit."[144] While neither of those constitutions included a bill of rights at that time, universal acceptance of arms in the hands of the populace was exemplified in an advertisement in the same *Gazette* for "gun locks" and "bar lead, shot and gun powder" at locations throughout the state.[145]

The proposed constitution, printed in the *Gazette* a few days after the above discussion,[146] evoked no further newspaper commentary. However, having arms was conservative compared to the right to revolution so widely accepted at the time. "Those who had resolution to demand their rights were found possessed of courage to defend them . . . having examined the primary rights of human nature," declared "Zeno."[147] "A people resolved to be free, in opposition to a court determined to reduce them to subjection" made the American Revolution, which had become "a foundation for future revolutions in other countries."[148]

People of the ink of "Zeno" would hardly require an explicit guarantee of the right to arms when they assumed armed revolution to be a right. In a further article supportive of the U.S. Constitution, which had no bill of rights at that time, the same writer noticed that "all people when uniting to withstand the encroachments of arbitrary power, are extremely jealous of their liberties."[149]

The Georgia Constitution was ratified on May 6, 1789. A month later, James Madison proposed the federal Bill of Rights in Congress. Like Massachusetts and Connecticut, Georgia failed to ratify the Bill of Rights until 1939. Yet there is no evidence that Georgians rejected its principles. Being a frontier state where every man carried a gun, Georgia had a living bill of rights, at least in regard to the right to bear arms.

CHAPTER 5

Charters Without Constitutions

"The Provinces of [Connecticut and Rhode Island]," complained British undersecretary William Knox in 1763, "are modeled upon the Ideas of corporate Towns; they . . . enact what Laws they please with[out] any Check or Controul, nor has the Crown any Hold, or scarcely any knowledge of them."[1] After independence was declared, these two colonies saw no need to adopt formal constitutions, but continued to rely on their royal charters to the extent they were consistent with independence.

CONNECTICUT

An Independent and Hardy Yeomanry

Connecticut's charter of 1662, which originated in town meetings, was reaffirmed by the General Assembly in October 1776 and remained operative until the adoption of a constitution and bill of rights in 1818.[2] The charter contained no list of the rights of individuals, hardly a surprise in that it was approved by Charles II and that few precedents existed for such a list until the English Declaration of Rights of 1689. Recognition in the Declaration of the rights to petition and to have arms were directed against the abuses of Charles II. Nonetheless, the charter of 1662 presupposed an armed people who the governor was authorized:

for their special Defence and Safety, to Assemble, Martial Array, and put in warlike Posture the Inhabitants of the said Colony, . . . and to encounter, expulse, repel and resist by Force of Arms, as well by Sea as by Land, and also to kill, slay and destroy by all fitting Ways, Enterprises, and Means whatsoever, all and every such Person or Persons as shall at any Time hereafter attempt or enterprize the Destruction, Invasion, Detriment, or Annoyance of the said Inhabitants or Plantation.[3]

All males ages sixteen through fifty were required to bear arms under the old militia law still in force in 1775.[4] When Gage disarmed Boston, Connecticut passed legislation to encourage the manufacture of firearms and gunpowder and established regulations for minutemen.[5] The Revolutionary press, led by the Hartford *Courant* and the New Haven *Post Boy*, called for the people to take arms and spread the alarm.

By contrast, under General Assembly enactments in 1775 and 1776, Tories were disarmed, deprived of property, and imprisoned.[6] A state of war meant that the enemy had none of the usual rights:

Even before the Declaration [of Independence] was signed, Connecticut prohibited freedom of speech. . . . The Committee of Safety took action for disarming the Tories or suspected Tories. In Petersham, for example, Loyalists were required to deliver all their arms to the selectmen; were not allowed to leave town without a pass signed by a majority of the Committee of Correspondence; nor were more than two allowed to meet together for any purpose than town meeting, public worship, or funerals.[7]

Disarmed and imprisoned Tories could confess error and be restored to favor.[8] Keeping and bearing arms was a right accorded to every good citizen. Not so with religion—everyone was taxed to support the Congregational Church.[9]

As published in 1784, the Militia Act declared that "the Defence and Security of all free States depends (under God) upon the Exertions of a well regulated and Disciplined Militia."[10] All males ages sixteen through forty-five were in the militia. Both militia infantrymen "and Householders under fifty-five Years of Age, shall, at all times be furnished at their own Expense, with a well fixed Musket," and horsemen with "a Case of good Pistols, a Sword or Cutlass."[11] The commander reviewed the required arms annually, including those of "Householders and others by Law obliged to keep Arms."[12]

Citizens were required to come armed to the watch and ward[13] and to pursue felons according to the hue and cry.[14] The only restrictions on arms other than traditional crimes were prohibitions on duelling[15] and on the unnecessary discharge of guns at night which created false alarms.[16]

In 1784, Dr. Richard Price published his *Observations on the Importance of the American Revolution*. The British philosopher, whose works sold widely in England and America, was well familiar with the theory of rights underlying the above laws. Price stated:

God forbid, that standing armies should ever find an establishment in America. . . . No wise people will trust their defence out of their own hands, or consent to hold their rights at the mercy of armed *slaves*. Free states ought to be bodies of armed *citizens*, and always ready to turn out, when properly called upon, to execute the laws, to quell riots, and to keep the peace. Such . . . are the citizens of America.[17]

Dr. Price had direct contacts with Connecticut, and with George Washington had been awarded the LL.B. from Yale College in 1781. Price believed that the ideal body politic of armed citizens existed in Connecticut: "The happiest state of man is the middle state between the *savage* and the *refined*. . . . Such is the state of society in CONNECTICUT, and some others of the American provinces; where the inhabitants consist, if I am rightly informed, of an independent and hardy YEOMANRY, all nearly on a level—trained to arms,—instructed in their rights."[18]

Confident in its reliance on an armed populace and not a paper bill of rights, Connecticut easily ratified the federal Constitution proposed in 1787. One writer argued that "by the proposed Constitution [the people] will lose no power, nor any right or privilege which they have ever held sacred and dear."[19] As for the claim that Congress could use the militia for a standing army, the writer argued: "The militia comprehends all the male inhabitants from sixteen to sixty years of age. . . . Against whom will they turn their swords? Against themselves!—to execute laws which are unconstitutional, unreasonable, and oppressive upon themselves! . . . The Constitution in this respect is certainly liberal. It puts the utmost degree of confidence in the people."[20]

Another writer contended that no declaration of rights was necessary because the Congress would have only limited, defined powers. *"There is no declaration of any kind to preserve the liberty of the press, etc.* Nor is liberty of conscience, or of matrimony, or of burial of the dead; it is enough that Congress have no power to prohibit either."[21] When the governor of North Carolina sent Connecticut governor Samuel Huntington a proposed bill of rights including guarantees for the press and arms, the latter responded: "A Bill of Rights in former times hath been judged necessary, but in this enlightened age, when it seems a self evident truth . . . that all right and authority in Government is derived from the People, and may be resumed whenever the safety or happiness of the People renders it necessary; is it necessary, or expedient, for them to form a Bill of Rights which seems at least to call in question a truth of such importance and which ought ever to be held indisputable?"[22]

The above philosophy was partly responsible for Connecticut's failure to adopt the federal Bill of Rights. Moreover, some Connecticut politicians looked askance at unqualified declarations of rights. As a member of Congress, Roger Sherman drafted a proposed bill of rights which failed to include explicit protection for the rights to bear arms and against unreasonable searches and seizures, although in militia debates he argued that "the people, if left to themselves, would provide such arms as are necessary."[23] Connecticut has been described as "a citadel of reaction and privilege" where "civil liberties were not recognized in any fundamental law."[24] Even so, in 1789 and 1790 the two legislative bodies managed to pass what became the first ten amendments, but not in the same session, nullifying that state's ratification.[25]

"To Bear Arms in a Coat": The Legacy of Noah Webster

Just as the Revolution ended, young Noah Webster began publishing political essays in Connecticut newspapers.[26] During the next half century, Webster became a leading advocate of the federal Constitution and authored the most renowned dictionary in the English-speaking world. Webster directly addressed the meaning of the right to keep and bear arms as understood in Connecticut and throughout America.

Webster lived in Philadelphia in 1787 while the federal constitutional convention met, and conversed with Franklin, Washington, Madison, and other convention delegates.[27] Two days before the convention ended, delegate Thomas FitzSimons asked Webster to write in support of the proposed constitution.[28] Webster responded with *An Examination of the Leading Principles of the Federal Constitution*, the first major pro-Constitution pamphlet.[29] Webster explained why the armed populace would remain sovereign under a constitution with an army but no bill of rights:

Another source of power in government is a military force. But this, to be efficient, must be superior to any force that exists among the people, or which they can command; for otherwise this force would be annihilated, on the first exercise of acts of oppression. Before a standing army can rule, the people must be disarmed; as they are in almost every Kingdom in Europe. The supreme power in America cannot enforce unjust laws by the sword; because the whole body of the people are armed, and constitute a force superior to any band of regular troops that can be, on any pretence, raised in the United States.[30]

Hamilton and Madison repeated the above argument in *The Federalist Papers*.[31] Like those writers, Webster contended that rights to arms and speech need not be spelled out. If a bill of rights was necessary, he sarcastically wrote in the *American Magazine*, then it should include a provision "that Congress shall never restrain any inhabitant of America from eating and drinking, at seasonable times, or prevent his lying on his right side, in a long winter's night, or even on his back, when he is fatigued by lying on his right."[32]

Webster's *A Compendious Dictionary of the English Language*, published in 1806, was only a step toward his magnum opus. This dictionary may be usefully applied to the terms "the right of the people to keep and bear arms." According to Webster, "people" means "persons in general,"[33] "bear" is "to carry,"[34] and "arms" are "weapons."[35]

In 1828, Webster published *An American Dictionary of the English Language*. Immediately adopted as the standard by Congress and the American people, Webster's *Dictionary* became the accepted norm even in England.[36] A linguistic analysis of the state and federal declarations on the right to bear arms may be appropriately based on this dictionary.

Several of the declarations state that "a well regulated militia" is "necessary to the security of a free state." "The militia of the country are the able bodied men," according to Webster.[37] "Regulated" means "adjusted by rule, method or forms; put in good order; subjected to rules or restrictions." Examples are "to *regulate* our moral conduct by the laws of God and society; to *regulate* our manners by the customary forms."[38] Thus, a well regulated militia includes all able-bodied men who regulate their training by customary methods.

As for "the right of the people to keep and bear arms," Webster defined "the people" as "the commonalty, as distinct from men of rank."[39] The term "bear" means "to carry" or "to wear; to bear as a mark of authority or distinction; as, to *bear* a sword, a badge, a name; to *bear* arms in a coat."[40]

Consistent with the meaning of "bear arms" as carrying weapons on the person, Webster defines "pistol" as "a small fire-arm, or the smallest fire-arm used. . . . Small pistols are carried in the pocket."[41] Generally, "arms" are "weapons of offense, or armor for defense and protection of the body."[42] "In *law*, arms are any thing which a man takes in his hand in anger, to strike or assault another."[43]

Even though these definitions of "arms" signify weapons carried by hand, Webster added that "*fire arms*, are such as may be charged with powder, as cannon, muskets, mortars, & c."[44] However, elsewhere Webster states: "The larger species of guns are called cannon; and the smaller species are called muskets, carbines, fowling pieces, & c. But one species of fire-arms, the pistol, is never called a gun."[45]

Webster left an inconclusive legacy on the meaning of the right to bear arms. His 1787 arguments suggest that the people could keep arms of any type necessary to overcome a standing army. However, the words used in the constitutional guarantees suggest that the right included only such arms as a person could "bear," that is, muskets, fowling pieces, pistols, and swords, and not cannon and heavy ordnance which one could not carry or wear. Whatever the scope of protected "arms," Webster did clarify the nature of the right to have arms by the commonality in a free state.

RHODE ISLAND

A Simple Republic

Two years of revolutionary war confirmed the fears of colonial undersecretary William Knox about the two colonies which had no need of a constitution. In 1777 he observed: "That the Constitutions under which the Charter Colonies have been settled are ill adapted to excite in the Inhabitants a Love of Monarchy, and the British Government, & a desire to continue connected with Great Britain, need not be proved. Rhode Island & Connecticut are simple Republics."[46] Knox's proposal that "the Arms of all the People should be taken away"[47] was particularly unrealistic in Rhode Island, a proven gateway for smuggling arms.

Just before Lexington, the *Newport Mercury* urged the readers to arm themselves, for "every Friend to his Country . . . will prepare himself to defend (Life, Liberty or Property) against every Invader."[48] In the following months, the *Mercury* reprinted all of the major patriot attacks on Gage for disarming the people of Boston. Perhaps Knox felt relieved when the British disarmed and burned Newport in 1776.

Rhode Island continued to rely on its colonial charter in the Revolution and until adoption of its first constitution in 1842. The Charter of 1663 based the security of the colony squarely on the armed populace. The governor was instructed to appoint officers to train the inhabitants in martial affairs.[49] The governor, his officers, and a majority of the freemen present at any general assembly had authority

to assemble, exercise in arms, martiall array, and putt in warlyke posture, the inhabitants of the sayd collonie, ffor theire speciall defence and safety; and to lead and conduct the sayd inhabitants, and to encounter, expulse, expell and resist, by force of armes, as well by sea as by land; and alsoe to kill, slay and destroy, by all fitting wayes, enterprizes and meanes, whatsoever, all and every such person or persons as shall, att any tyme hereafter, attempt or enterprize the destruction, invasion, detriment or annoyance of the sayd inhabitants or Plantations."[50]

In 1775, the people of Rhode Island were generally armed and organized into groups from plain mobs to independent militias.[51] The town of Providence implored nearby inhabitants to "hold yourself in readiness" and bring all weapons "you have by you" when the alarm sounds.[52] This was possible because of the traditional public policy of the colony. The Militia Act, reenacted several times during 1718–1798, provided that every citizen ages eighteen through forty-four must "provide himself with a good musket or firelock."[53] The horseman was to furnish himself with a pair of pistols and a saber.[54]

The public laws as printed in 1798 began with the Charter of 1663, which was reenacted "to secure them in the exercise of all their civil and religious rights."[55] Of all the laws passed in that century and still on the books then, none restricted the right to keep and bear arms. Even a broad prohibition on any Indian or slave from doing such things as going abroad after 9:00 P.M., or selling alcohol to them, did not mention arms.[56]

The offensive use of arms was restricted beyond the usual crimes of robbery and murder. Duelling was prohibited.[57] The sheriff was authorized to disperse twelve or more persons if they were "armed with clubs or other weapons" or thirty or more persons if they were riotously assembled. The sheriff could "require the aid of a sufficient number of persons in arms."[58]

Pranksters were confronted with a prohibition on unnecessarily firing "any gun, pistol, rocket, squib, or other fire-works, in any road, street, lane or tavern, or other public house, after sun setting and before sunrising."[59] More seriously, a fine was imposed "if any person shall fire any gun, musket, blunderbuss or pistol, loaded with a bullet or shot, in or across any road."[60]

Rights Which Cannot Be Abridged or Violated: The Convention of 1790

Unlike the other states, Rhode Island wanted no part of the federal government proposed in 1787. After refusing to call one seven times, in January 1790 the Rhode Island legislature finally voted to have a convention to consider ratification of the federal Constitution. The Constitution had been effective for a year and a half, and the federal Bill of Rights was ratified by six states by the end of that month.

Rhode Island newspapers were more apt to print news of neighboring states than of the federal government. The *Providence Gazette* printed nothing on the federal Bill of Rights in that period, but it did publish a proposed new bill of rights for Pennsylvania, which included a militia clause in a separate article from the following: "That the right of citizens to bear arms in defence of themselves and the State, and to assemble peaceably together . . . shall not be questioned."[61]

The convention met in March 1790 to consider ratification. Federalist leader Henry Marchant moved that the amendments recommended by Congress be read.[62] They were, including what became the Second

Amendment. A debate ensued on whether, as Madison proposed to Congress, States should be "precluded from making any Law respecting Religion or abridging the Rights of Consci[ence]."[63] Unlike the more general language of the other amendments, the First Amendment states that "Congress shall make no law." James Sheldon stated: "If it is right that Congress should not make any Laws respecting it no State ought to have the Right."[64] Marchant thought it was "enough for us to keep it out of the Gen[eral] Govt."[65]

Federalist Benjamin Bourne thought it improper to refer the federal Bill of Rights to a convention committee since it would have to be ratified by the state legislature. He inquired which states had ratified the Bill of Rights—six had at that point.[66]

Anti-federalist leaders Jonathan J. Hazard and Joseph Stanton, Jr., moved that the amendments proposed by New York and North Carolina be read, and they were along with those of Virginia.[67] The arms guarantee proposed by New York stated: "That the people have a right to keep and bear arms; that a well-regulated militia, including the body of the people *capable of bearing arms*, is the proper, natural, and safe defence of a free state."[68] Those of Virginia and North Carolina were identical, except that the well regulated militia was said to be "composed of the body of the people, trained to arms."[69]

In the conventions of the other states, the federalists had supported adoption of the Constitution without amendments, but by now their strategy was to support adoption of a bill of rights as an inducement to adoption of the Constitution. This explains the following:

Gov[ernor] Bradford says the Gentlemen have had an opportunity of Reading the Amend[men]ts in the Papers and others and much Time has been taken. Moves that the Committee be appointed. . . .
Moved by Mr. Champlin That the Committee be appointed from those who are opposed to the Constitution.[70]

The idea was to get the anti-federalists to suggest a bill of rights, and then to vote for the Constitution in hopes that the bill of rights would be adopted too.[71] A committee of ten, including Jonathan Hazard, was voted in.[72] The committee reported back, and the minutes reflect the following:

And the Business now begins—a Time of Expectation and the House very much crowded—Generals, Colonels, Delegates &c being obliged to Stand. The House now calling—Thus Life Passes and carries along the Tide of Time to land us in Eternity—of what consequence will then be all this Parade?
The SECRETARY reads the Report of the Committee.
The Bill of Rights read.[73]

The arms guarantee adopted by the committee was the New York language, verbatim.[74] This provision followed guarantees against cruel and unusual punishment and unreasonable search and seizure and in favor of the rights to assembly, petition, speech, and the press.[75]

The anti-federalists sought to stall a vote on the Constitution by referring the bill of rights to the people, while the federalists wanted the convention to adopt the bill of rights, hoping that it would then ratify the Constitution:

Job Comstock says this Business of high Importance—it has taken the Committee sometime to prepare the Bill of Rights—and moves that before the Bill of (40) Rights be discussed—Moves that the Bill of Rights and Amendment[s] be Referred to the People/at large/to have their Opinion and Sentim[en]ts thereon. . . .

Mr. Marchant observes That the Bill of Rights being agreed to it appears agreeable to our Minds—that it contains our professed Sentiments and is agreeable to the Constitutions of the United [States]—That We ought to make the Bill of Rights as perfect as possible. Moves that We now have a Vote whether we approve of this Bill of Rights.[76]

Comstock argued that "by adopting this Bill some Rights essential may be omitted," and Elisha Brown moved to refer the issue to the regular town meetings.[77] Marchant urged a convention vote because "we may declare that the People have such and such Rights and that when we adopt the Constitu[tion] it may appear that we claim such and such Rights Similar to what was done by New York and may go on to give instances and the Wishes of the People."[78]

The anti-federalists then maneuvered a vote to adjourn without voting on the Constitution.[79] The people in town meetings proceeded to discuss the Constitution and proposed bill of rights. Meanwhile, the U.S. Congress was threatening to boycott any shipping to or from Rhode Island.[80]

In May 1790, the delegates reconvened, and the federalists moved to adopt the Constitution with the bill of rights already agreed upon. The same committee met and suggested additional amendments.[81] This time the convention voted thirty-four to thirty-two to adopt the federal Constitution. The bill of rights formed the basis for Rhode Island's ratification, which declared that the following rights "cannot be abridged or violated":

I. That there are certain natural rights of which men, when they form a social compact, cannot deprive or divest their posterity,—among which are the enjoyment of life and liberty, with the means of acquiring, possessing, and protecting property, and pursuing and obtaining happiness and safety. . . .

XVII. That the people have a right to keep and bear arms; that a well-regulated militia, including the body of the people capable of bearing arms, is the proper, natural, and safe defence of a free state.[82]

The convention also recommended that the state legislature ratify what became the federal Bill of Rights, including the Second Amendment.[83] Two days before the legislature ratified the federal amendments, the *Providence Gazette* republished Rhode Island's proposed declaration of rights, including the clause "that the people have a right to keep and bear arms."[84] On June 7, 1790, Rhode Island became the ninth state to ratify the Bill of Rights.

In conclusion, Rhode Island and Connecticut were the only two states which adopted neither a constitution nor a bill of rights. These states joined four others which deemed a formal declaration unnecessary, even though the right to keep and bear arms flourished in all of the states. Nonetheless, with the ratification of the federal Bill of Rights, the days of the philosophy that a freeman had no need of a bill of rights were numbered, as the following two centuries would prove.

EPILOGUE:

State Constitutional Conventions in the Nineteenth and Twentieth Centuries

Rights such as press, assembly, and arms were considered fundamental in the states during the period from the Revolution through the adoption of the federal Bill of Rights. Only some of the states saw a need for a declaration of rights to be included in the state constitutions during that period. In the two centuries that have followed, most of the original states have adopted bills of rights for the first time or have strengthened protected rights.

Bill-of-rights provisions which explicitly or implicitly guarantee the right to keep and bear arms have been adopted in three epochs of American history. First, the antebellum period saw the adoption of the first bills of rights in several Northern states. Second, during Reconstruction, the Southern states amended their constitutions to expand protected rights, while other states hesitated to alter their bills of rights on the arms issue. Third, no further changes were made for almost a century until restrictive firearms legislation beginning in 1968 led to new arms guarantees. The following traces these developments.

TRIUMPH OF THE WRITTEN BILL OF RIGHTS: THE ANTEBELLUM PERIOD

Connecticut, 1818. Connecticut adopted its first constitution in 1818, and its bill of rights included the following: "Every citizen has a right to bear arms in defense of himself and the State."[1] The scant records which remain do not indicate that this right was controversial,[2] unlike freedom of religion, a guarantee which nearly led that constitution to defeat.[3] The arms guarantee remains an unaltered provision of the Connecticut Bill of Rights today.[4]

New York, 1828. The idea that a bill of rights was unnecessary was strongly expressed at the constitutional convention of New York in 1821. "Chief Justice Spencer thought much of the bill of rights redundant—perhaps, indeed, where rights are so well understood as in this country, it is useless to have any bill setting them forth."[5] P. R. Livingston argued that "a bill of rights is the mere repetition of the fundamental rights of this people, which have never been violated, and which, after forty years of practice under our constitution, we need not fear to see violated."[6] This was true of the right to keep and bear arms, which was still seen as a duty at that time. General Root wanted no voters who were armed only "with a broomstick, or club," but "they should be *armed and equipped according to law,* before they should be privileged to vote."[7]

As ratified in 1822, the New York Constitution mentioned speech and press, but contained no formal bill of rights.[8] However, in 1828, the New York legislature enacted its statutory Bill of Rights, which still includes the following: "A well regulated militia being necessary to the security of a free state, the right of the people to keep and bear arms cannot be infringed."[9]

Rhode Island, 1842. Rhode Island's Dorr Rebellion of 1841 sought the enfranchisement of the small freeholders. After suppressing the Dorr government by military force,[10] the charter government called a constitutional convention, which adopted many of the reforms demanded in what became the Constitution of 1842. A convention delegate spoke on behalf of the freeholders. "Who, but the old farmers, came forward most readily in the late difficulties? They left their hoes standing in the field beside their corn, and went directly to the depots, sending word for their wives to send their clothes, and for a boy to bring the old gun. The interests of these men, were the dearest interest of the state."[11]

The Constitution of 1842 began with a declaration that "the essential and unquestionable rights and principles hereinafter mentioned shall be established, maintained, and preserved, and shall be of paramount obligation in all legislative, judicial, and executive proceedings."[12] The list of rights which followed included these:

Sec. 22. The right of the people to keep and bear arms shall not be infringed.
Sec. 23. The enumeration of the foregoing rights shall not be construed to impair or deny others retained by the people.[13]

New Jersey, 1844. The lack of a bill of rights in New Jersey's 1776 constitution led to demands during the following decades that rights be recognized. The following words published in 1798 expressed this sentiment:

There are certain rights, when men enter into society they ought not to surrender—these are, the right of opinion, the right of property, and the right of the press—not only these, but all other rights ought to be accurately marked out and defined in the constitution. . . . But we are told that amidst all these defects the people have been happy and the country prosperous. . . . But as soon as the people begin to grow rich and populous, then corruption will flow in upon us, and the evils of the constitution be felt when perhaps it will be too late to remedy them.[14]

A constitutional convention which met in 1827 pointed out that the 1776 "temporary" constitution was adopted in a mere eight days and was never authorized by the people.[15] Among the defects cited were: "The Constitution imposes no limitations of power whatever upon the Legislature. . . . Laws infringing the liberties of the People [and] . . . the fundamental privileges of freemen might be enacted and carried into effect."[16]

Some delegates in the convention of 1844 opposed a bill of rights as unnecessary.[17] As Professor Charles R. Erdman notes: "But was life, liberty and property in such a precarious position in New Jersey from 1776 to 1844? A negative answer would be well supported by the history of the State under its first constitution. In fact a correspondent to the Newark Sentinel could say in 1844 that 'no people in the United States are freer from taxation nor whose rights of person and property are better secured' than those in New Jersey."[18]

Reflecting the above, there was not a single law on the books in those years restricting the right to keep and bear arms. Aside from a prohibition on duelling enacted after Aaron Burr killed Alexander Hamilton, the New Jersey legislature enacted no other restrictions until the twentieth century.

As adopted, the Constitution of 1844 contained an article entitled "Rights and Privileges." Free exercise of Judeo-Christian religions (but not others) was finally recognized.[19] Certain less controversial rights, such as due process of law and bearing arms, were not explicitly recognized. However, the bill of rights stated:

One. All men are by nature free and independent, and have certain natural and unalienable rights, among which are those of enjoying and *defending life and liberty*, acquiring, possessing, and *protecting property*, and of *pursuing and obtaining safety* and happiness. . . .

Nineteen. This enumeration of rights and privileges shall not be construed to impair or deny others retained by the people.[20]

The adoption of bills of rights in Connecticut, New York (albeit a statutory one), Rhode Island, and New Jersey signaled the triumph of the view that written, articulated guarantees were necessary, and the demise of the view that freemen had no need of a bill of rights. Further, the adoption of unenumerated rights provisions in Rhode Island and New Jersey was part of a trend in nineteenth-century constitution making which would be emulated by other states. While it already had a formal bill of rights, Maryland would become still another of the original states to adopt an unenumerated rights guarantee.

Maryland, 1851. The role of the armed citizen was still entrenched in the political fabric when the Maryland constitutional convention met in 1850–1851. Delegate Elias Brown recalled that "our forefathers were induced to take up arms, and to resist tyranny to obtain political rights for all!"[21] The guarantee of a well regulated militia was readopted without any debate.[22]

Joseph M. Parke of Carroll County moved the adoption of a new provision as follows: "This enumeration of rights shall not be construed to impair or deny others retained by the people."[23] When another delegate asked him "to specify what the nonenumerated rights were. . . . Mr. Parke said it was impossible for him to do so. He presumed that they were very numerous—so much so as to render it impossible to include them in the bill of rights."[24] Rejecting the argument that since "the bill of rights took away no rights, of course everything which was not taken away, remained," the convention adopted the amendment.[25]

There was one right that appears to have been taken for granted when Rhode Island, New Jersey, and Maryland adopted unenumerated rights guarantees. In *The Rights of an American Citizen* (1832), Benjamin L. Oliver stated: "Of those rights which are usually retained in organized society. . . . The first and most important of these rights, is that of self-defence."[26] Oliver analyzed "the right of the citizens to bear arms" as among "the rights reserved to the people of the United States; not being granted either to the general government, or to the state governments."[27] Of the unenumerated rights he stated:

There are some other rights, which are reserved to the people, though not mentioned in the general constitution. Among these is the right of self-defence, in cases where the danger is so imminent, that the person in jeopardy, may suffer irreparable injury, if he waits for the protection of the laws. . . . [A]s the compact between him and society is mutual, if society is unable to protect him, his natural right revives to protect himself.[28]

The right to keep and bear arms was already implicitly recognized in the guarantee of a well-regulated militia. Adoption of unenumerated rights provisions served as a reminder that lack of explicit lists of rights as fundamental as self-preservation would not be construed to impair or deny such rights.

RECONSTRUCTION AND THE EQUAL RIGHT OF FREEDMEN TO BEAR ARMS

Like the antebellum slave codes, the black codes passed by the Southern and border states after the War Between the States imposed disabilities on the freedmen, including the deprivation of arms. The federal Fourteenth Amendment was proposed in part to invalidate laws that members of Congress saw as violative of the individual right to keep and bear arms for self-defense.[29] This amendment recognized freed slaves as citizens, and guaranteed the same privileges and immunities to all citizens.

As a condition of reentry into the Union, the Southern states were required to ratify the Fourteenth Amendment and to adopt constitutions consistent with that amendment. Virginia, North Carolina, South Carolina, and Georgia initially rejected the amendment, but the disenfranchisement of ex-Confederates insured its ratification by those states in 1868 and 1869. Delaware and Maryland never having seceded, neither had any special obligations like those of the Southern states. Indeed, both rejected the Fourteenth Amendment in 1867; Delaware would not ratify it until 1901, and Maryland in 1959. New Jersey ratified in 1866, but rescinded its ratification in 1868.[30]

Maryland, 1867. As of 1860, the Maryland Code had no restriction of any kind on the peaceable bearing of arms, except for the following: "No slave shall carry any gun, or any other offensive weapon, from off his master's land, without a license from his said master, and any slave so offending shall be whipped."[31] In 1864, slavery was abolished in Maryland, and the following year the above and most other slave code provisions were repealed.[32] Thereafter, blacks and whites could lawfully keep and bear arms without any restrictions, although freed slaves were probably subject to being disarmed without warrant of law.

In 1866, the Fourteenth Amendment was proposed in the U.S. Congress with explanations that it would protect the individual right of freedmen and others to keep and bear arms for self-defense.[33] Maryland Senator Reverdy Johnson opposed adoption of the Fourteenth Amendment because it took away the power of the states to treat persons unequally.[34] Senator Johnson was aware that the Amendment was intended to overrule the Dred Scott precedent, which conceded that if blacks were citizens, they would be entitled "to keep and carry arms wherever they went."[35] Johnson had argued the Dred Scott case before the U.S. Supreme Court, contending that blacks should not be recognized as citizens.[36] In early 1867, the Maryland Senate rejected the Fourteenth Amendment.[37]

The debates in the Maryland constitutional convention of 1867 took place in the above context. The convention was considering a provision "that a well regulated militia is the proper and natural defense of a free government."[38] The following discussion ensued:

Mr. [Luther] Giddings moved to amend by adding after the word "government" the words, "and every citizen has the right to bear arms in defence of himself and the State."
Mr. [Henry F.] Garey moved to amend the amendment by inserting the word "white" after the word "every."
Mr. [Issac D.] Jones hoped the gentleman from Baltimore (Mr. Garey) would withdraw his amendment. Every citizen of the State means every white citizen, and none other.
Mr. Garey withdrew his amendment.[39]

Perhaps the amendment was prompted by the mass disarmings that took place in Baltimore early in the Civil War.[40] Giddings may have sought to protect freedmen who had been disarmed in Maryland. Garey and Jones clearly did not want nonwhites to have a right to bear arms.

Opposition to the proposed amendment was then expressed as follows: "Mr. [George W.] Brown thought it would be a dangerous thing to insert this declaration. If this broad declaration was put in the Bill of Rights, he did not see how you could disarm any man, drunk or sober, as he could throw himself on his reserved rights."[41]

Brown did not address the situation of those who bear arms for lawful purposes or explain why an intoxicated person could not be disarmed.[42] Brown may have feared that the guarantee would allow blacks the right to keep and bear arms, for just before this, he had "considered that a great wrong was done when slavery was abolished as it was."[43]

The debate then shifted to different premises:

Mr. Garey read from the constitution of the United States: "The right of the people to keep and bear arms shall not be infringed." He considered the proposed amendment entirely in accordance with the constitution of the United States, and that it should be adopted.
Mr. Jones said that for the very reason that it was in the constitution of the United States, he hoped it would not be inserted here. That was amply sufficient. We did not want any such declaration in the State of Maryland.[44]

At best, this reflects the often expressed antebellum view that the federal Second Amendment prohibits both federal and state infringement,[45] and thus a state guarantee is unnecessary. At worst, it reflects delegate Jones's campaign to prevent recognition of the right of freed slaves to bear arms. The day before, Jones had called emancipation "a violent, ruthless, outrageous act,"[46] and persuaded the convention to make a demand for compensation to former slaveowners a part of the Maryland Constitution.[47]

A proposal was then introduced to allay those who feared that a right to "bear" arms guarantee would allow blacks, drunks, or both to carry arms:

Mr. [John H.] Barnes offered the following amendment, to be inserted at the end of the article: "and the citizen shall not be deprived of the right to keep arms on his premises." Rejected.
The amendment of Mr. Giddings was then rejected.[48]

Delegate Barnes's proposal was already implicit in the Declaration of Rights since the members of the well regulated militia, which included all citizens, were entitled and required to keep arms on their premises. Barnes's amendment may have been rejected so that former slaves in Maryland could not keep arms in their homes.

The day after the above debate, a Baltimore newspaper charged that many of the convention delegates were proslavery.[49] Arguing for the equal right of blacks to suffrage, the editorial states:

Goldsmith, in the vicar of Wakefield, says: "The penal laws are in the hands of the rich. . . . " In Maryland, where a slaveocracy ruled, slaves were taxed less than any other property. But what shall be said of the laws against the free blacks? A free negro could not keep a dog or a gun. . . . This is a long series of laws touching directly upon the rights and freedom of the blacks.[50]

The right-to-bear-arms guarantee apparently failed to be made part of the Maryland Constitution in 1867 for the reason that the former slaveowners remained in power.

Virginia, 1867. Virginia, at that time under Radical Republican control, echoed very different sentiments. When more blacks than whites voted on the calling of a constitutional convention in 1867, landed interests advocated the discharge of black employees who voted the Radical ticket. One Radical threatened to resort to force before his children would go hungry, and "thanked God that the Negroes had learned to use guns, pistols, and ramrods."[51]

The Virginia convention of 1867–1868 readopted the provision of the Declaration of Rights of 1776 recognizing "a well regulated Militia, composed of the Body of the People, trained to Arms" under the descriptive label "RIGHT TO BEAR ARMS."[52] The formal militia, composed of all able-bodied males without regard to race, was provided for in a separate article.[53] Delegate John Hawnhurst stated: "The Bill of Rights is a declaration of individual rights, as against the Government. It is an assertion of certain rights that the Government shall not take away from the individual."[54] Radical Edward K. Snead added that "the rights declared in the Bill of Rights are natural and inherent rights, rights which previously existed."[55]

Discussion centered on the fact that the proposed federal Fourteenth Amendment would confer citizenship on freedmen. The delegates were well aware from the authorities upon which they relied that "citizenship" carried with it broad rights, including keeping and bearing arms.[56]

The convention also added a new provision to the Declaration of Rights as follows: "The rights enumerated in this Bill of Rights shall not be construed to limit other rights of the people not therein expressed."[57]

North Carolina, 1868 and 1875. North Carolina held its convention in 1868. The Bill of Rights Committee initially proposed that the 1776 language be readopted: "The people have a right to bear arms for the defence of the State."[58] However, as ratified, the 1868 Constitution repeated the language of the federal Second Amendment: "A well regulated militia, being necessary to the security of a free state, the right of the people to keep and bear arms, shall not be infringed."[59] This language clarifies the individual nature of the right, for there was no need in a state constitution to protect a right of the state to form militias from infringement by that same state. Militia issues and provisions were treated separately by that convention.[60] North Carolina governor William Holden spoke of "the constitutional right of all citizens to the possession of arms for proper purposes."[61]

At its convention of 1875, North Carolina added to the guarantee: "Nothing herein contained shall justify the practice of carrying concealed weapons, or prevent the Legislature from enacting penal statutes against said practice."[62] This express authority to regulate concealed weapons again indicated the individual nature of the main guarantee.

South Carolina, 1868 and 1895. The antebellum constitutions of South Carolina contained no bills of rights.[63] The slave code was the only serious interference with keeping and bearing arms. These provisions were reenacted at the end of the war[64] and were cited in debates in the U.S. Congress in support of adoption of the Fourteenth Amendment. Congressman George W. Julian (R., Ind.) complained: "Florida makes it a misdemeanor for colored men to carry weapons without a license to do so from a probate judge, and the punishment of the offense is whipping and the pillory. South Carolina has the same enactments. . . . Cunning legislative devices are being invented in most of the States to restore slavery in fact."[65]

A declaration of rights with the following was proposed at the South Carolina constitutional convention of 1868: "Every citizen has a right to keep and bear arms in defence of himself and the State, and this right shall never be questioned."[66] As reported from committee and as finally adopted, this was changed without objection to read, "the people have a right to keep and bear arms for the common defence."[67] The rights of "defending their lives and liberties . . . and protecting property," as well as all unenumerated rights, were also recognized.[68] Extensive debate centered on the additional clause providing that the military power shall always be subject to the civil authority,[69] a matter of controversy since the state was under military occupation at the time. C. C. Bowen, who had proposed the right-to-arms provision in its original form, argued: "I find men very zealous of the liberties of the people, now willing to put those liberties in the hands of the military. . . . [I]f a military officer has a sufficient number of bayonets to carry out his edict (declaring martial law), he may enforce it by simple force of arms, and yet have no right to do so."[70]

That the arms provision as adopted did not provide only a militia-related right is clear in that debate and provisions on the militia were covered elsewhere.[71] B. O. Duncan, who unsuccessfully opposed the clause subordinating the military to the civil authority,[72] moved that "the Legislature shall enact such laws as it may deem proper and necessary to punish the carrying of concealed deadly weapons."[73] The arms guarantee was considered a private right, for otherwise authority to prohibit the carrying of concealed weapons would have been unnecessary.

At the constitutional convention of 1895, delegate R. A. Meares introduced a resolution to amend the existing Declaration of Rights provision to add the following emphasized language: "The people have a right to keep and bear arms for the common defense, *or in aid of the civil power, when thereto legally summoned.*"[74] George S. Mower of the Declaration of Rights Committee moved to substitute the language of the federal Second Amendment.[75] This language was reported by the committee,[76] adopted by the convention,[77] and became part of the Constitution of 1895.[78] It remains part of the South Carolina Bill of Rights today.[79]

Georgia, 1868 and 1877. Georgia originally had no bill of rights, but the individual right to bear arms was interpreted as protected from state infringement by the federal Second Amendment.[80] The Georgia secession convention of 1861 adopted a Declaration of Fundamental Principles with the following: "The right of the people to keep and bear arms shall not be infringed."[81] The Confederate States Constitution ratified shortly thereafter included verbatim the old federal Bill of Rights, including the Second Amendment.[82] The postwar Georgia Constitution of 1865 adopted the same language.[83]

The arms guarantee was explained in 1866 in the *Loyal Georgian* (a Republican, black newspaper) in response to the following question:

Have colored persons a right to own and carry fire arms?

A Colored Citizen

Almost every day we are asked questions similar to the above. We answer certainly you have the same right to own and carry arms that other citizens have. . . .

Article II, of the amendments to the Constitution of the United States, gives the people the right to bear arms, and states that this right shall not be infringed. . . . All men, without distinction of color, have the right to keep and bear arms to defend their homes, families or themselves.[84]

The Reconstruction Convention of 1868 once again used the words of the Second Amendment, adding "but the General Assembly shall have the power to prescribe by law the manner in which arms may be borne."[85] When proposed in convention, the last part read, "borne by private persons,"[86] but the phrase was deleted.

The 1877 Georgia Constitution incorporated the following form which stands today: "The right of the people to keep and bear arms, shall not be infringed, but the General Assembly shall have power to prescribe the manner in which arms may be borne."[87] At the convention, Robert Toombs, chairman of the Committee of Final Revision, "moved to strike out all after the word 'infringed'."[88] Toombs argued that "the Legislature has no power to prescribe how the people shall bear arms; that they shall not carry them in their boots, or anywhere else that they want to. I think the people have the right to keep and bear arms as they choose for their protection."[89] Mr. Warren argued that the legislature should have power "to regulate the manner" of bearing arms, particularly "the indiscriminate bearing of concealed weapons,"[90] and successfully moved to lay Toombs' proposal on the table.[91]

The convention also rejected a proposal which would have authorized the legislature to "prescribe the manner *and place* in which arms may be borne."[92] Its intent was to "give the legislature power to prescribe where a man shall carry arms and where not."[93] Thus, the Georgia guarantee allowed for regulation of concealed arms, but not for prohibition on carrying arms per se.

Pennsylvania, 1873. While not under any federal constraint to do so, Pennsylvania had a constitutional convention in 1873, at which the delegates overwhelmingly defeated amendments to the arms guarantee which would have empowered the legislature to prohibit concealed weapons. The proposal would have added "openly" to the 1790 language as follows: "The right of the citizens openly to bear arms in defence of themselves and the State, shall not be questioned."[94]

Thomas Struthers, the proponent of the change, argued that persons charged with carrying arms secretly "fall back on the Constitution, which they say authorizes the bearing of arms, and therefore the act of Assembly is unconstitutional."[95] The chief spokesman for the opposition was Wayne MacVeagh, a frail man who contended:

To tell me that I am to walk the streets of this city at night without any protection whatever from ruffians, is to state something to which I will never agree. . . . Among other things that cannot be taken from a man, is the privilege he has to defend his life and to protect himself. Of course he is answerable to the fullest extent for the use of it, and your law against carrying concealed weapons does not interfere with the habit among the dangerous classes. . . . I believe in the right of self-defence of the weak against the strong.[96]

A question of whether laws against carrying concealed weapons are constitutional led to the following responses:

MR. MACVEAGH: . . . I understand the words in the old Constitution are used in the public sense of bearing arms in defence of person and life, as our ancestors did, and not for offensive purposes.

MR. [J. M.] BROOMALL. Will the gentleman tell me if the Legislature have a right to pass a law against carrying concealed deadly weapons, why they have not a right to pass a law against carrying open deadly weapons?

MR. MACVEAGH. If you put it upon that ground, I cannot see that the constitutional difficulty is avoided. I cannot see why the Constitution should prohibit a man from carrying weapons to defend himself unless he carries them openly, why you should require him to sling a revolver over his shoulder. If you mean that the militia shall be armed, you will find that provided for in another article.[97]

The practical pros and cons of carrying concealed arms were then debated, one side arguing that anticipation by criminals that law-abiding persons may be armed discourages attacks, and the other side insisting that there was no need to carry anything smaller than a rifle or shotgun. Everyone laughed when a delegate suggested mountain howitzers.[98] One delegate clarified that Pennsylvania law required showing of evil intent and argued that "it is constitutional to pass such laws in order to restrain persons from carrying concealed weapons with malicious intent."[99]

When proponents of the amendment urged passage to remove the doubts of judges as to the constitutionality of prohibitions on concealed weapons, the delegates voted the amendment down with 23 yeas and 54 nays.[100] Perhaps the most extended recorded debate in a state constitutional convention on the right to bear arms, the convention's action reaffirmed the importance of this freedom under the Pennsylvania Declaration of Rights.

TWENTIETH-CENTURY REACTIONS TO PROPOSED FIREARMS BANS

The westward expansion of new states throughout the nineteenth and early twentieth centuries resulted in the borrowing of arms guarantees from the original states and the creation of new ones.[101] Some of these guarantees were adopted routinely as part of fairly standardized bills of rights. Others, particularly in recent times, were adopted in response to proposed legislation[102] or judicial opinions supportive of prohibitions on firearms.[103]

For most of the twentieth century, none of the original thirteen states (fourteen including Vermont) saw any need to strengthen their arms guarantees or to adopt more explicit provisions. However, in the last twenty years numerous new restrictions have been enacted at the local, state, and federal levels. This led the states of Virginia, New Hampshire, and Delaware to adopt new provisions to protect the right to keep and bear arms. While more explicit, these guarantees reflect the same values taken for granted in all of the original states when they became independent over two hundred years ago.

Virginia, 1970. The idea that the free citizen had a right to keep and bear arms for protection both of the person and the community has existed in Virginia since first being settled in the seventeenth century.[104] The assassinations and urban unrest of the 1960s led to the proposal or enactment at the federal and state levels of numerous prohibitions on this right. In 1964, the Virginia General Assembly reacted to these developments by passing a resolution "concerning the inherent right of citizens of this Commonwealth to own and bear arms" which stated:

That the right to keep and bear arms guaranteed by the second amendment to the Constitution of the United States and which right is an inalienable part of our citizens' heritage in this State shall not be infringed; that any action taken by the General Assembly of Virginia to interfere with this right would strike at the basic liberty of our citizens; that no agency of this State or of any political subdivision should be given any power or seek any power which would prohibit the purchase or possession of firearms by any citizen of good standing for the purpose of personal defense, sport, recreation or other noncriminal activities; and that registration of arms, for which registration is not presently required, not be required, by legislative action of this body.[105]

In 1969, the Virginia Commission on Constitution Revision solicited and received public views, including a proposal "for a constitutional guarantee of the right to bear arms."[106] The Virginia General Assembly then adopted and the public ratified an amendment to Section 13 of the Declaration of Rights so that the section would read: "That a well regulated militia, composed of the body of the people, trained to arms, is the proper, natural, and safe defense of a free state, *therefore, the right of the people to keep and bear arms shall not be infringed.*"[107]

Delegate Lymen C. Harrell, Jr., chief spokesman in the House, explained that "this merely states something that has been a right and merely puts into the Virginia Constitution what is in the federal Constitution."[108] Delegate D. French Slaughter noted that it "confirms the historical parallel between the Article of the Virginia Constitution and the Second Amendment to the Constitution of the United States."[109] It is noteworthy that George Mason, author of the Virginia Declaration of Rights of 1776, also drafted the proposal that a federal bill of rights include that Declaration's militia guarantee and precede it with the words: "That the people have a right to keep and bear arms."[110]

Senator George F. Barnes began debates in the other house by noting that "not a person on this floor at the time we opened this session realized that these words were not in our state Constitution."[111] Barnes quoted Hubert H. Humphrey as stating: "Certainly one of the chief guarantees of freedom under any government, no matter how popular and respected, is the right of the citizen to keep and bear arms. This is not to say that firearms should not be carefully used and that definite safety rules and precautions should not be called into force. But the right of the citizen to bear arms is just one more guarantee against arbitrary government."[112]

Barnes then yielded to Senator M.M. Long, who revealed the real interests behind the new provision—sportsmen who wished to carry arms and all citizens who wished to keep arms in their homes—as follows:

The object and purpose of it is not to cripple law enforcement or anything of that sort. It is simply that the sportsmen of this State are very much interested in it. They think that they should have it since it is in the Constitution of thirty-five States and is guaranteed to the citizens by the second amendment to the Constitution of the United States. . . . Some citizens feel that they should be permitted to have arms in their homes, and they think that this will give them some protection.[113]

The people at large doubtlessly read the proposal as protecting a private right to keep arms in the home and to carry them, at least openly. Although it was placed with a militia guarantee, the arms guarantee was intended to preclude firearms prohibitions which applied to the general populace. While a right to keep and bear arms had always been assumed in Virginia, the public felt a need to adopt explicit language in the Declaration of Rights as amended in 1970.

New Hampshire, 1982. In 1975, the New Hampshire legislature passed and proposed to the electorate the following amendment to the constitution: "All persons have the right to keep and bear arms in defense of themselves, their families, their property and the state, but the legislature may prescribe the manner in which they may be borne and may prohibit convicted felons from carrying or possessing them." This first appeared in the House Journal as "relating to natural rights."[114]

Most of the debate centered on the extent of legislative power to regulate. Senator David Bradley explained the qualification as follows:

> That language, like the other language in here, is taken from other constitutional provisions in other states. It simply means that the right to bear arms is not an absolute right but may be regulated. The Legislature has now, we have laws which, for example, require the licensing of concealed loaded pistols. Without this kind of proviso, the ability of the state to have that kind of regulations would be in question and in jeopardy.[115]

Actually, no other state saw a need for explicit legislative power to disarm felons, but several authorized regulation of how arms are borne. Legislative empowerment to regulate bearing arms was objected to based on Massachusetts law which imposes a minimum mandatory one year sentence for unlicensed carrying of pistols:

> Sen. [William] SANBORN: . . . Under your proposed amendment the state legislature here could very easily pass a bill similar to the present restriction in Massachusetts where the Continental soldiers even have to have a tag hanging on them that they are licensed. Is that right?
>
> Sen. BRADLEY: I am not fully familiar with the Massachusetts law or the Massachusetts Constitution. But the Legislature would be able in the future, as they are presently, and always have been able to pass reasonable laws regulating the possessing of arms.
>
> Sen. SANBORN: You haven't read some of the items relative to the Bicentennial Celebration in Massachusetts that under the new law they just passed that they have to have permits even to carry an old empty musket?
>
> Sen. BRADLEY: No, I hadn't read that one, but I assume our Legislature would not be so foolish.[116]

Proponents continued to argue that without an explicit power to regulate the right, legislation which prohibited the bearing of arms by ordinary persons would be of doubtful constitutionality. Senator Robert Trowbridge stated that without the explicit legislative authority to regulate, the main guarantee "overrides all of those statutes. The Constitution prevails. Those statutes go out."[117]

This guarantee with the proviso was placed on the ballot for public vote in 1978. The results were 160,628 in favor and 87,807 against, which did not quite realize the necessary two-thirds majority needed to place the clause in the New Hampshire Constitution.[118]

In 1981, the guarantee was reintroduced and passed the legislature with the controversial language excised, so that it read: "All persons have the right to keep and bear arms in defense of themselves, their families, their property and the state." The only recorded discussion was the following comment by Senator Raymond Conley:

This Constitutional amendment reaffirms that all persons have the right to keep and bear arms in defense of themselves, their family, their property, and the state. . . . The federal courts, on several occasions, have interpreted the Second Amendment as imposing a limitation on the national government only and therefore does not speak to the States' rights. Thirty-seven states have Constitutional provisions guaranteeing the right to bear arms. Thirteen states have no Constitutional provisions and in the New England states only the state of New Hampshire has no such provisions.[119]

In 1982, the voters ratified the amendment and it became Part I, Article 2a of the New Hampshire Constitution. The ratification of this absolute version and the rejection in 1978 of the version with the words "the legislature may prescribe the manner in which they may be borne" suggests that some forms of legislative regulation of the right may be constitutionally suspect.

Delaware, 1987. The preamble of the Delaware Constitution of 1897 states that "all men have by nature the rights of . . . defending life and liberty, of acquiring and protecting reputation and property." Still in force, this provision may assume a right to have arms for defense and protection.

In 1987, an amendment to the Declaration of Rights was adopted which states: "A person has the right to keep and bear arms for the defense of self, family, home and state, and for hunting and recreational use." The official synopsis described it as "a constitutional amendment that explicitly protects the traditional lawful right to keep and bear arms."[120] This terminology implies that the right was already implicitly guaranteed by the Declaration of Rights.

The proposal passed the legislature almost unanimously in 1986 and again in 1987.[121] Adoption in both houses by a two-thirds margin in two consecutive sessions made the provision part of the Delaware Constitution.

Thus ends the saga of the second century of proclamations of a right to keep and bear arms under the state bills of rights. The 1768 Boston cry that "the inhabitants are to be disarmed" did not come true until Gage took decisive action in 1775. Lexington and Concord resulted in bills of rights guaranteeing a "well regulated militia," Boston resulted in recognition of the right to "keep" arms, and both prompted declarations of the right to "bear" arms.

Some states adopted bills of rights to formalize the liberties which government may not violate. In other states, the view prevailed that freemen had no need of a bill of rights. The right of individuals to keep and bear arms went unquestioned in those days, and there were no laws on the books which regulated the nonaggressive possession of firearms.

These ideals prompted the ratification of the Second Amendment. With the strong influence of both federal and state bills of rights, most of the remaining original states also adopted bills of rights. From the first Declaration of Rights, that of Virginia, which recognizes "the body of the people, trained to arms," to the most recent, Delaware's, which guarantees possession of arms "for the defense of self, family, home and state, and for hunting and recreational use," this controversial right has survived into the third century of the American body politic.

Notes

PREFACE

1. Comment, *Banning Handguns: Quilici v. Village of Morton Grove and the Second Amendment*, 60 WASH. UNIV. LAW QUARTERLY 1087, 1093 (1982).

2. Commonwealth v. Davis, 369 Mass. 886, 343 N.E.2d 847, 848 (1976).

3. 343 N.E.2d at 848–49.

4. One study by a leading authority on the history of the militia speculates concerning the intended meaning of the state guarantees as not recognizing any individual rights, but provides no original historical records to substantiate his thesis. See L. Cress, *An Armed Community: The Origins and Meaning of the Right to Bear Arms*, 71 JOUR. OF AMERICAN HISTORY 22, 29–30 (June 1984).

CHAPTER 1

1. Boston Chronicle, Sept. 19, 1768, at 363, col. 2.

2. An Act Declaring the Rights and Liberties of the Subject, 1 W. & M., Sess. 2, c.2 (1689).

3. *Id*.

4. Boston Evening Post, September 19, 1768, at 2, cols. 1–2.

5. *Id.*, September 26, 1768, Supplement, at 1, col. 1.

6. Boston Gazette, and Country Journal, September 26, 1768, at 3, cols. 1–2; Maryland Gazette (Annapolis), Oct. 20, 1768, at 3, col. 1; Georgia Gazette (Savannah), Nov. 2, 1768, at 1, col. 1.

7. Occupation of the Hall was particularly objectionable because it "contains many of the public Papers and the Town Arms." Boston Evening Post, October 3, 1768, at 3, col. 2 (includes an account of the invasion).

8. *Id*. at 4.

9. *Id*. at 3, col. 2.

10. Boston Gazette, and Country Journal, Oct. 3, 1768, at 2, col. 2.

11. Boston Evening Post, October 17, 1768, at 2, col. 3.

12. Boston Chronicle, Oct. 10, 1768, at 391, col. 3.

13. New York Journal, Oct. 20, 1768, at 2, col. 3.

14. *Id*., Feb. 2, 1769, at 2, col. 2.

15. Boston Gazette, and Country Journal, Oct. 17, 1768, at 2, col. 3.

16. BOSTON UNDER MILITARY RULE [1768–1769] AS REVEALED IN A JOURNAL OF THE TIMES, at xiii–ix (1971). All references below datelined Boston are from this column.

17. "Boston, Oct. 12," in New York Journal, Oct. 27, 1768, at 2, col. 3.

18. Boston Evening Post, Nov. 21, 1768, at 2, col. 3.

19. "Boston, Dec. 29," in *id*., Jan. 19, 1769, at 1, col. 2.

20. New York Journal, Apr. 13, 1769, at 4, col. 2.

21. Boston Gazette, and Country Journal, Nov. 7, 1768, at 2, col. 1 states: "Their being older and more numerous than we are, gives them no more Right to our Property, or to deprive us of the Disposal of it, than a Man's being armed, gives him a Right to take possession of every unarmed Person's Money, he meets on the King's Highway."

22. New York Journal, Mar. 23, 1769, at 2, col. 2.

23. "Boston, Jan. 18," in New York Journal, Supplement, Feb. 16, 1769, at 2, col. 2–3.

24. *Id*.

25. Boston Gazette, and Country Journal, Jan. 30, 1769, at 2, col.1 (signed "Shippen"); 1 THE WRITINGS OF SAMUEL ADAMS 299 (H. Cushing ed., 1904).

26. Boston Gazette, Feb. 27, 1769, at 3, col. 1; 1 THE WRITINGS OF SAMUEL ADAMS 317.

27. *Id*. at 317–18. Adams is quoting *verbatim* from 1 BLACKSTONE, COMMENTARIES *140–41, 143–44.

28. *Id*. at 318.

29. New York Journal, Supplement, Apr. 28, 1769, at 1, col. 2.

30. "Boston, March 17," in New York Journal, Supplement, Apr. 13, 1769, at 1, col. 3.

31. New York Journal, May 4, 1769, at 1, col. 3.

32. Massachusetts Gazette (Boston), June 15, 1769, at 1, col. 2; 1 THE WRITINGS OF SAMUEL ADAMS 344–45.

33. "Boston March 28," in New York Journal, Supplement, May 11, 1769, at 1, col. 1.

34. New York Journal, May 18, 1769, at 3, col. 2.

35. Massachusetts Gazette and Boston Weekly News-Letter, March 1, 1770, at 3, col. 2; June 21, 1770, Extraordinary Issue.

36. Boston Evening Post, March 12, 1770, at 2, col. 3.

37. *Id*., April 2, 1770, at 4, col. 1.

38. *Id*., April 30, 1770, at 4, cols. 1–2 (message from a House Committee to the Lieutenant Governor).

39. For example, Boston Evening Post, Feb. 5, 1770, at 3, col. 3 ("To be sold ... Gun Powder, Lead, Shot").

40. Massachusetts Gazette and Boston Weekly News-Letter, March 8, 1770, at 4, col. 2.

41. *Id.*, Apr. 6, 1770, at 1, col. 1.

42. Massachusetts Spy, Sept. 8, 1774, at 3, col. 3.

43. Massachusetts Gazette, and Boston Weekly News-Letter, Nov. 3, 1774, at 1, col. 1.

44. *Id.*, Nov. 10, 1774, at 2, col. 3.

45. *Id.* at 3, col. 1. In the Supplement to this issue, at 1, col.1, a writer deplored riots in New England, stating that "in the colonies south of New-England, there is no training up to military discipline, . . . there is no attempt by the populace to buy up arms and ammunition."

46. *Id.*, Dec. 1, 1774, at 2, col. 3. This reported the strength of the Boston militia at 10,000 men.

47. *Id.*, Dec. 29, 1774, at 2, col. 2.

48. *Id.* at 3, col. 1.

49. Connecticut Courant, Jan. 9, 1775, at 2, col. 2.

50. *Id.*, cols. 2–3.

51. New Hampshire Gazette and Historical Chronicle, Jan. 13, 1775, at 1, col. 1.

52. *Id.*

53. Massachusetts Gazette, Jan. 5, 1775, at 1, col. 1.

54. *Id.*, col. 2.

55. *Id.*, Jan. 19, 1775, at 2, col. 2.

56. Connecticut Courant, Jan. 16, 1775, at 2, col. 2.

57. *Id.*, col. 3.

58. *Id.*, Jan. 23, 1775, at 1, col. 3.

59. *Id.*, Jan. 30, 1775, at 1, col. 3.

60. Essex Gazette, Jan. 17, 1775, at 4, col. 1.

61. Essex Gazette, Feb. 28, 1775, at 4, col. 1.

62. *Id.*

63. Massachusetts Gazette; and Boston Weekly News-Letter, March 17, 1775, at 3, col. 1.

64. *Id.*

65. *Id.*, col. 2.

66. Connecticut Courant, Mar. 13, 1775, at 1, col. 3.

67. *Id.*

68. *Id.*, Apr. 3, 1775, at 2, col. 2.

69. Newport Mercury (R.I.), Apr. 10, 1775, at 2, col. 1.

70. Essex Gazette, April 25, 1775, at 3, col. 3.

71. Attested Copy of Proceedings Between Gage and Selectmen, Apr. 22, 1775, in Connecticut Courant, July 17, 1775, at 1, col. 3, and 4, col. 1.

72. *Id.* at 4, col. 2 (Apr. 23, 1775).

73. *Id.*

74. *Id.*, col. 3.

75. R. FROTHINGHAM, HISTORY OF THE SIEGE OF BOSTON 95 (1903).

76. *Id.* at 95 n.1.

77. Attested Copy of the Proceedings between Gage and Selectmen, Apr. 30, 1775, in Connecticut Courant, July 17, 1775, at 4, col. 3.

78. Connecticut Courant, May 8, 1775, at 2, col. 1.

79. *Id.* at 3, col. 1.

80. Connecticut Journal and New-Haven Post-Boy, May 19, 1775, at 6, col. 2.

81. Connecticut Courant, June 19, 1775, at 4, col. 2.

82. Connecticut Journal and New-Haven Post Boy, June 21, 1775, at 3, cols. 1–2.

83. Pennsylvania Evening Post, June 27, 1775, at 1, cols. 1–2.

84. Connecticut Courant, July 17, 1775, at 4, col. 1.

85. *Id.* at 2, col. 1. The Continental Congress adopted an address "To the People of Ireland" which complained that "the citizens petitioned the General for permission to leave the town, and he promised, on surrending their arms, to permit them to depart with their other effects; they accordingly surrended their arms, and the General violated his faith." *Id.*, Aug. 21, 1775, at 1, col. 3.

86. Virginia Gazette (Williamsburg), Aug. 5, 1775, at 2, col. 1.

87. *Id.*, June 24, 1775, at 1, col. 1; Maryland Gazette (Annapolis), July 20, 1775, at 1, col. 2.

88. For example, *Revolutionary Correspondence From 1775 to 1782*, 6 COLLECTIONS OF THE RHODE ISLAND HISTORICAL SOCIETY 132 (Providence 1867); J. JACKSON, WITH THE BRITISH ARMY IN PHILADELPHIA, 1777–1778, at 20 (1979).

89. 1 SOURCES OF AMERICAN INDEPENDENCE 176 (H. Peckman ed. 1978).

CHAPTER 2

1. J. SELSAM, THE PENNSYLVANIA CONSTITUTION OF 1776 at 175–76 (1936).

2. Pennsylvania Gazette (Philadelphia), June 12, 1776, at 2.

3. J. SELSAM, THE PENNSYLVANIA CONSTITUTION 148.

4. THE PROCEEDINGS RELATIVE TO CALLING THE CONVENTIONS OF 1776 AND 1790, at 48 (Harrisburg 1825) [hereafter cited "PROCEEDINGS"].

5. *Id.* at 49.

6. R. RYERSON, THE REVOLUTION IS NOW BEGUN: THE RADICAL COMMITTEES OF PHILADELPHIA, 1765–1776, at 117–18, 240 (1978).

7. *Id.* at 113–15, 167, 241.

8. ALEXANDER GRAYDON, MEMOIRS OF HIS OWN TIME 286–87 (Philadelphia 1846).

9. J. ADAMS, DIARY AND AUTOBIOGRAPHY 391 (1961).

10. B. KONKLE, GEORGE BRYAN AND THE CONSTITUTION OF PENNSYLVANIA 119 (Philadelphia 1922).

11. *Id.* at 121.

12. *Id.* at 117 n.1.

13. *Id.*

14. *Infra*, next topic heading.

15. A. GRAYDON, MEMOIRS 287.

16. *Id.* at 288.

17. J. SELSAM, THE PENNSYLVANIA CONSTITUTION 207 n.6.

18. PA. DEC. OF RIGHTS, Art. XIII (1776); PROCEEDINGS 56.

19. Pennsylvania Evening Post (Philadelphia), Aug. 20, 1776, at 413.

20. 22 B. FRANKLIN, PAPERS 514 n.2, 3 (1982).

21. Pennsylvania Evening Post, Sept. 26, 28, Oct. 8, 10, 15, 17, 19, 22, 24, 1776.

22. *Id.*, Oct. 24, 1776, at 531, col. 1.

23. *Id.* at col. 2.

24. *Id.*, Oct. 31, 1776, at 546.

25. PA. CONST., Art. II, Section 5 (1776); PROCEEDINGS 57.

26. Pennsylvania Evening Post, Oct. 10, 1776, at 503.

27. PA. CONST., Art. I, Section 43 (1776); PROCEEDINGS 64.

28. Pennsylvania Evening Post, Oct. 22, 1776, at 526–27.

29. *Id.* at 527, col. 1.

30. *Id.*, Nov. 5, 1776, at 554, cols. 1–2.

31. J. SELSAM, THE PENNSYLVANIA CONSTITUTION 178–79.

32. VA. DEC. OF RIGHTS, Art. XIII (1776).

33. PA. DEC. OF RIGHTS, Art. XIII (1776).

34. J. SELSAM, THE PENNSYLVANIA CONSTITUTION 182–83.

35. J. ADAMS, DIARY AND AUTOBIOGRAPHY 391 (1961).

36. 2 T. PAINE, COMPLETE WRITINGS 1085 (1969).

37. *Id.* at 45.

38. *Id.* at 35.

39. *Id.*, 2, at 57.

40. *Id.* at 53.

41. *Id.*, 1, at 85. A frequently repeated British order criticized by Paine provided: "all inhabitants who shall be found with arms, not having an officer with them, shall be immediately taken and hung up." *Id.* at 65.

42. *Id.* at 69.

43. *Id.* at 274.

44. *Id.* at 373–74.

45. 6 P. FORCE, AMERICAN ARCHIVES 965.

46. ACTS OF THE GENERAL ASSEMBLY OF THE COMMONWEALTH OF PENNSYLVANIA, ENACTED INTO LAWS, SINCE THE DECLARATION OF INDEPENDENCE ON THE FOURTH DAY OF JULY, A.D. 1776, at 22.

47. ACTS OF THE GENERAL ASSEMBLY OF THE COMMONWEALTH OF PENNSYLVANIA [1775–1781] at 347 (Philadelphia 1782).

48. PROCEEDINGS 87.

49. AN ABRIDGMENT OF THE LAWS OF PENNSYLVANIA, 1700–1811, at 173 (Philadelphia 1811).

50. *Id.* at 174.

51. *Id.* at 208.

52. ACTS OF THE GENERAL ASSEMBLY 193 (1782).

53. *Id.*

54. *See* AN ABRIDGMENT OF THE LAWS OF PENNSYLVANIA, 1700–1811 (Philadelphia 1811).

55. PROCEEDINGS 152.

56. *Id.* at 153–54. Members included William Findley, Edmond Hand, Henry Miller, James Wilson, William Irvine, William Lewis, James Ross, Charles Smith and Alexander Addison.

57. A. GRAYDON, MEMOIRS 351–56.

58. 2 DOCUMENTARY HISTORY OF THE RATIFICATION OF THE CON-STITUTION 336 (M. Jensen ed. 1976).

59. *Id.* at 623–24, 639. The Dissent of Minority bore clear marks of the 1776 Pennsylvania Declaration and Constitution on the rights to bear arms and to hunt. In fact, dissident leaders Smilie and Findlay were vigorous followers of Justice George Bryan, leader of the Pennsylvania constitutional convention of 1776. B. KONKLE, GEORGE BRYAN AND THE CONSTITUTION OF PENN-SYLVANIA 258. Justice Bryan played a key role in agitating for amendments to the proposed federal constitution, and his son George, author of the Dissent, also wrote the anti-federalist *Centinel* series which demanded a federal bill of rights. *Id.* at 309–38.

60. 1 ANNALS OF CONG. 434 (June 8, 1789). The proposed amendments were published in the Federal Gazette (Philadelphia), June 16, 1789, at 2, col. 2. Two days later it was explained that "the people are confirmed by the next article in their right to keep and bear their private arms." *Id.*, June 18, 1789, at 2, col. 1.

61. PROCEEDINGS 163.

62. *E.g.*, Providence Gazette & Country Journal, Jan. 30, 1790, at 1.

63. PROCEEDINGS 380.

64. On their role at the state convention, see A. GRAYDON, MEMOIRS 355–56.

65. PROCEEDINGS 173, 175.

66. *Id.* at 258.

67. *Id.* at 225, 263.

68. *Id.* at 270–71.

69. *Id.* at 274.

70. PA. DEC. OF RIGHTS, Art. XXI; PROCEEDINGS 305.

71. PA. DEC. OF RIGHTS, Art. VI, Section 2; PROCEEDINGS 302.

72. 1 THE PAPERS OF JAMES IREDELL 79 (1976).

73. 1 R. CONNER, HISTORY OF NORTH CAROLINA 324 (Chicago 1919).

74. *Id.* at 421.

75. *Id.* at 354–55.

76. *Id.* at 360.

77. *Id.* at 362.

78. North Carolina Gazette (Newbern), July 7, 1775, at 2, col. 3. A week later, the Gazette published the Address and Declaration of the Provincial Congress of South Carolina, which stated, "solely for the Preservation and in Defense of our Lives, Liberties, and Properties we have been impelled to associate, and to take up Arms . . . Our taking up Arms is the Result of dire Necessity, and in compliance with the first Law of Nature." *Id.*, July 14, 1775, at 1, col. 1.

79. 10 COLONIAL RECORDS OF NORTH CAROLINA 144–45 (W. Saunders ed. 1890).

80. *Id.* at 150.

81. *Id.* at 162.

82. *Id.* at 314.

83. *Id.* at 446.

84. *Id.* at 447.

85. JOURNAL OF PROCEEDINGS OF THE PROVINCIAL CONGRESS OF NORTH CAROLINA 32 (1776).

86. 10 COLONIAL RECORDS OF NORTH CAROLINA 870a.

87. *Id*. at 870b.

88. VA. DEC. OF RIGHTS, ART. XIII (1776).

89. PA. DEC. OF RIGHTS, ART. XIII (1776).

90. 10 COLONIAL RECORDS OF NORTH CAROLINA 918–19. The committee included "Willie Jones, Thomas Person, and Griffith Rutherford, radical leaders; Allen Jones, Thomas Jones, Samuel Ashe, and Archibald Maclaine, conservative leaders; Richard Caswell and Cornelius Harnett, who may be classed as moderates." 1 R. CONNER, HISTORY OF NORTH CAROLINA 412.

91. North Carolina Gazette, July 7, 1775, at 2, col. 3.

92. The committee was appointed on Nov. 13 and reported the Bill of Rights on Dec. 12, and the convention passed it on Dec. 17, 1776. 1 R. CONNOR, HISTORY OF NORTH CAROLINA 413. The debate took place on Dec. 14, 16, and 17, 1776. J. SEAWELL JONES, A DEFENSE OF THE REVOLUTIONARY HISTORY OF NORTH CAROLINA 286 (Raleigh 1834).

93. PROCEEDINGS AND DEBATES OF THE CONVENTION OF NORTH CAROLINA [1835], at 318 (Raleigh 1836).

94. *Id*. at 391.

95. 1 THE PAPERS OF JAMES IREDELL 425.

96. JOURNAL OF PROCEEDINGS OF THE PROVINCIAL CONGRESS OF NORTH CAROLINA 3–4 (1776).

97. *Id*., Art. XXV. The provision described the state boundaries, and provided that titles of individuals holding under previous laws would remain valid.

98. STATUTES OF THE STATE OF NORTH CAROLINA 591 (Edenton 1791).

99. *Id*. at 592.

100. A COLLECTION OF THE STATUTES OF THE PARLIAMENT OF ENGLAND IN FORCE IN THE STATE OF NORTH CAROLINA 60, 95 (Newbern 1792). State v. Huntley, 25 N.C. 418, 422–23 (1843) states: "The offense of riding or going armed with unusual and dangerous weapons to the terror of the people, is an offense at common law and is indictable in this state. A man may carry a gun for any lawful purpose of business or amusement. . . . It is the wicked purpose, and the mischievous result, which essentially constitute the crime."

101. A COLLECTION OF THE STATUTES 6, 398.

102. STATUTES OF THE STATE 242.

103. *Id*. at 587–88.

104. *See* LAWS OF THE STATE OF NORTH CAROLINA (Raleigh 1821).

105. STATUTES OF THE STATE 93.

106. *Id*. at 152–53.

107. *Id*.

108. 22 STATE RECORDS OF NORTH CAROLINA 663 (W. Clark ed. 1907).

109. 2 R. CONNER, HISTORY OF NORTH CAROLINA 33.

110. *Id*. at 34.

111. 4 J. ELLIOT, DEBATES IN THE SEVERAL STATE CONVENTIONS 149 (1838).

112. *Id*. at 185.

113. *Id*. at 216.

114. *Id*. at 226.

115. *Id*. at 244. This is identical to the Virginia provision. *Id*., 3, at 659.

116. *Id*., 4, at 245. This, too, is identical with the Virginia proposal. *Id*., 3, at 660.

117. *Id*., 1, at 333.

118. Ira Allen, *Autobiography* (1799), in J. WILBUR, IRA ALLEN: FOUNDER OF VERMONT, 1751–1814, at 17 (Boston: Houghton Mifflin, 1928).

119. *Id*. at 31.

120. *Id*. at 39.

121. *Id*. at 40.

122. IRA ALLEN, NATURAL AND POLITICAL HISTORY OF THE STATE OF VERMONT 49 (London: J. W. Myers, 1798).

123. *Id*.

124. *Id*. at 50.

125. *Id*. at 60.

126. *Id*. at 73–78.

127. J. WILBUR, IRA ALLEN 85.

128. *Id*. at 87.

129. *Id*.

130. VERMONT STATE PAPERS 70 (Middlebury: J. W. Copeland, 1823) (William Slade compl.).

131. D. CHIPMAN, A MEMOIR OF THOMAS CRITTENDEN, THE FIRST GOVERNOR OF VERMONT 27 (Middlebury 1849).

132. P. White, *Address on the Windsor Convention*, 1 COLLECTIONS (Vermont Historical Society) 63 (1870).

133. B. KONKLE, GEORGE BRYAN AND THE CONSTITUTION OF PENNSYLVANIA 117 n. 1 (Philadelphia 1922).

134. VT. CONST., Art. I, Sec. 15 (1777); PA. DEC. OF RIGHTS, Art. XIII (1776).

135. VT. CONST., Art. XXXIX (1777); PA. CONST., Art. I, Sec. 43 (1776).

136. J. WILBUR, IRA ALLEN 11–12.

137. VT. CONST., Art. I, Sec. 18 (1787).

138. VT. CONST., Art. I, Sec. 16 (1796).

139. See *Proceedings of the First and Second Councils of Censors*, in VERMONT STATE PAPERS, *passim* (1823).

140. *The Laws from the Year 1779 to 1786, Inclusive*, in VERMONT STATE PAPERS 307.

141. STATUTES OF THE STATE OF VERMONT, PASSED FEBRUARY AND MARCH 1789, at 97 (1789).

142. *Id* at 95–96.

143. IRA ALLEN, PARTICULARS OF THE CAPTURE OF THE OLIVE BRANCH, LADEN WITH A CARGO OF ARMS *passim* (London: J. W. Myers, 1798).

144. *Id*. at 6.

145. *Id*. at 141–42.

146. *Id*. at 146.

147. *Id*. at 245.

148. *Id*. at 246.

149. *Id.* at 403.

150. See IRA ALLEN, THE OLIVE BRANCH (Philadelphia 1805).

151. 2 J. ADAMS, LEGAL PAPERS 106, 116–117 (1965).

152. *Id.* at 108.

153. *Id.* at 125.

154. *Id.* at 143.

155. 13 and 14 Car. 2, c. 11, Section 5(2) (1662).

156. *Id.*, c. 3, Section 14.

157. *Id.*, c. 33, Sections 15, 19. These acts are discussed in 2 J. ADAMS, LEGAL PAPERS 108–109.

158. *Id.* at 326.

159. *Id.* at 331.

160. *Id.* Emphasis added.

161. *Id.*, 3, at 242.

162. *Id.* at 149. Pain argued for the Crown that due to the abusive conduct of the soldiers, "the most peaceable among us had <*thought*> found it necessary to arm themselves with heavy Walking Sticks or Weapons of Defense when they went abroad." *Id.* at 274. Samuel Adams argued in the press that one of the slain "was leaning upon his stick when he fell, which certainly was not a *threatening* posture: It may be supposed that he had as good right, *by the law of the land*, to carry a stick for his own and his neighbor's defence, in a time of danger, as the Soldier who shot him had, to be arm'd with musquet and ball, for the defence of himself and his friend the Centinel." 2 S. ADAMS, WORKS 119 (1906).

163. 2 J. ADAMS, LEGAL PAPERS 84.

164. *Id.* at 248.

165. *Id.* at 285.

166. *Id.*, 1 at 160.

167. *Id.* at n. 16.

168. *Id.* at 137.

169. 4 J. ADAMS, WORKS 215–16 (1851).

170. 3 S. ADAMS, WRITINGS 172 (1907).

171. JOURNAL OF THE CONVENTION FOR FRAMING A CONSTITUTION OF GOVERNMENT FOR THE STATE OF MASSACHUSETTS BAY (1779–1780), at 41 (1832).

172. *Id.* See 2 J. ADAMS, DIARY AND AUTOBIOGRAPHY 401 (1961). No records of debates were kept, although in the convention of 1820–1821 some members remembered the speeches of Samuel and John Adams in 1779. JOURNAL OF DEBATES TO REVISE THE CONSTITUTION OF MASSACHUSETTS 430, 435 (1853).

The portion of Art. XVII concerning the danger of armies to liberty and the subordination of military to civil authority, was commented on by ABBE DE MABLY, REMARKS CONCERNING THE GOVERNMENT AND THE LAWS OF THE UNITED STATES OF AMERICA: IN FOUR LETTERS, ADDRESSED TO MR. ADAMS 162–64 (1785) as follows: "These points neglected, the times will reproduce a Sylla, a Marius, a Caesar, a Cromwell, or a Valstein." After Adams responded by quoting promilitia and antiarmy provisions from the other state constitutions (*id.*, at 162–63), Mably wrote: "You must expect that your people, of whom the laws have so clearly established the sovereignty, may prove difficult to manage, because they will perceive of their power. Armed in the defence of their country, they will become jealous of their dignity." *Id.* at 166.

173. THE POPULAR SOURCES OF POLITICAL AUTHORITY: DOCUMENTS ON THE MASSACHUSETTS CONSTITUTION OF 1780, at 574 (1966).

174. *Id.* at 624.

175. MASS. DEC. OF RIGHTS, Arts. I and XVII (1780).

176. William Gordon wrote the most extensive articles on the constitution in the series "To the Freemen of the Massachusetts Bay." References to Adams and the convention are included in the Independent Chronicle, May 4, 1780.

177. Independent Chronicle, June 29, 1780, at 4, col. 3.

178. Adams' copy of DEI DELITTIE DELLA PENE (Haarlem and Paris 1780) is among his books in the Boston Public Library. 1 J. ADAMS, DIARY AND AUTOBIOGRAPHY 353 n.2, 442 n.23.

179. *Id.* at 352. Of Adams' opening statement in the Boston Massacre trial of 1770, his son, John Quincy Adams, later reported "the electrical effect produced upon the jury and upon the immense and excited auditory, by the first sentence with which he opened his defense, which was [a] citation from the then recently published work of Beccaria." 2 J. ADAMS, WORKS 238–39 (1856).

180. 3 J. ADAMS, DIARY AND AUTOBIOGRAPHY 194.

181. This is from one of John Adams's own copies of the work now located at the Boston Public Library Rare Book Collection. BECCARIA, AN ESSAY ON CRIMES AND PUNISHMENTS 161–162 (London 1775). Adams's Coat of Arms and name appears on the first page, and the title page contains the following handwritten note: "Thomas B. Adams. From his Father. 1800."

182. 3 J. ADAMS, DIARY AND AUTOBIOGRAPHY 358–59.

183. 1 J. ADAMS, A DEFENCE OF THE CONSTITUTIONS OF GOVERN-MENT OF THE UNITED STATES OF AMERICA 163 (1787–1788).

184. *Id.* at 168. "The vast bodies of citizens in arms, both elders and youth," characterized Harrington's commonwealth. J. HARRINGTON, POLITICAL WORKS 696 (J. Pocock ed. 1977). "Men accustomed to their arms and their liberties will never endure the yoke." *Id.* at 443. Sir Henry Vance the Younger, in an exposition of Harrington's writings, defined "free Citizen[s]" as those who "have deserved to be trusted with the keeping or bearing Their own Armes in the publick defence." *Id.* at 109.

185. A. SIDNEY, DISCOURSES CONCERNING GOVERNMENT 157 (London 1698).

186. T. HOBBES, LEVIATHAN 88 (1964).

187. *Id.* at 85.

188. J. LOCKE, OF CIVIL GOVERNMENT 174 (1955).

189. *Id.* at 114–15.

190. 3 J. ADAMS, A DEFENCE OF THE CONSTITUTIONS OF GOVERN-MENT OF THE UNITED STATES OF AMERICA 471–72 (1787–1788).

191. *Id.* at 475.

192. MASS. DEC. OF RIGHTS, Arts. I and XVII (1780).

193. 1 THE PERPETUAL LAWS OF THE COMMONWEALTH OF MASSA-CHUSETTS, FROM THE ESTABLISHMENT OF ITS CONSTITUTION IN THE

YEAR 1780, TO THE END OF THE YEAR 1800, at 288 (1801) [hereafter "PER-PETUAL LAWS"].

194. 1 PERPETUAL LAWS 346.

195. 1 PERPETUAL LAWS 366. Emphasis added.

196. 2 J. ELLIOT, DEBATES IN THE SEVERAL STATE CONVENTIONS 38 (1836).

197. *From the Boston Independent Chronicle,* Philadelphia Independent Gazetteer, Aug. 20, 1789, at 2, col. 2. Emphasis added.

198. Massachusetts Centinel (Boston), July 4, 1789, at 1, col. 2.

199. Senate Journal, MS by Sam A. Otis, Virginia State Library, Executive Communications, Box 13 (Sept. 9, 1789), at 1.

200. Militia Act (1793), 2 PERPETUAL LAWS 172–73.

201. *Id.* at 178.

202. *Id.* at 181.

203. *Id.* at 178.

204. 2 Edw. III, c. 3 (1328).

205. Act of 1795, 2 PERPETUAL LAWS 259. Emphasis added.

206. Rex v. Knight, 90 Eng. Rep. 330, 87 Eng. Rep. 75, 76. (K. B. 1686).

207. *See* An Act for Keeping Watches and Wards in Towns (1796), 2 PERPETUAL ACTS 409.

208. 4 S. ADAMS, WORKS 402 (1906).

209. *Id* at 403.

210. *Id.*

211. W. SUMNER, AN INQUIRY INTO THE IMPORTANCE OF THE MILITIA TO A FREE COMMONWEALTH IN A LETTER . . . TO JOHN ADAMS . . . WITH HIS ANSWER 4 (Boston 1823).

212. *Id.* at 16–17.

213. *Id.* at 21.

214. *Id.* at 39–40.

215. *Id.* at 69–70.

CHAPTER 3

1. 1 MASON, PAPERS 215–16 (Rutland ed. 1970).

2. JOURNAL OF PROCEEDINGS OF CONVENTION HELD AT RICHMOND 10 (1775).

3. *Id.* at 11.

4. *Id.* at 17 (1775).

5. PROCEEDINGS OF THE CONVENTION OF DELEGATES 100–02 (1776).

6. 1 JEFFERSON, PAPERS 344–45 (Boyd ed. 1951).

7. *Id.* at 353.

8. *Id.* at 347.

9. *Id.,* 2, at 443–44.

10. *Id.,* 1, at 362–63.

11. *Id* at 377.

12. Probably because its principles were taken for granted, the Declaration of Rights occasioned virtually no public debate. The chief exception was the free

exercise of religion clause which sparked some controversy. Virginia Gazette (Williamsburg), Oct. 18, Nov. 1, 8, 1776, at 1.

Aside from news of the armed conflict, the main firearms-related matters reported in the press concerned the production and acquisition of arms and ammunition. "A friend to the American cause" wrote that "every man, after he is furnished with the ingredients [saltpetre and sulphur], may make, or cause to be made, a pound and a half of good gunpowder," in one day; the formula followed. *Id.*, Feb. 16, 1776, Supp. at 2.

13. JEFFERSON, LIVING THOUGHTS 42 (J. Dewey ed. 1963) ("Aristotle, Cicero, Locke, Sidney, & c."). *See* ARISTOTLE, POLITICS 79 (T. Sinclair trans. 1962) ("the farmers have no arms . . . mak[ing] them virtually the servants of those who do possess arms"); CICERO, SELECTED POLITICAL SPEECHES 222 (M. Grant trans. 1969) ("a man who has used arms in self-defense is not regarded as having carried them with a homicidal aim."); J. LOCKE, OF CIVIL GOVERNMENT 114–15 (1955) (the people have not "disarmed themselves, and armed [a legislator], to make prey of them when he pleases."); A. SIDNEY, DISCOURSES CONCERNING GOVERNMENT 157 (1698) (in a popular government "every man is armed and disciplined").

14. THE COMMONPLACE BOOK OF THOMAS JEFFERSON 4 (G. Chinard ed. 1926). This is a condensed version.

15. JEFFERSON, COMMONPLACE BOOK, No. 53, Jefferson Papers, Library of Congress.

16. In *id.* at Nos. 30–78, Jefferson copied from COKE, THIRD INSTITUTE. The above quotation is from COKE at 161–62.

17. 1 MONTESQUIEU, THE SPIRIT OF THE LAWS 36 (T. Nugent transl. 1899); *id.* 2, at 64. In No. 797 of the COMMONPLACE BOOK (Jeff. Papers), Jefferson copied portions of a page where Montesquieu opposed "severe punishments" for "trifling" matters. Jefferson read, but did not copy, the following: "Hence it follows, that the laws of an Italian republic [Venice], where bearing fire-arms is punished as a capital crime and where it is not more fatal to make an ill use of them than to carry them, is not agreeable to the nature of things." 2 MONTESQUIEU 79–80.

18. Compare translation from 1 MONTESQUIEU 57–58 with THE COMMONPLACE BOOK (Chinard ed.) 261. Chinard compares this quotation with the anti-standing army provisions in Jefferson's proposed Virginia Constitution, *id.*, and with the militia clause of the Virginia Declaration of Rights, in JEFFERSON, PENSÉES CHOISIES DE MONTESQUIEU 34 (Chinard ed. 1925).

19. THE COMMONPLACE BOOK (Chinard ed.) 314; BECCARIA, ON CRIMES AND PUNISHMENTS 87–88 (H. Paolucci transl. 1963).

20. W. EDEN, PRINCIPLES OF PENAL LAW 301 (1772).

21. *Id.* at 210–11.

22. *Id.* at 213–14. Eden added:

> This idea is finely expressed by Cicero in his oration for Milo. "And indeed, gentlemen, there exists a law, not written down anywhere but inborn in our hearts. . . . I refer to the law which lays it down that, if our lives are endangered by plots or violence or armed robbers

or enemies, any and every method of protecting ourselves is morally right. When weapons reduce them to silence, the laws no longer expect one to await their pronouncements. For people who decide to wait for these will have to wait for justice, too—and meantime they must suffer injustice first."

Latin translation from CICERO, SELECTED POLITICAL SPEECHES 222 (M. Grant transl. 1969). For related passages copied by Jefferson, see THE COMMONPLACE BOOK (Chinard ed.) 325–26.

23. THE COMMONPLACE BOOK (Chinard ed.) 7; E. DUMBAULD, THOMAS JEFFERSON AND THE LAW 134–36, 236–37 (1978). *See* COMMITTEE OF REVISORS APPOINTED BY THE GENERAL ASSEMBLY IN 1776, at 3 (Richmond 1784).

24. E. DUMBAULD, THOMAS JEFFERSON AND THE LAW, at 134.

25. 2 JEFFERSON, PAPERS 350.

26. *Id*. at 251. *See* 9 HENING, STATUTES 267–69.

27. Act of 1757, 7 HENING 95.

28. Acts of 1784, 9 HENING 476, and 1785, 12 HENING 9. Jefferson's Bill for Establishing a Manufactory of Arms which defined "arms" as muskets, carbines, pistols, and swords passed in 1779. 3 JEFFERSON, PAPERS 132, 135.

29. 2 JEFFERSON, PAPERS 444.

30. *Id*. at 443–44. Emphasis added.

31. Act of 1772, 8 HENING 593.

32. NOAH WEBSTER, AN AMERICAN DICTIONARY OF THE ENGLISH LANGUAGE (New York, 1828) (definition of "gun": "But one species of firearms, the pistol, is never called a gun.")

33. 2 JEFFERSON, PAPERS 444.

34. *Id*.

35. 2 JEFFERSON, PAPERS 492, 505.

36. E. DUMBAULD, THOMAS JEFFERSON AND THE LAW 237, n.19.

37. 2 JEFFERSON, PAPERS 496.

38. *Id*.

39. *Id*. at 519. Emphasis added.

40. 2 Edw. III, c.3 (1328).

41. E. DUMBAULD, THOMAS JEFFERSON AND THE LAW 237.

42. COKE, THIRD INSTITUTE 160–62.

43. *Id*. at 168; JEFFERSON, COMMONPLACE BOOK, No. 60, Jefferson Papers, Library of Congress.

44. *See* Wilkes v. Jackson, 12 Va. (2 Hen. & M.) 355, 359–60 (1808).

45. Rex v. Knight, 87 Eng. Rep. 75, 76, 90 Eng. Rep. 330 (K.B. 1686).

46. *Id*.

47. The Acts of 1748 (6 HENING 109–10) and 1792 (12 HENING 123) stated: "No negro or mulatto shall keep or carry any gun, powder, shot, club, or other weapon whatever [under penalty of 39 lashes] . . . *provided nonetheless*, that every free negro or mulatto, being a housekeeper, may be permitted to keep one gun, powder and shot," and a bond or free negro may "keep and use" a gun by license at frontier plantations.

48. 2 JEFFERSON, PAPERS 663. "No slave shall keep any arms whatever or

pass unless with written orders from his master or employer, or in his company with arms from one place to another." Act of 1785, 12 HENING 182.

49. "The great object is, that every man be armed," contended Patrick Henry. 3 J. ELLIOT, DEBATES IN THE SEVERAL STATE CONVENTIONS 386 (1836). George Mason warned against "disarm[ing] the people; that it was the best and most effectual way to enslave them." *Id.* at 380. Zachriah Johnson defended the proposed federal constitution: "The people are not to be disarmed of their weapons." *Id.* at 646.

50. VA. DEC. OF RIGHTS, ART. XIII (1776).

51. PA. DEC. OF RIGHTS, Art. XIII (1776); N.C. DEC. OF RIGHTS, Art. XVII (1776); VT. DEC. OF RIGHTS, Art. XV (1777); MASS. DEC. OF RIGHTS, Art. XVII (1780).

52. 3 MASON, PAPERS 1068–71 (Rutland ed. 1970).

53. 3 J. ELLIOT, DEBATES IN THE SEVERAL STATE CONVENTIONS 657 (1836).

54. *Id.* at 656.

55. *James Madison's Autobiography*, 2 WM. & MARY Q. 191, 208 (1945).

56. L. CARR & D. JORDAN, MARYLAND'S REVOLUTION OF GOVERNMENT, 1689–1692, at 5 (1974).

57. 8 MARYLAND ARCHIVES 218 (Baltimore: Maryland Historical Society, 1883–1964).

58. *Id.* at 56–57, 65.

59. M. HALL *et al.* eds., THE GLORIOUS REVOLUTION IN AMERICA 184 (1964).

60. *Id.* at 178.

61. 1 W. & M., Sess. 2, c.2 (1689).

62. *Id.*

63. 29 MARYLAND ARCHIVES 224.

64. *Id.* 13, at 557; 22, at 565.

65. *Id.* 52 at 454.

66. T. HANLEY, CHARLES CARROLL OF CARROLLTON 90 (1970).

67. Slaves were disarmed since the Act of 1715, but there were no provisions on Catholics or Papists. *See* LAWS OF MARYLAND (Annapolis: Jonas Green, 1765); LAWS OF MARYLAND MADE SINCE 1763 (Annapolis: Frederick Green, 1787).

68. T. HANLEY, CHARLES CARROLL OF CARROLLTON 138.

69. A COUNTRY GENTLEMAN, CONSIDERATIONS ON THE PENAL LAWS AGAINST ROMAN CATHOLICS IN ENGLAND AND THE NEW ACQUIRED COLONIES IN AMERICA 54 (London: R. & J. Dodsley, 1764).

70. T. HANDLEY, CHARLES CARROLL OF CARROLLTON 182–85; R. HOFFMAN, A SPIRIT OF DISSENSION: ECONOMICS, POLITICS, AND THE REVOLUTION IN MARYLAND 108–9 (1973).

71. Maryland Gazette (Annapolis), Oct. 13, 1768, at 2, col. 2.

72. *Id.*, Oct. 20, 1768, at 3, col. 1.

73. PROCEEDINGS OF THE CONVENTION OF THE PROVINCE OF MARYLAND 7 (Annapolis: Frederick Green, 1775).

74. W. EDDIS, LETTERS FROM AMERICA 100 (1969). [emphasis added]

75. *Id.*, at 113.

76. PROCEEDINGS OF THE CONVENTION 13. A large portion of this journal concerns the encouragement of the manufacture, purchase, acquisition, keeping, bearing, and using arms for the revolutionary cause.

77. Maryland Gazette, May 11, 1775, at 2, col. 2.

78. *Id.*, June 15, 1775, at 1, col. 1.

79. *Id.*, June 22, 1775, at 1, col. 1.

80. *Id.*, Aug. 17, 1775, at 2, col. 2.

81. *Id.*, Aug. 24, 1775, at 1, cols. 1–2. There never seemed to be enough arms, and advertisements such as the following were typical: "Wanted immediately, a number of hands who are acquainted in the different branches of the manufacture of firearms." *Id.*, at 3, col. 1.

82. D. SKAGGS, ROOTS OF MARYLAND DEMOCRACY, 1753–1776, at 220 (1973).

83. *Id.* at 184.

84. *Id.* at 224.

85. *Id.* at 225.

86. *Id.*

87. R. HOFFMAN, A SPIRIT OF DISSENSION 170.

88. *Id.* at 171.

89. *Id.*

90. D. SKAGGS, ROOTS OF MARYLAND DEMOCRACY 227–28.

91. *Id.* at 190–95.

92. *Id.* at 185.

93. *Id.* at 191.

94. *Id.* at 190–91.

95. PROCEEDINGS OF THE PROVINCE OF MARYLAND 29 (Annapolis 1776).

96. *Id.* at 39.

97. *Id.* at 49.

98. *Id.* at 50–58 (Oct. 31–Nov. 3, 1776). The Delaware Declaration of Rights was published in the *Maryland Gazette,* Oct. 1, 1776, at 1. Maryland's militia clause would be almost identical with that of Delaware.

99. MD. DEC. OF RIGHTS, Art. VIII (1776).

100. *Id.*, Art. XXXIII.

101. *Id.*, Art. XXV.

102. *Id.*, Art. XXVI. The Declaration was published in the Maryland Gazette on Nov. 14, 1776, at 3. No public commentary on the Declaration was published in the Gazette through the end of the year, while the war dominated the news.

103. THE GENERAL PUBLIC STATUTORY LAW AND PUBLIC LOCAL LAW OF THE STATE OF MARYLAND, FROM THE YEAR 1692–1839 INCLUSIVE, at 31 (Baltimore: John D. Toy, 1840).

104. 1 J. ELLIOT, DEBATES IN THE SEVERAL STATE CONVENTIONS 372 (Philadelphia 1836).

105. *Id.* at 382.

106. William Paca, Samuel Chase, and Robert Goldsborough. *Id.*, 2, at 549.

107. *Id.* at 550.

108. *Id.*

109. *Id.* at 552.

110. *Id*. at 553.

111. *Id*. at 555.

112. *Id*., 1, at 324.

113. *Id*. at 340. Maryland ratified on Dec. 19, 1789, second only to New Jersey. The Maryland Gazette followed the progress of the amendments in Congress, from Madison's introduction of them (June 18, at 1); debate on what became the Second Amendment (June 25, at 1–2); and the final version of the Bill of Rights (Sept. 3, at 2). It published no political commentary on the meaning of the amendments.

114. 3 DOCUMENTARY HISTORY OF THE RATIFICATION OF THE CON-STITUTION 37 (M. Jensen ed. 1978).

115. *Id*. at 37, 115.

116. *Id*. at 38–39.

117. PROCEEDINGS OF THE CONVENTION OF THE DELAWARE STATE 12 (Wilmington: James Adams, 1776). The other members were Richard Bassett, Jacob Moore, Charles Ridgley, John Evans, Alexander Porter, James Sykes, John Jones, James Rench, and William Polk.

118. *Id*. at 13.

119. *Id*. at 15.

120. B. KONKLE, GEORGE BRYAN AND THE CONSTITUTION OF PENN-SYLVANIA 124 n.1 (Philadelphia 1922).

121. *Id*. at 119.

122. *Id*. at 124 n.1.

123. Pennsylvania Evening Post, Aug. 20, 1776, at 413.

124. PROCEEDINGS OF THE CONVENTION OF THE PROVINCE OF MARYLAND (Annapolis 1776) (Aug. 27, 1776).

125. PROCEEDINGS OF THE CONVENTION OF THE DELAWARE STATE 16 *ff*.

126. LETTERS TO AND FROM CAESAR RODNEY, 1756–1784, at 119 (Philadelphia 1933).

127. DEL. DEC. OF RIGHTS, Art. XVIII (1776).

128. MD. DEC. OF RIGHTS, Art. XXV (1776).

129. VA. DEC. OF RIGHTS, Art. XIII (1776).

130. DEL. DEC. OF RIGHTS, Arts. XIX, XX (1776); PA. DEC. OF RIGHTS, Art. XIII (1776).

131. PA. DEC. OF RIGHTS, Art. XIII (1776).

132. PROCEEDINGS OF THE CONVENTION OF THE DELAWARE STATE 20, 40.

133. *Id*. at 36.

134. *Id*. at 40.

135. DEL. DEC. OF RIGHTS, Art. III (1776).

136. Authored by "Philo-Alethias, Delaware," Maryland Gazette, Oct. 31, 1776, at 3, col.1.

137. LAWS OF THE GOVERNMENT OF NEW-CASTLE, KENT AND SUSSEX UPON DELAWARE 171 (Philadelphia: B. Franklin, 1741).

138. LAWS OF THE GOVERNMENT OF NEW-CASTLE, KENT AND SUSSEX UPON DELAWARE 12 (Philadelphia 1763).

139. LAWS OF THE GOVERNMENT 152 (1741).

140. *Id*. at 178.

141. HAROLD B. HANCOCK, THE LOYALISTS OF REVOLUTIONARY DELAWARE 28 (London 1977).

142. *Id*. at 41.

143. *Id*. at 48.

144. *Id*. at 49–50.

145. *Id*. at 55.

146. PROCEEDINGS OF THE CONVENTION OF THE DELAWARE STATE 12.

147. *Id*. at 36.

148. H. HANCOCK, THE LOYALISTS OF REVOLUTIONARY DELAWARE 57.

149. *Id*. at 63 and 137 n.5.

150. *Id*. at 77.

151. *Id*.

152. *Id*.

153. *Id*. at 90–91.

154. *Id*. at 110.

155. *Id*. at 112.

156. *Id*. at 113.

157. 3 DOCUMENTARY HISTORY OF THE RATIFICATION OF THE CONSTITUTION 41.

158. *Id*. at 62.

159. *Id*. at 66.

160. *Id*. at 71, 74.

161. *Id*. at 63.

162. *Id*. at 97.

163. *Id*.

164. *Id*. at 102.

165. *Id*. at 63.

166. TIMOLEON [JAMES TILTON], THE BIOGRAPHICAL HISTORY OF DIONYSIUS, TYRANT OF DELAWARE 22 (Philadelphia 1778).

167. *Id*. at 26.

168. *Id*. at 29.

169. LAWS OF THE STATE OF DELAWARE, 1700–1797, at 968 (New Castle: Samuel and John Adams, 1797).

170. MINUTES OF THE CONVENTION OF THE DELAWARE STATE 12–13 (1791). Members of the 1776 convention are identified in PROCEEDINGS OF THE CONVENTION OF THE DELAWARE STATE 6 (1776).

171. MINUTES OF THE CONVENTION OF THE DELAWARE STATE 18.

172. *Id*. at 22 (Dec. 17, 1791).

173. DEL. DEC. OF RIGHTS, Art. XVIII (1776).

174. PA. DEC. OF RIGHTS, Art. XXI (1790).

175. H. HANCOCK, THE LOYALISTS OF REVOLUTIONARY DELAWARE 48–50.

176. 3 DOCUMENTARY HISTORY OF THE RATIFICATION 62, 97.

177. MINUTES OF THE GRAND COMMITTEE OF THE WHOLE CONVEN-

TION OF THE STATE OF DELAWARE 12 (Wilmington: James Adams, 1792) (Dec. 20, 1791).

178. 3 DOCUMENTARY HISTORY OF THE RATIFICATION 62, 97.

179. DEL. CONST., Art. I, Section 17 (1792).

180. MINUTES OF THE CONVENTION OF THE DELAWARE STATE 42–43.

181. MINUTES OF THE GRAND COMMITTEE OF THE WHOLE 13.

182. LAWS OF THE STATE OF DELAWARE 104 (1797).

183. *Id.* at 1136.

184. New-Hampshire Gazette and Historical Chronicle (Portsmouth), Jan. 6, 1775, at 1, col. 1 (Governor's Proclamation); M. BROWN, FIREARMS IN COLONIAL AMERICA: THE IMPACT ON HISTORY AND TECHNOLOGY, 1492–1792, at 295 (1980).

185. New-Hampshire Gazette, Jan. 13, 1775, at 1, col. 1.

186. *Id.*, Feb. 24, 1775, at 1, col. 1.

187. *Id.*, Jan. 27, 1775, at 1, col. 3.

188. 6 W. SWINDLER, SOURCES AND DOCUMENTS OF U.S. CONSTITUTIONS 342 (1973–1979).

189. CONSTITUTIONS OF NEW HAMPSHIRE 155 (undated microfilm, Library of Congress).

190. AN ADDRESS OF THE CONVENTION . . . TO THE INHABITANTS 10 (Exeter, N.H. 1782).

191. *Id.* at 14.

192. R. RUTLAND, THE BIRTH OF THE BILL OF RIGHTS 81 (1962); 1 DOCUMENTARY HISTORY OF THE FIRST FEDERAL ELECTIONS 858–59 (M. Jensen ed. 1976).

193. N.H. CONST., Pt. I, Art. XIII (1784).

194. *Id.*, Art. XIII.

195. *Id.*, Art. VI.

196. *Id.*, Art. XXX.

197. THE PERPETUAL LAWS OF THE STATE OF NEW HAMPSHIRE, at 115 (Portsmouth 1789).

198. *Id.* at 116. Certain government officials, students, Quakers, Indians, and Negroes were excepted from the militia.

199. *Id.* at 117.

200. *Id.*

201. *Id.*

202. *Id.* at 184.

203. *Id.* at 184–85.

204. N. EISEMAN, THE RATIFICATION OF THE FEDERAL CONSTITUTION BY THE STATE OF NEW HAMPSHIRE 22 (1983).

205. *Id.* at 23.

206. *Id.* at 22.

207. *Id.* at 5.

208. *Id.* at 6.

209. *Id.* at 5.

210. 16 DOCUMENTARY HISTORY OF THE RATIFICATION OF THE CONSTITUTION 179 (J. Kaminski ed. 1986).

211. Besides Sullivan, the federalists on the committee included John Lang-

don, Bartlett (Josiah or Thomas), Benjamin Bellows, Samual Livermore, Benjamin West, Francis Worcester, and John Pickering. Anti-federalists were Atherton, Joseph Badger, Thomas Dow, Smith (Ebenezer or Jonathan), Abel Parker, William Hooper, and Charles Barrett. *Id.* at 79.

212. J. WALKER, A HISTORY OF THE NEW HAMPSHIRE CONVENTION 40 (Boston 1888).

213. 1 J. ELLIOT, DEBATES IN THE SEVERAL STATE CONVENTIONS 326 (Philadelphia 1836).

214. *Id.*

215. J. WALKER, A HISTORY OF THE NEW HAMPSHIRE CONVENTION 40.

216. *Id.* at 41.

217. *Id.* at 42.

218. 1 DOCUMENTARY HISTORY OF THE FIRST FEDERAL ELECTIONS 839–40 (M. Jensen ed. 1976). However, the federalists too supported an armed population. The New Hampshire Spy, Mar. 10, 1789, reported that the state was "engaged in organizing her militia, which is by far the best disciplined in the United States." *Id.* at 840.

219. 3 J. ELLIOT, DEBATES IN THE SEVERAL STATE CONVENTIONS 659 (1836), and *id.*, 1, at 327–38.

220. JOURNAL OF THE CONVENTION WHICH ASSEMBLED IN CONCORD, TO REVISE THE CONSTITUTION OF NEW HAMPSHIRE, 1791–1792, at 43 (Concord 1876).

CHAPTER 4

1. New York Packet and American Advertiser, Jan. 4, 1776, at 1, col. 4, and 4, col. 4.

2. *Id.*, Aug. 26, 1776, at 2, cols. 2–3.

3. *E.g.*, *Id.*, Jan. 18, 1776, at 3, col. 4.

4. *Id.*, Apr. 4, 1776, at 2, col. 1.

5. *Id.*, cols. 1–2.

6. *Id.*, Apr. 18, 1776, at 1, col. 4.

7. *Id.* at 2, col. 1.

8. *Id.*

9. New York Gazette and Weekly Advertiser, Sept. 30, 1776 and thereafter.

10. *Constitution of 1777*, in REPORTS OF THE PROCEEDINGS AND DEBATES OF THE CONVENTION OF 1821, at 691–95 (Albany 1821) [hereafter cited as *Constitution of 1777*].

11. T. ROOSEVELT, GOUVERNEUR MORRIS 51 (Boston 1898).

12. 1 JOURNALS OF THE PROVINCIAL CONGRESS, PROVINCIAL CONVENTION, COMMITTEE OF SAFETY AND COUNCIL OF SAFETY OF THE STATE OF NEW YORK 552 (Albany 1842).

13. William Smith, William Duer, Governeur Morris, Robert R. Livingston, John Broome, John M. Scott, John Jay, John S. Hobart, Abraham Yates, Henry Wisner, Sr., Samuel Townsend, Charles DeWitt, and Robert Yates. *Id. See Constitution of 1777*, at 692–94.

14. *Constitution of 1777* 692–94.

15. For accounts of the framing of the New York Constitution, *see* G. DAN-GERFIELD, CHANCELLOR ROBERT R. LIVINGSTON 88 (1960); G. PELLEW, JOHN JAY 74 (Boston 1898); 1 H. FLANDERS, THE LIVES AND TIMES OF THE CHIEF JUSTICES OF THE SUPREME COURT 200 ff. (Philadelphia 1869); 1 J. SPARKS, THE LIFE OF GOUVERNEUR MORRIS 123 (Boston 1832); C. LIN-COLN, THE CONSTITUTIONAL HISTORY OF NEW YORK 487–559 (Rochester 1906).

16. B. MASON, THE ROAD TO INDEPENDENCE: THE REVOLUTIONARY MOVEMENT IN NEW YORK, 1773–1777, at 229 (1966).

17. G. PELLEW, JOHN JAY 76–77.

18. *Id*. at 40.

19. N.Y. CONST., Art. XL (1777).

20. 1 JOURNALS OF THE PROVINCIAL CONGRESS, at 892.

21. G. PELLEW, JOHN JAY 87.

22. *Id*. at 88.

23. D. GREENBERG, CRIME AND LAW ENFORCEMENT IN THE COL-ONY OF NEW YORK, 1691–1776, at 232 (1974).

24. BECCARIA, AN ESSAY ON CRIMES AND PUNISHMENTS 170–71 (Phil-adelphia: A. Bell, 1778). The New York edition is advertised in *New York Gazetteer*, Oct. 28, 1773, but no copy is extant.

25. 1 LAWS OF THE STATE OF NEW YORK, COMPRISING THE CON-STITUTION, AND THE ACTS OF THE LEGISLATURE, SINCE THE REVO-LUTION, FROM THE FIRST TO THE FIFTEENTH SESSION, INCLUSIVE 336 (New York 1792).

26. *Id*. at 227–29.

27. *Id*. at 188.

28. *Id*. at 189.

29. *Id*. at 289, 291.

30. *Id*. at 491.

31. New York Journal, and Daily Patriotic Register, June 13, 1788, at 2, cols. 1–2.

32. *Compare* 1 JOURNALS OF THE PROVINCIAL CONGRESS 552, *with* 2 J. ELLIOT, DEBATES IN THE SEVERAL STATE CONVENTIONS 206–7 (1836).

33. *The Federalist, No. 29*, in THE FEDERALIST PAPERS 184–85 (Arlington House ed. n.d.). In a seditious libel prosecution in 1803–1804, Hamilton asserted: "Never can tyranny be introduced into this country by arms. . . . The spirit of the country with arms in their hands, and disciplined as a militia, would render it impossible." 1 THE LAW PRACTICE OF ALEXANDER HAMILTON 831 (J. Goebel ed. 1964).

34. THE ANTIFEDERALIST PAPERS 75 (M. Borden ed. 1965).

35. 2 J. ELLIOT, DEBATES IN THE SEVERAL STATE CONVENTIONS 401.

36. *Id*., 1, at 328.

37. *Id*. at 327, 329.

38. New York Packet, June 23, 1789, at 2, cols. 1–2.

39. 12 MADISON PAPERS 239–40 (C. Hobson & R. Rutland eds. 1979).

40. *Id*. at 257.

41. N.J. Const., Art. XVIII (1776).

42. *Id*., Art. XXII.

43. C. ERDMAN, THE NEW JERSEY CONSTITUTION OF 1776, at 32 (Princeton 1929).

44. *Id.* at 33.

45. *Id.* at 36.

46. *Id.* at 47.

47. *Id.*

48. W. GRIFFITH, EUMENES: BEING A COLLECTION OF PAPERS WRITTEN FOR THE PURPOSE OF EXHIBITING SOME OF THE MORE PROMINENT ERRORS AND OMISSIONS OF THE CONSTITUTION OF NEW JERSEY 9 (Trenton 1799). Griffith never mentions lack of a bill of rights as an unwarranted omission.

49. C. ERDMAN, THE NEW JERSEY CONSTITUTION 48 n.20.

50. T. ROOSEVELT, GOUVERNEUR MORRIS 51 (Boston 1898).

51. K. COLEMAN, THE AMERICAN REVOLUTION IN GEORGIA, 1763–1789, at 79 (1958).

52. JOURNAL OF THE VOTES AND PROCEEDINGS OF THE CONVENTION OF NEW JERSEY, JUNE 10–AUGUST 21, 1776 *passim* (Burlington 1776). On the constitution, see *id.* at 49–51.

53. 1 BLACKSTONE, COMMENTARIES *140–44 (St. Geo. Tucker ed. 1803).

54. JOURNAL OF THE VOTES AND PROCEEDINGS 47–48. Seizing arms from and arresting tories took place in all the colonies, but the above reference to taking arms from pacifists is unusual. From the beginning of the war, George Washington discussed the need to purchase arms from private individuals. 5 THE WRITINGS OF GEORGE WASHINGTON 19 (Fitzpatrick ed. 1932–1940). "I did not think myself Authorized to seize upon any Arms the property of private Person; but if they can be collected and the owners satisfied for them, it would be of very essential service." *Id.*, 9, at 274–75.

55. The New-York Gazette and The Weekly Mercury (Newark, N.J.), Nov. 2, 1776, at 3, col. 1–2.

56. *Id.*, Oct. 5, 1776, at 2, col. 2.

57. *Id.*, Oct. 26, 1776, at 1 , col. 2.

58. 10 THE WRITINGS OF GEORGE WASHINGTON 90.

59. ACTS OF THE COUNCIL AND GENERAL ASSEMBLY OF THE STATE OF NEW-JERSEY 166 (Trenton 1784).

60. *Id.* at 168.

61. *Id.* at 169.

62. *Id.* at 180.

63. ACTS OF THE GENERAL ASSEMBLY OF THE PROVINCE OF NEW-JERSEY 235 (Burlington 1776).

64. LAWS OF THE STATE OF NEW JERSEY 19–21 (1800).

65. *Id.* at 308.

66. Hamilton's losing of the duel has been attributed to his use of a pistol with a hair-set trigger, which he intended to use to obtain an unfair advantage contrary to the *code duello*. M. Lindsay, *The Burr-Hamilton Duelling Pistols*, in AMERICA: THE MEN AND THEIR GUNS THAT MADE HER GREAT 15–19 (C. Boddington ed. 1981).

67. 3 DOCUMENTARY HISTORY OF THE RATIFICATION OF THE CONSTITUTION 125 (M. Jensen ed. 1978).

68. *Id.* at 120.

69. *Id.* at 154–55.

70. R. WEIGLEY, THE PARTISAN WAR: THE SOUTH CAROLINA CAMPAIGN OF 1780–1782 (1970).

71. 1 J. DRAYTON, MEMOIRS OF THE AMERICAN REVOLUTION . . . AS RELATING TO SOUTH CAROLINA 12 (Charleston 1821).

72. *Id.* at 166.

73. North Carolina Gazette (Newbern), July 14, 1775, at 1, col. 1.

74. EXTRACTS FROM THE JOURNALS OF THE PROVINCIAL CONGRESS 121 (Charlestown 1776).

75. 1 J. DRAYTON, MEMOIRS OF THE AMERICAN REVOLUTION 216.

76. EXTRACTS FROM THE JOURNALS 54.

77. *Id.* at 26–27. The committee included Charles Cotesworth Pinckney, John Rutledge, Charles Pinckney, Henry Laurens, Christopher Gadsden, Rawlins Lowndes, Arthur Middleton, Henry Middleton, Thomas Bee, Thomas Lynch, Jr., and Thomas Heyward, Jr.

78. *Id.* at 82.

79. *Id.* at 137–38.

80. 1 J. DRAYTON, MEMOIRS OF THE AMERICAN REVOLUTION 378.

81. *Id.*, 2, at 255.

82. *Id.* at 266.

83. *Id.* at 267.

84. THE PUBLIC LAWS OF THE STATE OF SOUTH CAROLINA, FROM ITS FIRST ESTABLISHMENT AS A BRITISH PROVINCE TO THE YEAR 1790, INCLUSIVE, Appendix 13 (Philadelphia 1790).

85. *Id.* at 14.

86. EXTRACTS FROM JOURNALS 97.

87. *Id.*

88. 1 J. DRAYTON, MEMOIRS OF THE AMERICAN REVOLUTION 300.

89. *Id.* at 301.

90. *Id.* at 302.

91. THE PUBLIC LAWS 174.

92. *Id.*

93. *Id.* at 168. Similarly, "their using and carrying wooden swords and other mischievous and dangerous weapons" out of the plantation was prohibited, and "if he or they be armed with such offensive weapons aforesaid, him or them [white persons] to disarm, take up and whip." *Id.* at 172. Striking a white person, even in self-defense, was punishable, "and for the 3d offense [he] shall suffer death." *Id.* at 169.

94. *Id.* at 168.

95. *Id.*

96. *Id.* at 205.

97. *Id.* at 207.

98. *Id.*

99. *See* A BILL FOR ESTABLISHING THE CONSTITUTION OF THE STATE OF SOUTH CAROLINA 1 (Charleston: Peter Timothy 1777) (Constitution of 1776 "temporary only").

100. S.C. CONST., Arts. XLI, LII, and XLIII (1778).

101. *Id.*, Art. XXXVIII.

102. 4 J. ELLIOT, THE DEBATES IN THE SEVERAL STATE CONVENTIONS 316 (1836).

103. Charles Cotesworth Pinckney, Charles Pinckney, and John Rutledge.

104. *See id.* at 338–39. The seven included Charles Cotesworth Pinckney, John Rutledge, Charles Pinckney, Henry Laurens, Christopher Gadsden, Thomas Bee, and Thomas Heyward.

105. *Id.* at 341.

106. *Id.* at 337.

107. JOURNAL OF THE CONSTITUTIONAL CONVENTION OF SOUTH CAROLINA, MAY 10, 1790–JUNE 3, 1790, at 1 (F. Hutson ed. 1946) (C.C. Pinckney, Gadsden, Bee, Heyward, C. Pinckney, *et al.*).

108. *Id.* at 31. C.C. Pinckney and the usual names composed a Committee of Arrangements. *Id.* at 23. Resolutions were referred to that committee "in order that they become a part of the Bill of Rights." *Id.* at 25. Yet none of the resolutions paralleled the usual bill of rights provisions of the day.

109. S.C. Const. Arts. VIII; IX, Sec. 6 (1790).

110. *See* PUBLIC LAWS OF THE SENATE OF SOUTH CAROLINA . . . DOWN TO THE YEAR 1790 (Philadelphia 1790).

111. 3 DOCUMENTARY HISTORY OF THE RATIFICATION OF THE CONSTITUTION 201 (M. Jensen ed. 1978).

112. K. COLEMAN, THE AMERICAN REVOLUTION IN GEORGIA 76–77 (1958).

113. *Id.* at 80.

114. THE CONSTITUTION OF THE STATE OF GEORGIA i (Savannah 1777).

115. Committee members included: Button Gwinnett, William Belcher, Joseph Wood, Josiah Lewis, John-Adam Treutlen, Henry Jones, and George Wells. *Id.*

116. *Id.* at i–ii.

117. *Id.* at 1.

118. GA. CONST., Arts. LIX, LX, and LXI (1777).

119. *Id.*, Art. XXXV.

120. K. COLEMAN, THE AMERICAN REVOLUTION IN GEORGIA 87.

121. 3 DOCUMENTARY HISTORY 205.

122. K. COLEMAN, THE AMERICAN REVOLUTION IN GEORGIA 89.

123. *Id.* at 119; 3 DOCUMENTARY HISTORY 204.

124. K. COLEMAN, THE AMERICAN REVOLUTION IN GEORGIA 94.

125. DIGEST OF THE LAWS OF THE STATE OF GEORGIA 241 (Savannah 1802).

126. *Id.*

127. *Id.* at 241–42.

128. *Id.* at 263.

129. *Id.* at 350.

130. *Id.* at 423.

131. *Id.*

132. *Id.* at 424.

133. *Id.*

134. *Id.* at 432.

135. *Id.* at 433.

136. *Id.* at 437.
137. 3 DOCUMENTARY HISTORY 223.
138. *Id.* at 247.
139. *Id.*
140. *See* THE CONSTITUTION OF THE STATE OF GEORGIA, RATIFIED THE 6th OF MAY 1789, at 3 (Augusta 1789).
141. GA. CONST., Art. IV, Sec. 3, 4 (1789).
142. *Id.*, Art. IV, Sec. 5.
143. Georgia State Gazette or Independent Register (Augusta), Jan. 10, 1789, at 1, col.1.
144. *Id.*, col. 2.
145. *Id.* at 4, col. 3.
146. *Id.*, Jan. 24, 1789, at 3.
147. *Id.*, Jan. 31, 1789, at 1, col. 1.
148. *Id.*, col.2.
149. *Id.*, Feb. 7, 1789, at 1, col. 1–2.

CHAPTER 5

1. 1 SOURCES OF AMERICAN INDEPENDENCE 150 (H. Peckham ed. 1978).
2. D. ROTH & F. MEYER, FROM REVOLUTION TO CONSTITUTION: CONNECTICUT 1763 TO 1818, at 25 (1975); M. CARY, THE CONNECTICUT CONSTITUTION 2–3 (1900).
3. 1 B. POORE, THE FEDERAL AND STATE CONSTITUTIONS 256 (1877).
4. R. Hinman, *A General View of Connecticut at the Commencement of the Revolutionary War* (1842), in CHRONOLOGY AND DOCUMENTARY HANDBOOK OF THE STATE OF CONNECTICUT 49–50 (M. French ed. 1973).
5. PUBLIC RECORDS OF THE COLONY OF CONNECTICUT, FROM MAY, 1775, TO JUNE, 1776, INCLUSIVE, at 17, 291 (Hartford, n.d.). Council of Safety minutes mostly concern manufacture of gunpowder and plans of resistance. *Id.* at 451 *ff.* In 1775 Connecticut had numerous gunsmiths, and a state bounty of five shillings per firearm greatly encouraged manufacture. D. ROTH, CONNECTICUT: A BICENTENNIAL HISTORY 101 (1979).
6. D. ROTH & F. MEYER, FROM REVOLUTION TO CONSTITUTION 82.
7. J. ADAMS, NEW ENGLAND IN THE REPUBLIC 1776–1850 at 63 (1926).
8. Connecticut Courant, April 1, 1776, at 3, cols. 2–3.
9. D. ROTH & F. MEYERS, FROM REVOLUTION TO CONSTITUTION 49.
10. ACTS AND LAWS OF THE STATE OF CONNECTICUT 144 (Hartford 1784).
11. *Id.* at 150.
12. *Id.* at 151.
13. *Id.* at 156.
14. *Id.* at 22.
15. *Id.* at 43.
16. *Id.* at 8. Slaves were required to have passes, but were not specifically disarmed. *Id.* at 233 *ff.*

17. R. PRICE, OBSERVATIONS ON THE IMPORTANCE OF THE AMERI-
CAN REVOLUTION 16 (London and Boston, 1784).

18. *Id*. at 58. Price also wrote:

> Britain, indeed, consisting as it does of *unarmed* inhabitants, and
> threatened as it is by ambitious and powerful neighbors, cannot hope
> to maintain its existence long after becoming open to invasion by
> loosing its naval superiority.—But this is not the case with the Amer-
> ican states. . . . They are all a well-trained *militia*; and the successful
> resistance which, in their infancy and without a naval force, they
> have made to the invasion of the first *European* power, will probably
> discourage and prevent all future invasions. *Id*. at 63.

19. 3 DOCUMENTARY HISTORY OF THE RATIFICATION OF THE CON-
STITUTION 389 (M. Jensen ed. 1978).

20. *Id*. at 389. This was in response to the claim that "this looks too much
like Baron Stuben's *militia*, by which a *standing army* was meant and intended."
Id. at 378.

21. *Id*. at 489–90.

22. 2 DOCUMENTARY HISTORY OF THE FIRST FEDERAL ELECTIONS,
1788–1790 at 13 (G. DenBoer ed. 1984).

23. Compare *The Bill of Rights: The Roger Sherman Draft*, THIS CONSTITUTION
36 (Spring/Summer 1988) *with* 2 ANNALS OF CONGRESS 1808 (Dec. 16, 1790).

24. T. LE DUC, CONNECTICUT AND THE FIRST TEN AMENDMENTS TO
THE FEDERAL CONSTITUTION 1 (Washington, D.C. 1937). "The spirit of
tolerance and of personal liberty embodied in those [proposed 12 amendments
to the federal Constitution] was contrary to the traditions and practices of the
State, and one would not expect that they would have a sympathetic reception."
Id. at 1–2.

25. *Id*. at 2–4.

26. R. ROLLINS, THE LONG JOURNEY OF NOAH WEBSTER 13 (1980).

27. *Id*. at 51–52.

28. *Id*. at 52–53.

29. Published in Philadelphia on Oct. 17, 1787, long extracts of this work were
reprinted in the New Haven Gazette, Nov. 29, 1787. 13 DOCUMENTARY HIS-
TORY OF THE RATIFICATION OF THE CONSTITUTION 405–6 (J. Kaminski
and G. Saladino eds. 1981).

30. N. WEBSTER, AN EXAMINATION OF THE LEADING PRINCIPLES OF
THE FEDERAL CONSTITUTION 43 (Philadelphia: Prichard & Hall, 1787).

31. *The Federalist*, Nos. 29 (Hamilton) and 45 (Madison), in THE FEDERALIST
PAPERS 185, 299 (Arlington House ed. n.d.).

32. J. MORGAN, NOAH WEBSTER 114 (New York 1975).

33. N. WEBSTER, A COMPENDIOUS DICTIONARY OF THE ENGLISH
LANGUAGE 220 (New Haven 1806).

34. *Id*. at 26.

35. *Id*. at 18.

36. N. WEBSTER, ON BEING AMERICAN: SELECTED WRITINGS, 1783–
1828, at 166 (H. Babbidge ed. 1967).

37. N. WEBSTER, AN AMERICAN DICTIONARY OF THE ENGLISH LANGUAGE (New York 1828) ("militia").

38. *Id*. ("regulated").

39. *Id*. ("people," 3).

40. *Id*. ("bear", 2 and 3).

41. *Id*. ("pistol").

42. *Id*. ("arms," 1).

43. *Id*. ("arms," 4).

44. *Id*. ("arms," end).

45. *Id*. ("gun").

46. 1 SOURCES OF AMERICAN INDEPENDENCE 165 (H. Peckham ed. 1978).

47. *Id*. at 176.

48. Newport Mercury, Mar. 27, 1775, at 2, col. 3.

49. B. POORE, THE FEDERAL AND STATE CONSTITUTIONS 1600 (1877).

50. *Id*.

51. D. LOVEJOY, RHODE ISLAND POLITICS AND THE AMERICAN REVOLUTION, 1760–1776, at 173, 188 (1958).

52. Newport Mercury, Aug. 14, 1775, at 3, col. 2.

53. PUBLIC LAWS OF THE STATE OF RHODE ISLAND 429–30 (Providence 1798).

54. *Id*. at 426.

55. *Id*. at 5.

56. *Id*. at 612–14.

57. *Id*. at 593.

58. *Id*. at 583.

59. *Id*. at 568.

60. *Id*.

61. Providence Gazette & Country Journal, Jan. 30, 1790, at 1.

62. THEODORE FOSTER, MINUTES OF THE CONVENTION HELD AT SOUTH KINGSTOWN, RHODE ISLAND, IN MARCH 1790, at 58 (T. Foster ed. 1929).

63. *Id*. Madison's proposals of June 8, 1789, included the following: "No state shall violate the equal rights of conscience, or the freedom of the press, or the trial by jury in criminal cases."

64. *Id*.

65. *Id*.

66. *Id*. at 58–59.

67. *Id*. at 59.

68. 1 J. ELLIOT, DEBATES IN THE SEVERAL STATE CONVENTIONS 328 (1836).

69. *Id*., 3, at 659; 4, at 244.

70. MINUTES OF THE CONVENTION 60.

71. *Id*., n.77.

72. Other members were Ray Sands, Joshua Barker, Judge Stephen Steere, John Sayles, James Sheldon, Thomas Allen, Samuel Pearce, General Arnold, and Pardon Mawney. *Id*. at 60.

73. *Id*. at 61.

74. *Id.* at 95.

75. *Id.*

76. *Id.* at 62.

77. *Id.* at 77.

78. *Id.* at 78.

79. *Id.* at 23.

80. J. KAMINSKI, *"Outcast" Rhode Island—The Absent State*, THIS CONSTI-TUTION, No. 15, at 36–37 (Summer 1987). *See* F. BATES, RHODE ISLAND AND THE FORMATION OF THE UNION 149–200 (1898).

81. MINUTES OF THE CONVENTION 25.

82. 1 J. ELLIOT, DEBATES IN THE SEVERAL STATE CONVENTIONS 334–35 (1836). Rhode Island also suggested several amendments pertaining to state powers. *Id.* at 336–37.

83. MINUTES OF THE CONVENTION 26.

84. Providence Gazette and Country Journal, June 5, 1790, at 23.

EPILOGUE

1. CONN. CONST., Art. I, Section 18 (1818).

2. The language as adopted was the same as was originally reported by Chairman Edwards of the Bill of Rights Committee. JOURNAL OF PROCEED-INGS OF CONVENTION 16, 20 (Hartford 1901).

3. The constitution passed by a margin of 13,918 to 12,364. *Id.* at 118. On support for an established church in Connecticut as the major objection to a constitution, *see* J. STEADFAST, AN ADDRESS TO THE PEOPLE OF CON-NECTICUT ON . . . THE PROPOSITION FOR A NEW CONSTITUTION (Hart-ford 1804).

4. CONN. CONST., Art. I, Section 15 (1965).

5. REPORTS OF THE PROCEEDINGS AND DEBATES OF THE CONSTI-TUTION OF 1821, at 163 (Albany 1821).

6. *Id.* at 171.

7. *Id.* at 210. Col. Young also "was willing to require that, in addition to militia duty, the person performing it should be a resident, and be duly armed and equipped." *Id.* at 213.

8. N.Y. CONST., Art. VII, (1822).

9. "This provision appears in the Declaration of Rights of William and Mary (1689 Para. 7), in the United States Constitution (2d amendment) and in the Revised Statutes of 1828 (Pt. 1, Ch. 4, Section 3)." REPORT OF BOARD OF STATUTORY CONSOLIDATION 440 (1907).

10. 8 W. SWINDLER, SOURCES AND DOCUMENTS 351–52 (1973–74).

11. JOURNAL OF THE CONVENTION . . . RHODE ISLAND 48 (1842).

12. R.I. Const., Art. I, preamble (1842).

13. *Id.*, Art. I.

14. C. ERDMAN, THE NEW JERSEY CONSTITUTION OF 1776, at 99 (1929), quoting The Federalist (Trenton), March 27, 1798.

15. MEMORIAL OF THE CONVENTION OF DELEGATES ASSEMBLED AT TRENTON ON THE 22d OF AUGUST 1827, ON THE SUBJECT OF REVISING AND AMENDING THE CONSTITUTION OF NEW JERSEY at 2–3 (n.d.).

16. *Id.* at 5.

17. PROCEEDINGS OF THE NEW JERSEY CONSTITUTIONAL CONVEN-
TION OF 1844, at 139 (Trenton 1942).

18. C. ERDMAN, THE NEW JERSEY CONSTITUTION 99, quoting Sentinel
of Freedom, March 5, 1844.

19. N.J. CONST., Art. I, Section 3 (1844).

20. *Id.* (emphasis added).

21. DEBATES AND PROCEEDINGS OF THE MARYLAND REFORM CON-
VENTION TO REVISE THE STATE CONSTITUTION 188 (Annapolis 1851).

22. *Id.* at 201.

23. *Id.* at 225.

24. *Id.* at 225–26.

25. *Id.* at 226. The provision became MD. CONST., Art. I, Section 42.

26. B. OLIVER, THE RIGHTS OF AN AMERICAN CITIZEN 40 (1832).

27. *Id.* at 174, 176.

28. *Id.* at 186.

29. S. HALBROOK, THAT EVERY MAN BE ARMED: THE EVOLUTION
OF A CONSTITUTIONAL RIGHT 107–153 (1984).

30. WE THE STATES 91 (Richmond 1964). Explaining the Fourteenth
Amendment, the Committee on Federal Relations of the Massachusetts General
Court cited the Second Amendment "right of the people to keep and bear arms"
as "one of the amendments of the Constitution [which] grew out of a jealousy
for the rights of the people, and is in the direction, more or less direct, of a
guarantee of human rights." MASS. H.R. DOC. No. 149, at 3 (1867).

31. THE MARYLAND CODE 454 (Baltimore 1860).

32. 3 SUPPLEMENT TO THE CODE OF MARYLAND 52 (Baltimore 1865).

33. S. HALBROOK, THAT EVERY MAN BE ARMED 107–153.

34. *Id.* at 113–14.

35. Scott v. Sanford, 60 U.S. (19 How.) 393, 417 (1857).

36. S. HALBROOK, THAT EVERY MAN BE ARMED 114.

37. WE THE STATES 91 (Richmond 1964).

38. PERLMAN, DEBATES OF THE MARYLAND CONVENTION OF 1867,
at 79, 151 (Baltimore 1867).

39. *Id.* at 150–51.

40. E. POLLARD, THE LOST CAUSE 117, 125 (1867).

41. PERLMAN, DEBATES OF THE MARYLAND CONVENTION 151.

42. Similarly, Congressman Washington C. Whittorne (D., Tenn.) argued
against adoption of the Civil Rights Act of 1871 that "if a police officer of the
city of Richmond or New York should find a drunken negro or white man upon
the streets with a loaded pistol flourishing it, & c., and . . . he takes it away, the
officer may be sued, because the right to bear arms is secured by the Constitution." CONG. GLOBE, 42nd Cong., 1st Sess., pt. 1, 337 (Mar. 29, 1871).

43. The Baltimore Gazette, May 29, 1867, at 4, col. 3.

44. *Id.,* May 30, 1867, at 4, col. 2.

45. S. HALBROOK, THAT EVERY MAN BE ARMED 92–107.

46. The Baltimore Gazette, May 29, 1867, at 4, col. 3.

47. MD. CONST., Art. III, Sec. 37 (1867). Jones was well known for his

authorship of the "emancipation compensation" amendment. See, for example, Maryland Journal (Towson), May 30, 1867, at 2, col. 1.

48. PERLMAN, DEBATES OF THE MARYLAND CONVENTION 151.

49. American and Commercial Advertiser (Baltimore), May 30, 1867, at 1, col. 4.

50. *Id*.

51. Richmond Times, April 18, 1867, in W. DUBOIS, BLACK RECONSTRUCTION IN AMERICA 541 (1935).

52. 1 VIRGINIA CONVENTION OF 1867–1868, DEBATES AND PROCEEDINGS 350 (1868).

53. *Id*. at 519. The Conservative members complained: "This Constitution further provides for a militia to be composed of *all male citizens . . .* without distinction of race or color." DOCUMENTS OF THE CONSTITUTIONAL CONVENTION OF THE STATE OF VIRGINIA 5–6 (Richmond 1867).

54. 1 VA. CONVENTION 421.

55. *Id*. at 634.

56. *Id*. at 535–40 (St. Geo. Tucker), 622 (Dred Scott decision), 356 and 403 (right of revolution).

57. DOCUMENTS OF THE CONSTITUTIONAL CONVENTION OF THE STATE OF VIRGINIA 109 (Richmond 1867). This provision is currently VA. CONST., Art. I, Section 17.

58. JOURNAL OF THE CONSTITUTIONAL CONVENTION (N.C.) 165, 212, 215, 229 (1868).

59. N.C. CONST., Art. I, Section 24 (1868).

60. For example, JOURNAL OF THE CONSTITUTIONAL CONVENTION 175, 485 (controversy on whether whites and blacks to be enrolled in the same militia companies).

61. Weekly Journal (Wilmington), Sept. 25, 1868. Far from being dependent on militia duties only, the right to bear arms was relied on to oppose militia abuses. State v. Kerner, 181 N.C. 574, 107 S.E. 222, 224 (1921).

62. JOURNAL OF CONVENTION OF STATE OF NORTH CAROLINA 261 (1875).

63. S.C. CONST. (1776, 1778, 1790, 1865).

64. South Carolina law punished by fine or corporal punishment the keeping of a firearm by a person of color without a permit, except that farmowners could keep a shotgun or rifle suitable for hunting. W. DUBOIS, BLACK RECONSTRUCTION IN AMERICA 172–73.

65. CONG. GLOBE, 39th Cong., lst Sess., pt. 4, 3210 (June 16, 1866).

66. PROCEEDINGS OF THE CONSTITUTIONAL CONVENTION OF SOUTH CAROLINA 85 (1868).

67. *Id*. at 258; S.C. CONST., Art. I, Section 28 (1868).

68. PROCEEDINGS OF THE CONSTITUTIONAL CONVENTION 257, 259.

69. *Id*. at 341–49.

70. *Id*. at 346–47.

71. *Id*. at 349–50, 407, 571, 671–75, 751–52.

72. *Id*. at 343.

73. *Id*. at 357.

74. JOURNAL OF THE CONSTITUTIONAL CONVENTION OF THE STATE OF SOUTH CAROLINA 135 (Columbia 1895).

75. *Id.* at 147.

76. The Committee included Mower, J.L.M. Irby, J.E. Ellerbe, J.O. Byrd, J.S. Cantey, J.M. Sullivan, W.H. Timmerman, George von Kolnitz, F.P. Taylor, W.T. Bobo, and W.R. Singletary. *Id.* at 20.

77. *Id.* at 277, 347.

78. S.C. DEC. OF RIGHTS, Section 26 (1895).

79. S.C. CONST., Art. I, Section 20 (1971).

80. Nunn v. State, 1 Ga. 243 (1846).

81. GA. CONST., Art. I, Section 6 (1861).

82. CONFED. CONST., Art. I, Section 9, Para. 13 (1861).

83. GA. CONST., Art. I, Section 4 (1865); JOUR. OF THE PROCEEDINGS OF THE CONVENTION (GA.) 182, 366 (1910).

84. The Loyal Georgian (Augusta), Feb. 3, 1866, at 3, col. 4.

85. GA. CONST., Art. I, Section 14 (1868).

86. JOURNAL OF PROCEEDINGS OF THE CONSTITUTIONAL CONVENTION (GA.) 168 (1868) (emphasis added).

87. GA. CONST., Art. I, Section 1, Para. 22 (1877); GA. CONST., Art. I, Section 1, Para. 8 (1983). The militia clause which had been in the 1868 Constitution was deleted from this section. JOURNAL OF THE CONSTITUTIONAL CONVENTION OF THE PEOPLE OF GEORGIA 80, 117 (Atlanta 1877). The clause reappeared in the militia article of the constitution as follows: "A well regulated militia being essential to the peace and security of the State, the General Assembly shall have authority to provide, by law, how the militia of this State shall be organized, officered, trained, armed and equipped—and of whom it shall consist." *Id.*, at 72.

88. *Id.* at 117. Toombs was "the most active leader of the Convention" and "the outstanding delegate on . . . the rights of individuals." E. WARE, A CONSTITUTIONAL HISTORY OF GEORGIA 160 & n.5 (1947).

89. S. SMALL, A STENOGRAPHIC REPORT OF THE PROCEEDINGS OF THE CONSTITUTIONAL CONVENTION HELD IN ATLANTA, GEORGIA, 1877, at 91 (1877).

90. *Id.*

91. JOURNAL OF THE CONSTITUTIONAL CONVENTION 117.

92. *Id.*

93. S. SMALL, A STENOGRAPHIC REPORT 91.

94. DEBATES OF THE CONVENTION TO AMEND THE CONSTITUTION OF PENNSYLVANIA 258 (Harrisburg 1873).

95. *Id.*

96. *Id.* at 258–59.

97. *Id.* at 259.

98. *Id.* at 259–60.

99. *Id.* at 260. The act was held to be constitutional because it only punished maliciously carrying a weapon with unlawful intent to harm another. Wright v. Commonwealth, 77 Pa. 470, 471 (1875).

100. DEBATES OF THE CONVENTION 261.

101. State v. Kessler, 289 Or. 359, 614 P.2d 94 (1980).

102. Illinois adopted an arms guarantee in 1970 in response to proposed handgun bans, but the Supreme Court of that state nonetheless upheld the Morton Grove ban, America's first. Kalodimos v. Village of Morton Grove, 470 N.E.2d 266 (Ill. 1984).

103. A more explicit arms guarantee passed in Maine in 1987, in reaction to a state supreme court opinion which was thought to emasculate the arms guarantee of 1819. State v. Friel, 508 A.2d 123, 125–26 (Me. 1986), *cert. denied* 107 S.Ct. 156 (1986).

104. W. SHEA, THE VIRGINIA MILITIA IN THE SEVENTEENTH CENTURY 31–32 (1983).

105. JOURNAL OF THE SENATE (VA.) 250–251, 472 (1964). The resolution also stated:

> The right of the citizen is entwined in the very roots of the founding of this Commonwealth when it was not only the individual's right to bear arms but his duty to bear arms in the defense of his community—only slaves were forbidden by law to carry weapons— Thomas Jefferson deemed the right to bear arms worthy of inclusion in his drafts of the Virginia Constitution—and the rise or fall of the political rights of the citizen has been allied with the right to bear arms or the deprivation of such rights. *Id.*

106. THE CONSTITUTION OF VIRGINIA: REPORT OF THE COMMISSION ON CONSTITUTIONAL REVISION 507 (Charlottesville 1969). The proposal was from George S. Knight of Alexandria, who explained in an affidavit dated Oct. 2, 1986 in the author's possession: "As commonly understood in the 1969–1970 period by members of the general public in Virginia, "the right of the people to keep and bear arms' expresses a personal right of private individuals to keep firearms (including rifles, shotguns, pistols, and revolvers) and other commonly possessed arms in their homes, businesses, and other premises, and to bear or carry arms for lawful purposes, including defense of self, family, and the Commonwealth."

107. PROCEEDINGS AND DEBATES OF THE HOUSE OF DELEGATES PERTAINING TO AMENDMENT OF THE CONSTITUTION, EXTRA SESSION 1969/ 1970, at 473 (1970). Emphasis added.

108. *Id.* at 474.

109. *Id.* at 775.

110. 3 J. ELLIOT, DEBATES IN THE SEVERAL STATE CONVENTIONS ON THE ADOPTION OF THE FEDERAL CONSTITUTION 659 (1836); 3 G. MASON, PAPERS 1070–71 (1970).

111. PROCEEDINGS AND DEBATES OF THE SENATE OF VIRGINIA PERTAINING TO AMENDMENT OF THE CONSTITUTION, EXTRA SESSION 1969/ 1970 at 391 (1970).

112. *Id.* at 392.

113. *Id.* at 393.

114. N.H. HOUSE JOUR. 45 (1975).

115. N.H. SENATE JOUR. 604 (1975).

116. *Id.*

117. *Id.* 605–06.

118. Letter from Daniel Gray, Committee Research Staff, New Hampshire House of Rep., April 6, 1987, in author's possession.

119. N.H. SENATE JOUR. 470–71 (1981).

120. H.B. 554, Del. House of Rep., 113rd General Assembly (1986).

121. 113rd General Assembly of Del., 2d Sess., House (May 22, 1986), Senate (June 25, 1986); 114th General Assembly of Del., 1st Sess., House (April 2, 1987), Senate (April 16, 1987).

Selected Bibliography

I. PRIMARY SOURCES

Newspapers

Boston Chronicle, 1768
Boston Evening Post, 1768–1770
Boston Gazette, and Country Journal, 1768–1775
Connecticut Courant, 1775
Essex Gazette, 1775
Georgia State Gazette, 1789
Maryland Gazette, 1768, 1775
Massachusetts Gazette, 1768–1775
Massachusetts Spy, 1774–1775
New York Journal, 1768–1769
New York Packet, 1776
Pennsylvania Evening Post, 1775–1776
Virginia Gazette, 1775–1776

Constitutional Conventions

DEBATES OF THE CONVENTION TO AMEND THE CONSTITUTION OF PENNSYLVANIA (Harrisburg 1873).
EISEMAN, N. THE RATIFICATION OF THE FEDERAL CONSTITUTION BY THE STATE OF NEW HAMPSHIRE (1983).
ELLIOT, J. DEBATES IN THE SEVERAL STATE CONVENTIONS (1838).
FOSTER, THEODORE. MINUTES OF THE CONVENTION HELD AT SOUTH KINGSTOWN, RHODE ISLAND, IN MARCH 1790 (Providence 1929).
JOURNAL OF THE CONSTITUTIONAL CONVENTION OF THE PEOPLE OF GEORGIA (Atlanta 1877).

JOURNAL OF THE CONVENTION FOR FRAMING A CONSTITUTION OF GOVERNMENT FOR THE STATE OF MASSACHUSETTS BAY (1779–1780) (1832).

JOURNAL OF PROCEEDINGS OF THE PROVINCIAL CONGRESS OF NORTH CAROLINA (1776).

JOURNALS OF THE PROVINCIAL CONGRESS, PROVINCIAL CONVENTION, COMMITTEE OF SAFETY AND COUNCIL OF SAFETY OF THE STATE OF NEW YORK (Albany 1842).

MINUTES OF THE CONVENTION OF THE DELAWARE STATE (1791).

PERLMAN. DEBATES OF THE MARYLAND CONVENTION OF 1867 (Baltimore 1867).

PROCEEDINGS AND DEBATES OF THE SENATE OF VIRGINIA PERTAINING TO AMENDMENT OF THE CONSTITUTION, EXTRA SESSION 1969/1970 (1970).

PROCEEDINGS OF THE CONSTITUTIONAL CONVENTION OF SOUTH CAROLINA (1868).

PROCEEDINGS OF THE CONVENTION OF THE DELAWARE STATE (Wilmington: James Adams, 1776).

PROCEEDINGS OF THE CONVENTION OF THE PROVINCE OF MARYLAND (Annapolis 1776).

PROCEEDINGS RELATIVE TO CALLING THE CONVENTIONS OF 1776 AND 1790 (Harrisburg 1825).

Books and Published Sources

ADAMS, J. A DEFENCE OF THE CONSTITUTIONS OF GOVERNMENT OF THE UNITED STATES OF AMERICA (1787–1788).

ADAMS, J. LEGAL PAPERS (1965).

ALLEN, IRA. PARTICULARS OF THE CAPTURE OF THE OLIVE BRANCH (London: J. W. Meyers, 1798).

BECCARIA, C. AN ESSAY ON CRIMES AND PUNISHMENTS (London 1775).

BOSTON UNDER MILITARY RULE [1768–1769] AS REVEALED IN A JOURNAL OF THE TIMES (O. Dickerson compl. 1971).

COLONIAL RECORDS OF NORTH CAROLINA (W. Saunders ed. 1890).

THE COMMONPLACE BOOK OF THOMAS JEFFERSON (G. Chinard ed. 1926).

DOCUMENTARY HISTORY OF THE RATIFICATION OF THE CONSTITUTION (various editors 1976–1986).

FROTHINGHAM, R. HISTORY OF THE SIEGE OF BOSTON (Boston 1903).

GRAYDON, ALEXANDER. MEMOIRS OF HIS OWN TIME (Philadelphia 1846).

JEFFERSON, T. PAPERS (Boyd ed. 1951).

MADISON, J. PAPERS (C. Hobson & R. Rutland eds. 1979).

MARYLAND ARCHIVES (Baltimore: Maryland Historical Society, 1883–1964).

MASON, G. PAPERS (Rutland ed. 1970).

PAINE, T. COMPLETE WRITINGS (1969).

POPULAR SOURCES OF POLITICAL AUTHORITY: DOCUMENTS ON THE MASSACHUSETTS CONSTITUTION OF 1780 (1966).

PRICE, R. OBSERVATIONS ON THE IMPORTANCE OF THE AMERICAN REVOLUTION (London and Boston, 1784).

SOURCES OF AMERICAN INDEPENDENCE (H. Peckman ed. 1978).
SUMNER, W. AN INQUIRY INTO THE IMPORTANCE OF THE MILITIA TO
    A FREE COMMONWEALTH (Boston 1823).
WRITINGS OF SAMUEL ADAMS (H. Cushing ed. 1904).

II. SECONDARY SOURCES

CONNER, R. HISTORY OF NORTH CAROLINA (Chicago 1919).
THE CONSTITUTION OF THE STATE OF GEORGIA (Savannah 1777).
DRAYTON, J. MEMOIRS OF THE AMERICAN REVOLUTION, FROM ITS
    COMMENCEMENT TO THE YEAR 1776, INCLUSIVE; AS RELATING
    TO SOUTH CAROLINA (Charleston 1821).
DUMBAULD, E. THOMAS JEFFERSON AND THE LAW (1978).
ERDMAN, C. THE NEW JERSEY CONSTITUTION OF 1776 (Princeton 1929).
HALBROOK, S. THAT EVERY MAN BE ARMED: THE EVOLUTION OF A
    CONSTITUTIONAL RIGHT (1984).
HALL, M. THE GLORIOUS REVOLUTION IN AMERICA (1964).
HANCOCK, HAROLD B. THE LOYALISTS OF REVOLUTIONARY DELA-
    WARE (London 1977).
KONKLE, B. GEORGE BRYAN AND THE CONSTITUTION OF PENNSYL-
    VANIA (Philadelphia 1922).
LOVEJOY, D. RHODE ISLAND POLITICS AND THE AMERICAN REVOLU-
    TION, 1760–1776 (1958).
OLIVER, B. THE RIGHTS OF AN AMERICAN CITIZEN (1832).
POORE, B. THE FEDERAL AND STATE CONSTITUTIONS (1877).
RUTLAND, R. THE BIRTH OF THE BILL OF RIGHTS (1962).
SELSAM, J. THE PENNSYLVANIA CONSTITUTION OF 1776 (1936).
SKAGGS, D. ROOTS OF MARYLAND DEMOCRACY, 1753–1776 (1973).
SWINDLER, W. SOURCES AND DOCUMENTS OF U.S. CONSTITUTIONS
    (1973–1979).
WILBUR, I. IRA ALLEN: FOUNDER OF VERMONT, 1751–1814 (Boston: Hough-
    ton Mifflin, 1928).

Index

About the Author

STEPHEN P. HALBROOK, an Attorney at Law, is a member of the
Virginia and D.C. Bars, the U.S. Supreme Court Bar, and several federal
appellate court bars. His previous books include: *That Every Man Should
Be Armed: The Evolution of a Constitutional Right and Social Philosophy*.
Halbrook has written articles that appeared in the *Journal of Air Law and
Commerce, George Mason University Law Review, Vermont Law Review, Law
and Contemporary Problems*, and various Congressional Reports.